The
Reference Shelf®

Sports in America

The Reference Shelf
Volume 85 • Number 4
H. W. Wilson
A Division of EBSCO Information Services
Ipswich, Massachusetts
2013

GREY HOUSE PUBLISHING

The Reference Shelf

The books in this series contain reprints of articles, excerpts from books, addresses on current issues, and studies of social trends in the United States and other countries. There are six separately bound numbers in each volume, all of which are usually published in the same calendar year. Numbers one through five are each devoted to a single subject, providing background information and discussion from various points of view and concluding with an index and comprehensive bibliography that lists books, pamphlets, and articles on the subject. The final number of each volume is a collection of recent speeches. Books in the series may be purchased individually or on subscription.

Library of Congress Cataloging-in-Publication Data

Library of Congress Cataloging-in-Publication Data
Sports in America.
    pages cm. -- (The reference shelf ; volume 85, number 4)
  Includes bibliographical references and index.
  ISBN 978-0-8242-1215-5 (issue 4, pbk.) -- ISBN 978-0-8242-1211-7 (volume 85)
1. Sports--United States--History.
  GV583.S68525 2013
  796.0973--dc23

                                                                        2013019515

Cover: McDonough's Anthony Chase, left, and Eric Marsh, right, combine to stop Hammond quarterback Josh Whaley during the play off game at McDonough on November 19, 2010. McDonough defeated Hammond 28-18 to advance to the state semi finals. (©Washington Post/Getty Images)

The Reference Shelf, 2013, published by Grey House Publishing, Inc., Amenia, NY, under exclusive license from EBSCO Information Services, Inc.

Printed in the United States of America

Contents

3

The Big Business of Collegiate Sports

4

The Concussion Culture

5

The Doping Era

6

The Rise of Fantasy Sports

Preface

An Introduction to American Sports Culture and History:
The Case of Lance Armstrong

This overview of sports in American culture and history involves three overarching questions. The first—What is the nature of sports heroism?—centers on the connection between the personal integrity of athletes and the social triumph of their feats. Conversely, the second question—Can anything involving the games and play of sports be considered tragic?—centers on the connection between the personal duplicity of athletes and the social corruption represented in their actions. The line between the two questions is not always clear, especially when sports transcend their competitive boundaries and the connection between personal motivations and social effects become complex. In the ensuing ambiguities is a third overarching question, which centers on the connection between the personal rhetoric of athletes and the general nature of social control: Is it ever truly possible to get behind the masks of public figures?

A single case in modern American culture serves to illuminate the three questions: the biography, triumphs, corruption, and potential redemption of Lance Armstrong, whose story is a kind of encompassing "perfect storm." The question of integrity and triumph leads, in Armstrong's case, to the idea that, by importing into American culture a sport not part of the nation's mainstream trinity—football, baseball, and basketball—while exporting an American presence in that sport to the rest of the world (most notably France), Armstrong became a kind of heroic embodiment of the American Dream. Indeed, Armstrong lived, as he called it during his two-part interview with Oprah Winfrey (which was taped on January 14, 2013, and aired on January 17 and 18), "this mythic perfect story." However, Armstrong's quick clarification, "and it wasn't true" (*Telegraph*), leads straight to the second question addressed herein.

The connection between duplicity and corruption is as complex in Armstrong's case as the connection between integrity and triumph. What, in particular, does the case suggest about how Americans philosophically view competition in the pursuit of a "level playing field"? Perhaps even more hauntingly, Armstrong's persona evokes the third question about rhetoric and control, especially given the seemingly all-access, Internet-driven information age. A picture tells a thousand words: in anticipating Armstrong's upcoming sixth Tour de France in 2004, *Sports Illustrated*, a magazine that had celebrated Armstrong as its 2002 Sportsman of the Year, featured a two-page photograph of the cyclist quiescently lying on his back on a grassy field. With the caption, "What, me worry?," Armstrong is shown with his legs crossed and a broad smile on his face as he rests his head on his folded arms. Walking toward Armstrong in the background, though, is a solitary, older Frenchman, his intrusive gaze not only slightly disrupting the photograph's triumphant ethos but suggesting only now—post-Oprah interview—that the world would discover Armstrong's secrets as slowly and surely as the man's gait.

Integrity, Triumph, and Heroism

In their ideal state, sports embody nothing short of the American Dream, defined and driven by the principle of fair competition. This dream may be taken as involving the *pursuit* of winning, not winning itself; the word *compete* affirms as much, deriving from Latin and meaning "to strive for (something) together with another."[1] Cooperation is fine, but when the twin sanctions of fortune and fame are at stake, human motivations and actions can get messy. At one point, Armstrong's friend, Michele Ferrari, the physician notorious for dispensing performance-enhancing drugs to high-profile athletes and who was banned by the US Anti-Doping Agency, minced no words in observing, "Lance wishes to swallow the world" (qtd. in Coyle 7).

Americans have always found a kind of heroism in winning itself, but Armstrong's astonishing level of personal success seemed to eclipse the common definition of winning. Even though Armstrong's chosen sport, cycling, is not part of the American "trinity" of popular sports, Armstrong's seeming transformation from youthful braggart to cancer patient, athlete, and humble servant fighting to fund cancer research seemed to so embody the American Dream that the public was swept along. Armstrong's heroism, in fact, was almost governmentally sanctioned (he rode for the US Postal Service team), and he was featured on the cover of *Sports Illustrated* eleven times (one after his last Tour de France victory). In 2005, at his good-bye speech atop the podium after winning his seventh Tour de France, Armstrong closed—in words he remarked during his interview with Oprah were regrettable—"Finally, the last thing I'll say to the people who don't believe in cycling—the cynics, the skeptics—I'm sorry you can't dream big and I'm sorry you don't believe in miracles" (qtd. in Bayless). The irony of Armstrong's comment still stings, for Armstrong himself, clearly enough, did not believe in miracles.

The implications of Armstrong's triumphs sweep across sports culture and history. Winning has become everything in the American sports landscape. In football, Green Bay Packers coach Vince Lombardi left no doubt: "There is no room for second place. There is only one place in my game, and that's first place" ("What It Takes"). In baseball, the ostracized Pete Rose once said in almost Faustian imagery, "I'd walk through hell in a gasoline suit to play baseball" (Banks 128). And, in basketball, coach of the 1980s Los Angeles Lakers Pat Riley summarized, "There is winning and misery and even when we win I'm miserable" (qtd. in Hirsch). At his height, Armstrong seemed to embrace these attitudes, a dubious status questioned even in 2001 by three-time Tour de France winner Greg LeMond (the only American now acknowledged with the title): "If Lance is clean, it is the greatest comeback in the history of sports. If he isn't, it would be the greatest fraud" (qtd. in Magnuson).

Duplicity, Corruption, and Tragedy

At first blush, to categorize anything about sports as "tragic" would seem distorted. Except in a few cases (such as in automobile racing), nobody dies in sports, and death is traditionally part of tragedy. The concept of "tragedy," though, is not necessarily linked to death but to the irrational: *tragedy* is derived from Greek words meaning, *goat song*.[2] How tragedy is manifest in human actions varies, but the quality of "acting in two opposing ways" that is central to duplicity[3] is a start in considering the issue: taken in rational terms, one thing cannot be two things at once. Enter Lance Armstrong.

Whether or not Armstrong is a sympathetic character is a complex issue. The argument that Armstrong's drug use was only in keeping with a culture of duplicity is a valid one; as one indication, of the ten fastest finishers in the 2005 Tour de France, only three have not been linked to doping as of 2013 (McLean). Furthermore, to win the Tour de France seven times in a row entails a level of dedication few possess; his dedication included his dogged rationality when staring into cameras and, more intrepidly, filing lawsuits against those who would impugn his innocence. Additionally, Armstrong's 2001 autobiography, *It's Not about the Bike* (2000), made him a best-selling author. His follow-up books were also successful. Interestingly, after the Oprah interview and in the wake of Armstrong's disclosures, the Manly Library in Sydney, Australia, moved Armstrong's writings to its fiction section ("Lance Armstrong Books").

The implications of Armstrong's case for American sports history and culture reach, in particular, to the institution of the Olympics, for nowhere is the potential for tragedy as clearly on display. Beyond the general politicizing of the Games, ruptures in the Olympic spirit of fair competition are conspicuous. The line drawn between professionalism and amateurism meant, for example, that Jim Thorpe had his 1912 decathlon and pentathlon medals stripped for playing semiprofessional baseball; the medals were posthumously restored in 1983. In 1972, incompetence, if not corruption, in officiating was on display when referees allowed the final play of the gold-medal basketball game between the United States and the Soviet Union to be replayed twice, with the Soviets earning gold; the US team never accepted its silver medals. Finally, the use of performance-enhancing drugs became front-page news at the 1988 Seoul Olympics when Jamaican-born sprinter Ben Johnson (representing Canada) defeated American rival Carl Lewis in the 100-meter dash. When Johnson tested positive for anabolic steroids, the headline on *Sports Illustrated*'s October 3, 1988, cover screamed, "Busted!" Whatever the issues, the tensions running through these stories underlie Armstrong's case, for he interrupted his professional efforts to win a bronze medal (which was later stripped) at the 2000 Games.

Rhetoric, Control, and Acting

Beyond its humor, the Manly Library's reclassification of Armstrong's books raises questions about the relationship between athletes and audiences: Can either know or even control the other? Athletes seek endorsements derived from the approval of audiences, and audiences seek social identity and even a kind of status from the achievement of "their" athletes. This symbiotic relationship is nowhere more apparent than in commercials. In 1993, Charles Barkley found himself in a media storm when he disclaimed for a Nike advertisement, "I am not a role model." The statement is often used out of context; Barkley was merely arguing that parents, not athletes, must lead their children. Meanwhile, probing the mentality of fans (a word, one must remember, abbreviated from "fanatics") suggests how sports create at least a sense of cultural ownership. In a continuing series of commercials playing on the superstitions of fans, one of Bud Light's 2013 Super Bowl advertisements featured two men who carry a thread-worn recliner through the streets of New Orleans in order to have a mystic, played by musician Stevie Wonder, place a hex on it. The commercial's O. Henry ending reveals that the "lucky chair" belongs to a friend who cheers for a rival team. In the irrational minds of such fans, correlation is causation.

In attempting to "swallow the world," Armstrong sought to enjoy Barkley's detachment while controlling how fans perceived him. As he commented in the Oprah interview, "I was a bully in the sense that I tried to control the narrative" (*Telegraph*). Armstrong's rhetorical tactics were never subtle. In a commercial for Nike that ran from 2001 until his downfall, he is shown getting tested for drugs, going through his day, and then riding his bike through rain and the gloom of night. In a defiant voice-over that came to typify his rhetoric, he asserts, "This is my body, and I can do whatever I want to it. I can push it, study it, tweak it, listen to it. Everybody wants to know what I'm on. What am I on? I'm on bike, busting my ass, six hours a day. What are you on?" In response to Armstrong's revelation of drug use, the sadder-but-wiser press asked the questions that much of the rest of the nation was thinking. As journalist and longtime Armstrong defender Rick Reilly wrote about Armstrong's admission and apology in his interview with Winfrey, "When he says he's sorry now, how do we know he's not still lying? How do we know it's not just another great performance by the all-time leader in them?" Riley's question was more than rhetorical, and the only sure answer coming from the interview was that Armstrong revealed nothing beyond barren facts.

What, then, does Armstrong's case suggest about the general connection between rhetoric and control? In a 2005 deposition, Armstrong commented about what being caught doping would mean: "Everything I do off of the bike would go away, too. And don't think for a second I don't understand that. . . . All of that would be erased" (qtd. in Schrotenboer). From a humanist view, to be "erased" is central to tragedy. In light of the second part of the Oprah interview, *Sports Illustrated* writer S. L. Price coupled the whole matter with the concurrent, curious case of Notre Dame football player Manti Te'o, who was "catfished" (i.e., to be fooled by an Internet ruse) into believing a fictional character to be real. Te'o discovered that real love and death cannot be erased so easily as hanging up the phone or deleting an email. Meanwhile, Americans discovered that same week that what they had believed to be the multifaceted persona of Armstrong was only multimirrored. Referring to Armstrong's tearful recollection during the second Oprah interview about telling his son to stop defending his honor, Price skewered, "Are we certain Lance Armstrong even has a 13-year-old son?" (54). Perhaps, then, Armstrong should be characterized in the information age not as Christopher Marlowe's Dr. Faustus but as Ben Jonson's mountebank Volpone. After peeling away the layers of beliefs, language, and actions that constitute a person's humanity, one finds at the core of Armstrong not LeMond's characterization of a fraud but, rather, a shape-shifting thespian who, once the curtain drops, simply moves on to his next performance, the previous role forgotten by his audience. To be sure, Armstrong will count on his audience's short-term memory for the rest of his life.

Precedent and Hope

One truth emerges from Armstrong's case: sports will endure. In Shakespeare's *King Lear*, Edgar comments, "the worst is not / So long as we can say 'This is the worst'" (4.1.27–28). Armstrong's breathtaking duplicity seems to answer Edgar's definition, but even a cursory survey of American sports history—across blurry categories of corruption and widely different sports—suggests episodes that, at the time, seemed equally radical and final. In other words, cheating, lying, and corruption have long been a part of American sports. For example, the 1950–51 City College of New York men's basketball team conspired with gamblers to "shave" points in manipulating margins of victory. In 1994, Tonya Harding's then-husband, Jeff Gillooly, joined with two others in attempting to break rival skater Nancy Kerrigan's right leg. Further-more, the legendary phrase, "Say it ain't so, Joe"—a young boy's plea to White Sox outfielder "Shoeless" Joe Jackson, hoping the latter would confirm that he had not participated in fixing the 1919 World Series—became part of the American lexicon. Then and now, however, the truth has a way of inexorably surfacing. In 2001, Notre Dame football coach George O'Leary resigned because he had lied on his resume about his credentials. In 1980, Boston Marathon runner Rosie Ruiz appeared a little too fresh when, after taking a subway, she crossed the finish line first. In 2001, unscrupulous adults falsified Little League sensation Danny Almonte's age (he was fourteen when the maximum age was twelve).

Given the repeated and consistent failures of athletes and institutions through-out American sports history, one wonders why sports continue to compel and even inspire the public. The question is, ultimately, as inscrutable as trying to define human nature itself. Maybe the appeal is the tie between sports and the innocence of youth. Maybe it is the simple wonder of what skilled athletes can do with their minds and bodies. Maybe it is an underlying sense of civic, if not cultural, identity. Whatever the answer, logic need not apply: In sports, miracles sometimes really do happen, there sometimes really is "no *I* in *team*," and hope sometimes really is rewarded. Chief Justice Earl Warren once commented, "I always turn to the sports section first. The sports section records people's accomplishments; the front page nothing but man's failures" (Quinn 76). Warren is right: If human limitations and corruptions can somehow just be ignored, then one can find in American sports nothing short of the triumphant human spirit that can fashion heroic order from life's all-too-frequent tragic chaos.

Notes

1. *Shorter Oxford English Dictionary on Historical Principles*, 5th ed, s.v. "compete."
2. *Shorter Oxford English Dictionary on Historical Principles*, 5th ed, s.v. "tragedy."
3. *Shorter Oxford English Dictionary on Historical Principles*, 5th ed, s.v. "duplicity."

1

Youth Sports

Petaluma, California's Danny Marzo (12) celebrates with teammates after hitting a walk-off, solo home run in the eighth of an elimination baseball game against Parsippany, New Jersey, at the Little League World Series tournament in South Williamsport, Pennsylvania., Monday, August 20, 2012. Petaluma won 5–4.

The Perks and Pitfalls of Youth Sports

Youth sports grew out of the rapid industrialization of the United States from the 1880s through the first decades of the 1900s. During this time period, child labor was outlawed, leading to a large number of children with little to do during the hours after their daily schooling finished. Thus, adults in some American cities began organizing structured competitive games for children, and these gradually developed into youth leagues for games such as baseball, football, hockey, tennis, and soccer. The early sporting leagues shared an identical mission with the modern leagues that follow in their footsteps, conferring on children the physical, social, and psychological benefits of engaging in competitive athletics.

In the twenty-first century, youth sports are an American obsession, constituting a $5 billion industry in 2010. Census estimates indicate that between 30 and 40 million American children between the ages of five and eighteen are involved in organized sports. The physical and psychological benefits of playing team sports have been extensively documented and explored as youth sports culture developed in the United States. While most Americans feel involvement in youth sports is a wholesome, healthy, and beneficial activity, in some cases, adult obsession has come at the physical and psychological expense of youth athletes; this unfortunate downside to the culture has led some to call for regulation.

The Physical Benefits of Youth Sports

According to the President's Council on Physical Fitness and Sports, the percentage of overweight youth from ages six to eleven has quadrupled since the early 1970s and has tripled for children between the ages of twelve and nineteen. Lack of physical activity is one of the most important contributors to this trend, and only an estimated 18 percent of American children engage in the recommended sixty minutes of physical activity per day. Some research suggests that excessive attention to video games and television are factors that contribute to a growing sedentary lifestyle among American youth and thereby contribute to obesity and other health problems.

Through participation in youth sports, children may avoid the inactivity that contributes to childhood obesity. It is also generally believed that participation in youth sports helps children to develop muscular coordination and reflexes, among a variety of other benefits. The National Alliance of Youth Sports (NAYS) says that participation in amateur athletics promotes an appreciation for the benefits of physical fitness that can turn into healthy patterns later in life, resulting in adults who continue to engage in sports or other regular exercise.

While the anecdotal physical fitness angle of youth sports is accepted and has been repeated widely by organizations that promote youth sports involvement, there have been few attempts to investigate these claims quantitatively. A 2011 research study published in *Current Sports Medicine Reports* indicates that children involved in sports are more likely to eat fruits and vegetables and to drink milk than children not involved in sports. Conversely, the study also found that youth athletes are also more likely to consume unhealthy snack food and sugary drinks, the two primary causes of childhood obesity. Overall, youth sports participation has a negligible effect on moderating obesity because snack and junk food are accepted parts of sports culture and because children do not couple increased physical activity with healthier diet choices.

The Emotional, Psychological, and Social Benefits of Youth Sports

In addition to providing a potentially positive contribution to overall fitness and athletic ability, participation in youth sports has been tied to a plethora of social and psychological benefits. One of the primary psychological benefits associated with youth sports is the development of interpersonal skills. Youth athletes can develop a sense of belonging as a member of the team that may translate into greater ability to experience a sense of group membership and cooperation in other areas of life.

A 2006 University of Maryland study found that student athletes are 15 percent more likely than nonathletes to be involved in their communities and to take time for civic engagements, including participating in voting and volunteer activities. The study similarly found that male athletes were 8 percent more likely and female athletes 16 percent more likely to feel comfortable with public speaking. Overall, this study provides some quantitative evidence to support the belief that participation in sports can translate to success in group membership and cooperation, skills that have a variety of functions in society.

A 2000 study on the effects of high school athletic participation on economic outcomes indicated that student athletes earn more money than nonathletes of similar IQ and educational level. The study found that high school athletes have a 25 to 35 percent higher level of educational attainment after high school and that, on average, they earn from 12 to 15 percent more than nonathletes having similar levels of intelligence and educational attainment.

After a thorough examination of their findings, the researchers determined that youth athletics functions to create higher adult performance through a number of separate but interrelated effects. For one, youth sports serve as a form of training in which the benefits of continued effort and an industrious attitude toward goal achievement are demonstrated in simple, easily comprehensible athletic accomplishment. This training may function later to encourage individuals to invest energy and effort into activities that have less immediate and clear-cut rewards, because the individuals have come to have faith in the function of the underlying work ethic they learned in part from youth sports.

In addition, the researchers suggest that youth sports participation can build self-esteem as individuals learn to believe in their ability to handle challenges, which can likewise translate into success in advancing in a later career. In a healthy sporting environment individuals may also learn about the positive experiences that can be gained through failure and through learning from one's mistakes. It is often argued among supporters of youth sports that athletic activities teach both resiliency, by demonstrating to children that losses are part of normal life experience, and how to continue moving toward goals after suffering setbacks.

Further, proponents of youth sports have often argued that these activities teach individuals discipline and learning to adhere to rules-based systems. The ability to work within the structure of a specific system, such as within the rules of a team sport, may translate to a more developed capacity to understand and work within the rules of a corporation or other role. The discipline required to participate in competitive sports relates directly to the both the self-discipline required to complete personal goals and the ability to understand the dynamics of how to work under the authority of another. Similarly, many children have the opportunity in youth sports leagues to become leaders and may use this opportunity to learn how to motivate and manage others to achieve a common goal.

Investment in Children

The men and women who become coaches of youth sports leagues can play important roles in guiding the development of hundreds or even thousands of children. Coaches can become role models and have the opportunity both to model healthy, positive mental attitudes and to provide mentoring to the children on their teams. In the best cases, coaches supplement and enhance the positive lessons that children learn from their parents and serve to reinforce important skills that can be applied to many life activities. In the worst scenarios, coaches can be overly dominant and even insulting, causing potential psychological harm to children.

Because the relationship between a coach and an athlete can have a major effect on young athletes, significant research has attempted to examine the qualities that contribute to effective coaching relationships. Research released in 2009 by sports psychologists at the University of Washington examined the "mastery climate," in which coaches stress positive interactions with athletes and focus on teamwork and personal goals, as compared to the "ego climate," which stresses team victory and personal responsibility for the team's success. The report indicates that coaches who manage to create a mastery climate retain more of their athletes from season to season and foster a relatively stable and beneficial psychological environment.

The Potential Hazards of Youth Sports

There is a common American stereotype of coaches or parents whose own hopes of "going pro" or getting a scholarship were thwarted and who, in order to compensate for their own perceived failures, become obsessed with the sporting activities of their children or players on their team. This stereotype is common because it occurs repeatedly in youth sports culture and is part of the formula that can transform the beneficial activity of sports into a physically and psychologically detrimental experience.

In general, pushing children in youth sports in hopes that they will develop into college or professional athletes is an illusory goal. Fewer than one in one hundred youth sports players will play in college, and less than 2 percent of those athletes will receive tuition assistance. The chances of transitioning from collegiate sports to professional sports are even less promising. Even the most gifted athletes in the nation's youth leagues have less than a 1 percent chance of becoming professional players, regardless of the coaching or parenting they receive.

Participation in sports can become an obsessive activity that has an unfortunate tendency to feed into existing emotional dysfunctions. Statistically, when asked about their reasons for participating in sports, only 13 percent of boys and 4 percent of girls listed winning the game as their primary motivation, and most listed "achieving personal goals" and "having fun" as their foremost priority. Parents and coaches are often more focused on competitive success, and this can lead to placing unhealthy pressures on child athletes. A 2012 survey headed by the Minnesota Amateur Sports Commission indicated that more than 45 percent of amateur sports players reported being insulted or called names by their coaches.

An estimated one-third of repetitive stress injuries among youth are amateur-sports related. While injuries are a normal part of sporting activities, repetitive stress injuries are completely avoidable given appropriate time to recuperate. Pitchers urged to pitch too often or soccer players who are put on the field with a knee injury run an increased risk of suffering an injury that could become serious; furthermore, the benefits of pushing oneself beyond one's physical limits are not in evidence.

A related issue is the degree to which the positive psychological benefits of sports are tied to performance. In the ideal scenario, children develop better coordination and fitness while participating in a supportive environment that encourages each player regardless of their personal skill levels. In the real world, children can sometimes experience reduced self-esteem when they feel that their personal physical limitations disappoint his or her parents, coaches, or other team members. Surveys suggest that between 15 and 25 percent of youth sports participants feel picked on by fellow team members, and many players also reported experiencing shame or depression regarding mistakes made during a game.

Parents must learn to moderate their expectations when encouraging children to engage in sports. It is important for parents to realize that the positive benefits of sports are not dependent on competitive success but are the product of positive experiences in team and personal achievement gained while engaging in safe physical activity. Most coaches recommend that parents remember the extreme unlikelihood that their child, regardless of skill, will matriculate into collegiate or professional sports and to recognize that the ultimate goal of participation must be enjoyment and a healthy lifestyle. Parents are also cautioned to pay attention to their children's wishes and to realize that the same physical benefits gained through youth sports can be found in alternative athletic activities; also, similar psychological benefits can be gained through other types of group activities, from the Boy and Girl Scouts to community drama or dance clubs.

Straight Outta Compton

By Jeff Benedict and Armen Keteyian
Sports Illustrated, December 2, 2011

A top student and football star in South Central L.A., Kitam Hamm is one of a growing number of high school athletes who face life-and-death decisions every day as they try to survive in gang-infested communities.

The iPhone beside Kitam Hamm's bed vibrates at 6:15 on a recent morning, stirring him awake. A car alarm pulses in the alley and police sirens scream past, noises so familiar that they go unnoticed. Squinting, Hamm flips on the light. Letters from college football recruiters—all neatly taped to the wall next to his bed—come into focus: Stanford, Harvard, Princeton, UCLA, Columbia and seven more. They are the first thing the 18-year-old Hamm sees every morning, a daily reminder that he's one step closer to making it out of Compton, California.

In a neighborhood with at least three rival gangs, Hamm's every move is orchestrated, right down to what he wears and which route he takes to school. Hamm's 12-unit apartment complex is surrounded by a black iron fence and has a single secured entrance. It sits in a neighborhood where the streets are lined with billboards, walls with graffiti and small businesses secured by bars and gates. For Hamm, dropping his guard can be the difference between life and death.

Hamm's parents, Donyetta and Kitam Sr., were 21 and already had three daughters when Kitam Jr. was born. By then Kitam Sr., once affiliated with the Bloods, had cut his gang ties, and Donyetta had seen her brother, who had been a Crip, sentenced to life in prison without parole for his role in a murder at a liquor store. These experiences galvanized the Hamms, both now 39, to do everything possible to protect their son from the influences of the street.

"We live in Blood territory, and there have been a lot of murders here," says Donyetta. "We don't let Kitam go anywhere without permission. He comes home from football practice, and we eat together as a family every night. Then he does homework. He's not allowed out after dark. He has a very structured life."

That structure has enabled Hamm to excel on the football field and in the classroom. A 5'9", 170-pound running back and safety at Compton High, Hamm has a sprinter's speed and bench-presses 315 pounds. Despite missing four games with an ankle injury, Hamm rushed for 602 yards, scored 11 touchdowns and had 31 solo tackles for the 3–7 Tarbabes. Hamm is on pace to graduate with a 3.8 GPA, ranks 44th in a senior class of 514 and plans to take prelaw courses in college.

Protecting a child from gang violence isn't easy in Compton, a city of 96,000 that was called the murder capital of the US in the 1990s. Compton is currently home to 34 active street gangs—often several on the same block—and more than 1,000 gang members.

"I started talking to Kitam about gangs in elementary school because that's when you get introduced to them," says Kitam Sr., who started running with the Bloods when he was 13. "Having a father in the home makes a big difference. A lot of kids here don't have dads, and a gang becomes their only family. I told Kitam early on that before I allow a gang to take you out, I'll take you out first. The only gang Kitam belongs to is the Hamm family."

The latest FBI figures show that gang activity in the US is growing at an alarming rate, with more than one million active gang members, up from 800,000 in 2005. In Los Angeles the situation is particularly dire, with scores of gangs vying for territory and influence in close proximity to one another. With so many gang members around, it can be almost impossible for high school athletes to avoid them and their influence.

"The presence of large numbers of gang members in high schools creates pressures for many nongang members, including athletes," says Scott Decker, director of the School of Criminology and Criminal Justice at Arizona State and co-author of a soon-to-be-released study funded by the US Justice Department about gang members in college athletics. "Students in Los Angeles schools face increased pressure to join gangs, and find their lives affected by gangs. Athletes are often targets [to recruit as members] because of the visibility and prestige they can bring to gangs."

In their study Decker and co-author Geoff Alpert, a criminal justice professor at South Carolina, conclude that universities don't properly check the backgrounds of their recruits. The study, which was conducted among 120 BCS conference schools and 10 other universities with Division I basketball programs, found that nearly 70% of campus police chiefs and athletic directors who responded believed gang members were participating in athletics at either their schools or another institution.

To further explore the issue of gangs and sports, SI partnered with CBS News and went to Compton, the birthplace of the Bloods and the Crips and a recruiting hot spot for college football and basketball players. On a recent drive through the city's streets, Sgt. Brandon Dean, a supervisor in the L.A. County Sheriff's office assigned to the gang unit in Compton, pointed out that many popular perceptions about gangs date back to the 1980s and '90s and no longer fit the reality. The days of two powerful gangs carving up territory and marking it with colors are long gone.

"Today in Southern California there are hundreds of Crip gangs and hundreds of Blood gangs," said Dean. "Not all Blood gangs and all Crip gangs get along. You have shootings that occur between a Crip gang and another Crip gang." In addition to this fragmentation, Dean said, there has been a large influx of Latino gangs, some of which have ties to drug cartels.

With so many smaller gangs operating in such a congested area, it's common to have multiple rival gangs occupying opposite sides of the same street or different stretches of the same block. "Everything is intermingled," Dean said. It's a situation that makes any young male vulnerable to being mistaken as a member of a rival gang.

"A lot of kids in this neighborhood are gifted athletes," said Dean as he drove past a cul-de-sac where graffiti from three gangs marked walls and fences, and teens hung out drinking and smoking in the middle of the afternoon. "Unfortunately, some get involved in a gang and commit crimes. Others get involved in the sense that they are mistaken as gang members and ultimately get shot and killed as a result."

It's all part of the new world of gangs, in which the long-held tradition of leaving athletes alone no longer applies. In the last four years Hamm has seen nine friends, including several athletes, die as a result of gang violence. Hamm's experience is common in Compton.

"My deepest fear is my environment," says Alphonso Marsh, a senior cornerback and Division I recruit at Compton's Dominguez High, which is trying to use its football program to steer players away from gangs. "I lost my godbrother. He was killed in 2009 by some boys on the street. He was 17."

The 2009 shooting of wide receiver Dannie Farber, one of the top high school players in the Los Angeles area, underscores the danger that athletes can face every day. During a routine visit to a Compton fast-food restaurant, Farber was approached by a gang member who asked him, "Where you from, cuz?" When Farber stood up and replied, "What?" the gang member shot him four times in a senseless killing that reverberated throughout the city.

Two years later Kitam Hamm faced an eerily similar situation. One afternoon last spring as he stepped off a city bus across the street from his family's apartment, two young men approached. One had a gun.

"Where you from, Blood?" the one with the gun asked, gang-speak for *What gang are you in?*

Hamm froze. He quickly remembered lessons his father had drilled into him: *Don't act hard. Remain calm. Give the right answer.*

"Nowhere," Hamm told the armed man. "I ain't from nowhere," code for *I'm not in a gang.*

That answer saved his life. The gangster stared Hamm down, then tucked his gun in his waistband and moved on. Hamm collapsed on the bus-stop bench, knowing he had truly just dodged a bullet.

Hamm starts his day by confronting a question most teenage boys scarcely consider when getting ready for school: What should I wear? The answer is complicated when your street is a border between rival street gangs. Colors, particularly of shirts and baseball caps, signify affiliation and invite peril.

"I don't wear red because I might get accused of being a Blood," Hamm says. "And I don't wear blue because the Bloods might think I'm a Crip." On this day he chooses a plaid shirt and dark jeans.

It's almost 7:30 when Kitam Jr. slings his book bag over his shoulder, says goodbye to his mother and follows his dad to the car. Kitam Sr. drives his son to school every day. On this morning, with Leo Sayer singing *Oh Girl* on the radio, the two

In the last four years Hamm has seen nine friends, including several athletes, die as a result of gang violence. Hamm's experience is common in Compton.

Hamms discuss tackling techniques during the 10-minute commute to school. Kitam Jr. says he'd be able to hit even harder if he were heavier. "Size matters, don't get me wrong," his father says. "But if you're small *and you're strong*, you can still rock a person."

Kitam and his father have always had a special bond. Kitam Sr. has tried to teach his son right and wrong, how to excel in sports and how to survive on the streets. When Kitam Jr. was 12, his father started taking him to a neighborhood basketball court to play with older kids, forcing him to find ways to get his shot off against taller and stronger players. One day a man showed up in a hooded sweatshirt. Kitam Sr. suspected he had a gun. Moments later the man brandished a pistol and pointed it at one of the players. "Stay behind me," Kitam Sr. told his son. Then he put his hands up and stepped toward the armed man. "Please don't kill this guy in front of my son," he pleaded. "My son don't need to see this." After a tense pause, the man left and Kitam Sr. took Kitam Jr. home.

"If you want to know how bad and dirty it is, all you have to do is pay attention to where we live and how many guys are ending up dead," says Kitam Sr. "The gangs don't care about kids or how old or young you are. You have to stay away and not get caught up by being in the wrong place at the wrong time."

In another era Compton High was the home of baseball great Duke Snider and former NFL commissioner Pete Rozelle. Both were in the class of '44. Back then the school's racial composition reflected that of the city—almost exclusively white. Today, of Compton High's 2,400 students, 79% are Latino and 20% are African-American. The current Compton High was once a community college, and the 55-acre campus is now surrounded by a 10-foot-high security fence.

Inside the gates is an environment that is safe. It's a place where Hamm has no enemies and where lots of people look out for him. People like 45-year-old Anthony Johnson, one of numerous uniformed security guards on campus. Short and powerfully built, Johnson also doubles as Hamm's running backs coach. Hamm spots Johnson and stops to say hello. After a brief exchange, Johnson imparts some advice. "Be a stand-up young man in life," says Johnson. "Say what you mean. And work hard."

Hamm listens, especially in light of what has happened to Johnson's 23-year-old son, Brandon. In July, Brandon Johnson and two other men were arrested in connection with the killing of an 18-year-old in nearby Long Beach. Hamm had looked up to Brandon, who was one of the nation's top running backs for crosstown rival Dominguez High in 2006 and went on to play two seasons at the University of Washington. Today he sits in jail awaiting trial, having pleaded not guilty to murder.

"I try to avoid all [potentially bad] situations," Hamm says, making his way to his first class, physics and anatomy. "Around here one mistake can change your life forever."

That's something Hamm's parents have told him time and again. They also tell him *don't waste time—keep busy.* He thinks of that when he arrives at class and discovers that the janitor didn't remove the chairs from the tabletops after mopping the floor. Alone in the classroom, Hamm takes down all 35 chairs and arranges them neatly under tables. He finishes just as the other students file in and a substitute teacher gives them the period to study independently. A din of chatter quickly rises as a few kids break out snack food from their backpacks and youngsters cluster into three or four groups. Hamm sits off by himself, pulls out an essay due in another class and works on it for the entire period.

During third period Hamm is summoned to the guidance office. When he arrives, his guidance counselor, Araya Hiyabu, is holding an envelope. "This came today," he says, handing it to Hamm.

It's a package from Norries Wilson, football coach at Columbia. Though Kitam has heard before from the Ivy League school, Hiyabu stresses that this is a request that needs immediate attention. "They want an official transcript," Hiyabu says, adding that Hamm should make sure Compton head coach Brian Collins reviews the letter.

Hamm isn't afraid to tell college admissions officers about his roots. But he can't help thinking that they might not understand. His parents met when they were 15. As part of being affiliated with the Bloods, Kitam Sr. was selling drugs. Donyetta soon got pregnant with their first child, and at 16 was on welfare. That's when she put her foot down and told Kitam Sr. to end his involvement with gangs and crime.

By his own account, Kitam Sr. listened. "Donyetta changed my thinking," he says. "All my friends were going to jail. So it wasn't hard for me to walk away. But my dad used drugs and I didn't have the proper structure to teach me how to provide for my children. I just decided I wanted my kids to grow up and be part of a solution and not part of a problem."

By the time Kitam Jr. was born, his father had been working for three years unloading trucks at a warehouse. "That's how he provided for his family for years," says Donyetta. "He had to butt heads with a lot of gang members. He had numerous fights. But he was determined to be with me and our children. It's amazing he made it. We fought to be where we are today."

Today the Hamms are a model family. Their three daughters were solid students at Compton High, and two are now attending Fremont College in Los Angeles. Both Kitam Sr. and Donyetta work full time—he as an in-home health aide and she as the manager of the apartment complex where they live. Her compensation consists of free rent, which enables them to squeak by on a combined annual income of $21,000. They qualify for food stamps but refuse them. "My pride won't let me stand in that line," Donyetta says.

If Kitam Sr. and Donyetta both took second jobs, they'd earn more. But then they wouldn't be there for Kitam. "Our job right now is keeping Kitam safe," Donyetta says. "I don't want Kitam to be a statistic. I don't want to be the mother who puts on a shirt with my son's picture on it, and throws roses at his grave."

As he leaves his English class, Kitam knows he's got to figure out how to get across in his college admissions statement that he is a product of remarkable parents.

Lunch hour at Compton High easily could be mistaken for an outdoor party. Hundreds of students avoid the cafeteria, choosing instead to hang out in the sunny courtyard in the center of the campus. That's where Hamm ends up. But he's there just long enough to recruit a couple of friends to follow him to a meeting in a classroom just off the courtyard. It's being conducted by Traco Rachal from the Fellowship of Christian Athletes. When Hamm enters the room, Rachal, a former linebacker in the CFL who attended nearby Carson High, is reading from the Bible and speaking to 40 students. "Being tempted is not a sin," Rachal tells the students. "It's how you respond to temptation that matters."

The same guys who attended the Bible study class are in the football locker room with Hamm two hours later, suiting up. Football practice occupies the biggest chunk of Hamm's school day. That's by design. The time between school letting out and nightfall is when boys in Compton get into trouble. Football provides an alternative.

At 3 p.m. Hamm starts by getting his ankles taped. Both are sprained badly enough that his coach suggests he sit out. But Hamm declines. With just two games remaining in his high school career, he wants to take advantage of every opportunity. Even on the practice field.

Hamm spends much of the practice like a coach, encouraging the jayvee players, before scrimmaging with the varsity. It's 6:57 and dark by the time Hamm limps out of the locker room, spots his father parked curbside and sinks into the front seat of the car. At home Donyetta has the family's apartment immaculately clean, and the aroma of Mexican food is wafting from the oven.

There is no dining table in the Hamm home. Instead, the family members eat dinner on their laps in front of the television. Plates in hand, Kitam, his parents and one of his sisters and her two-year-old daughter take their places on the sofa.

Suddenly Kitam gets a text message. It's from Minnesota Vikings wide receiver Greg Camarillo. The two have been friends since Greg's brother Jeff taught and coached Kitam in seventh and eighth grade. That was around the same time that Greg started his NFL career with the San Diego Chargers. Together the Camarillo brothers decided to launch Charging Forward, a program that encourages and rewards student-athletes who excel in academics. They based the program in Compton.

The Camarillos aren't from Compton, but their father, Albert, a renowned history professor at Stanford, was born and raised there. At his father's urging, Jeff began his teaching career in Compton and—inspired in part by Greg—came up with the idea for Charging Forward.

Hamm was one of the first boys to join Charging Forward. He immediately became one of Greg and Jeff's favorites. "In 11 years I've spent in education, I have rarely encountered a kid like Kitam," Jeff says.

Although Jeff has since moved back to Palo Alto to become the vice principal at East Palo Alto Academy, and Greg has been traded to Minnesota, they keep in close contact with Hamm, sending him football equipment, getting him tickets to NFL games in San Diego and encouraging him to keep his grades up. These days they are trying to help him through the recruiting process.

For the next hour Hamm sits on his bed, doing homework on his laptop and texting back and forth with Camarillo. The opportunity to keep up a dialogue with an NFL player who excelled scholastically helps makes it easy for Hamm to stay in at night.

"U think ur better at O or D?" Camarillo texts.

"I'm good on both. If I had to pick, probably defense."

"I sent u a package today. U should get it in about 3 days."

When Hamm signs off, he's inspired to write his college admission essay. First he puts in his earbuds and scrolls through his iTunes to his favorite song, *Bless the Broken Road*, by Rascal Flatts. He cranks up the volume and starts mouthing the words: *I set out on a narrow way many years ago, hoping I would find true love along the broken road....This much I know is true, that God blessed the broken road.*

With his parents in the next room, Hamm begins writing on a notepad. He opens with what it felt like when he first discovered a decade ago that his mother had Hodgkin's lymphoma. The words come easily:

> When I was 7 years old I found out what cancer was. Being so young I really didn't know how to handle the situation. Only thing I can remember is every time the subject came up people got quiet and tears started to fall.

He's interrupted when his bedroom door opens and Donyetta pokes her head in. "Can I see your personal statement?" she says.

Hesitant, he hands her his pad, afraid she might not like it. Donyetta has always kept quiet about her cancer, not wanting others to view her as weak. (The disease was in remission but came back 10 months ago. Donyetta is undergoing chemotherapy.)

"O.K.," she says after reading the essay. Then the two say good night.

Hamm, who surprised his mother on his 18th birthday by getting her name tattooed on his chest, turns to a visitor and says, "She asks why I don't tell her I love her. I'm just not an emotional person. But I love her. I want to be strong for her. My dad is scared he's going to lose her. If he loses her, I think he'll lose his mind."

It is a few minutes past midnight. Hamm is exhausted, physically and mentally. He sets the alarm on his iPhone for 6:15, turns out the light, clasps his hands, looks up and says a prayer before going to sleep: "God, please keep me safe."

Learning to Play and Playing to Learn: Organized Sports and Educational Outcome

By Ann Rosewater
Education Digest, September 1, 2009

Millions of children participate in sports. Sports make up the largest category of after-school activities available for children and youth. What happens in the context of sports matters—it may affect how and what children learn, how they interact with others (adults and peers) and who those others are, and their capacity to regulate their emotional and physical development over time.

High-quality organized sports are a gateway to academic achievement, better grades, improved chances of attending college, and success in the labor market—and these benefits are especially important for low-income youth. My report analyzes several distinct strands of research on the effects on youth of participation in organized sports.

Over the years, researchers have examined this core issue from any number of perspectives. Findings have varied, depending on the nature of their inquiries, whom they asked, and how they compiled their data. Sometimes researchers developed data that seemed to contradict previous research. But more often their data reinforced a straightforward conclusion: that high-quality organized sport engage students, teach them important skills, draw them into the task of learning, and connect them to fellow students and caring adults. An important result is a series of improved outcomes for students.

My report examines data on the impact of organized sports on the academic and intellectual achievement of students. The studies surveyed indicate that:

- Children and youth who participate in organized sports are higher achievers in terms of grades and dropout rates, as well as related measures of academic achievement, such as homework completion and educational aspirations.

- Physical activity, including participation in organized sports, produces intellectual and academic benefits that may have long-term positive effects on life chances.

- Participation in physical activity affects key brain functions critical to learning.

- Both boys and girls reap the achievement benefits of participation in organized sports.

- Participants in organized sports are more likely to attend college and to land better jobs with more responsibility and higher pay.

Regarding the impact of participation in organized sports on students' values and motivations, the data demonstrate that:

- Sports help children and youth feel better connected to school, attend regularly, and connect with a more positive peer network.

- Parents of high school students who participate more in sports have higher expectations for their children.

- Sports participation builds planning skills and provides the experience of failing and trying again (persistence)—experiences that provide a learning process that can translate to greater achievement in school.

Sports have an important effect on the development of children's peer networks. Research finds that:

- High school youth participating in organized sports view sports as providing a place to meet other young people "who had at least one shared interest."

- High school girls find participation in sports to be a way to break gender stereotypes, enhancing their sense of possibility.

- Sports participation contributes significantly to youth identity, especially in high school.

The effects of participating in organized sports are as good or better for children from low-income families as for children from families with more income. The data show that:

- For children who are on the margin (e.g., poor, learning disabled, obese, gay), sports participation can minimize feelings of difference and isolation and increase the likelihood of attending college.

- Participation in organized sports may provide an opportunity for low-income children that other youth take for granted; as a result, the effects on academics and grades are more pronounced for poor children.

- Sports participation is correlated with improved grades or test scores among African American and Latino students.

- African American and Latina female athletes reported better grades in high school and greater involvement with extracurricular activities than female non-athletes.

Opportunities to participate in organized sports are not evenly distributed across the student population. The data show that:

- Adolescents from more affluent families are more likely to participate in organized activities than adolescents from low-income families.

- Asian Americans and Latinos are less likely to participate in sports than other ethnic groups.

- Disparities in participation are more pronounced in activities, such as sports and lessons, that require financial investment.

- Opportunities dwindle as students move from elementary to middle and high schools.

- Boys have more opportunities to participate in organized sports than girls, and girls' opportunities to participate diminish more rapidly as they advance from elementary to high school.

Too many young people lack sufficient opportunities to participate in high-quality organized sports. The data show that:

- According to one study, about 75% of children from white middle class backgrounds participated in organized sports activities, while only 40% to 60% of low-income children of color did so.

- Urban girls, especially girls of color, often face higher barriers to participation, including outside jobs, cultural factors, and weaker parental support for sports involvement.

- Latino children report having fewer opportunities for safe outdoor play and are less physically active than white children.

Based on these findings, I offer a series of recommendations for policy, practice, and research to ensure that organized sports programs fulfill their promise and enable participants to reach their educational goals.

Recommendations for Practice, Policy, and Research

The recommendations cross three major categories critical to moving the sports-based youth development field toward a goal of improving educational outcomes for children and youth. The first two, program quality and equitable access to high-quality programs, are top priorities.

Careful evaluation of intentional improvements made in quality and access, and application of the findings of these assessments, will continue to advance these programs' quality and stability and the likelihood that more children will participate and reap the benefits.

1. Strengthen the Quality of Programs to Foster the Attributes That Lead to Positive Educational Outcomes.

Connect sports-based youth development programs more deliberately to schools and learning.

- Require school attendance and/or performance and offer supports to help students meet these requirements.

- Explore collaborations with other programs or the inclusion of other components such as tutoring, creative writing, or other academically oriented activities.

- Employ teachers and other school staff in sports programs and hold programs at or near school sites.
- Create ways for coaches to serve as liaisons to the schools, either by having school staff work in the program or by establishing expected and regular interactions between coaching staff/volunteers and schools.

Create a conduit for trained, enthusiastic volunteer coaches and mentors to serve in low-income communities where they are needed most.

- Increase the number of volunteers in organized after-school sports programs through Ameri-Corps, VISTA, and other volunteer initiatives.

Ensure that coaches are well prepared and supported to work with the youth in their programs.

- Be clear about coaches' multiple roles, including as supporters of the school system's academic goals, as mentors for participating youth, and as advisors for parents.
- Train coaches in principles of child and adolescent development, emotion regulation, and theories of learning.
- Communicate directly with schools about students' academic status and help students get academic help when needed.
- Invest in regular supervisory support for coaches to promote stability and continuity.

Organize sports activities in a way that encourages and supports sustained parent participation.

- Set games at times that parents are more likely to be available, such as on weekends.
- Regularly provide information to parents about available high-quality organized sports opportunities. Ensure that information is responsive to parents' cultural and linguistic needs.
- Use technology to communicate regularly with parents.
- Encourage parents, including mothers, to become coaches.
- Hold year-end events for parents and their children to celebrate successes together. Ensure that every young person is recognized for her or his participation.

Promote youth involvement in program design.

- Provide opportunities for children and youth to have a voice in determining the activities of interest to them.
- Support teens' capacity for independent decision making while providing adult guidance.
- Give older youth increasingly responsible roles in the sports activities, including coaching younger children.

- Promote peer relationships and peer learning through group or team activities, including team decision making.

Take steps to avoid risky behaviors.

- Directly address the increased risk of alcohol abuse among athletes by offering alcohol and drug education, creating an alcohol-free pledge or policy or other strategies.

2. Improve Access to and Sustained Participation in High-Quality Programs Particularly for Under-Served Children and Youth: Girls, Low-Income Children, and Youth of Color.

Ensure that federal programs that support after-school activities are adequately funded and incorporate high-quality organized sports opportunities. Such programs include:

- 21st Century Community Learning Centers Program, which supports the creation of community learning centers that provide academic enrichment opportunities during nonschool hours, particularly for students who attend high-poverty and low-performing schools. The program allows schools and community-based organizations to offer a broad array of enrichment activities, which can include sports.
- Carol M. White Physical Education Program, which provides grants to local education agencies and community organizations for physical education, including after-school programs.

Increase the number of high-quality programs in low-income communities.

- Broaden the view of education to incorporate after-school sports and other activities as an essential component. Frame after-school programs as "extended learning" with choices available that include high-quality organized sports.

Place programs in sites that children and parents can reach easily and safely.

- Ensure that affordable, preferably free, school or public transportation is available to sports programs to return children and youth home after the programs are completed.
- Expand and improve or create new sports environments that protect children and youth from the risks of unsafe neighborhoods.

Address financial barriers that preclude participation by low-income children.

- Provide free participation or, if fees are required, make them minimal.
- If fees must be charged, programs should offer and publicize scholarships, sliding fee scales, work opportunities, and other strategies that make participation affordable for the children and teens of low-income families.

Recognize and address parents' needs and values.

- Educate parents about the benefits of sports participation, particularly for girls. Make the case that participation in organized and structured activities is beneficial to child and adolescent development and that participation is more about learning skills and connecting to academics than about competition.

- Strengthen teachers', staff's, and coaches' sensitivity to parents' cultural experiences, values, and belief systems as a way to help parents see the benefits of their children's participation in sports.

- Educate parents about what makes a quality program. Strategies may include regularly providing information highlighting effective programs, offering a checklist for parents that identifies the components of quality programs, or developing a community-wide resource bank that enables parents to match their children's needs.

- Engage parents through informational meetings and other outreach methods that encourage their attendance. Sessions that provide meals, child care, and programs that engage the whole family in activities can provide useful inducements for parents and other family members to participate. Highlighting stories of children who succeed may provide useful images that help parents connect participation with results.

- Identify enrollment policies that will accommodate the mobility of low-income, minority, and immigrant families.

Develop specific strategies to promote persistent and engaged participation.

- Design programs to promote continuity of participation over time.

- Develop strategies to keep girls from dropping out of sports activities. Focus on girls in middle school, with special attention to girls of color, who have the highest attrition rates.

3. Increase Investment in Research and Evaluation to Improve Program Quality and Opportunities for Participation.

- Create and highlight models of quality at program, school-district, and city levels and study and replicate them. Look at differences in populations in terms of what makes programs most effective in improving educational outcomes.

- Design research to study what coaches do to promote emotion regulation and academic success. Follow the same line of inquiry as research on how teachers promote a positive learning climate.

- Evaluate programs with specific interventions designed to promote persistence and engagement in sports-based youth development programs, with special attention to middle school girls.

- Continue to examine the issues surrounding selection bias.

- Identify the characteristics of effective programs that enable them to attract and retain youth from groups with lower participation and higher attrition rates, such as girls, youth of color, and youth in low-income communities.

The educational benefits arising from participation in supervised and structured sports activities indicate the importance of ensuring that all children, especially those for whom participation has been limited, have these opportunities. Furthermore, the opportunities in which all children participate should build in the kinds of experiences and practices that researchers have found make a difference to their learning and success. While millions of America's children participate regularly in sports, there are many who do not, especially among low-income children, children of color, and girls.

With such enormous potential residing in youth sports, it is critical to learn from the current knowledge base and continue to build it to help ensure that young people reap all the benefits possible from their participation.

A Review of Organized Youth Sport in the United States

By Jay Albrecht and Bradford Strand
Youth First: The Journal of Youth Sports, Spring 2010

Approximately 44 million girls and boys currently participate in organized youth sport programs across the United States (National Council of Youth Sports [NCYS], 2008). Youth sport programming today involves the state-sponsored and privately-funded educational institutions, club-sport organizations, sport-medicine clinics, and personal training programs (DiFiori, 2002). In many instances, the chance to be involved with any of these programs offers the youth sport participant opportunities to compete in a sport on a year-round basis. Indeed, approximately 75 percent of the youth participating in organized sport activity are involved in more than one activity, and in some cases, multiple seasons (NCYS, 2008).

The growth of organized youth sport in the United States has been, in part, shaped by historical, cultural, and societal events. An example of such an event was the creation of the Young Men's Christian Association (YMCA), initially established during the mid 1800s with hopes that young men involved with the Industrial Revolution would use physical activity and sport as an alternative to promiscuous behavior (Young Men's Christian Association, 2008). Another notable event encouraging youth sport participation during the latter half of the 20th century was the 1972 Title IX Educational Amendment—a legal ramification that propagated youth sport participation, creating equal opportunity for boys and girls to compete in the United States (Jennings, 1981).

Since its inception, organized youth sport has grown in the United States, but not without important, and at times, serious implications, many of which have surfaced and become more apparent in the past 20 years. The need for qualified coaches over the past two decades has quadrupled, which in some manner explains today's interest of approximately 2.4 million adults, often parents, actively involved with coaching organized youth sport (Barfield et al., 2003; Koester, 2000; Quain, 1989). Injury and medical costs in youth sport, the use of performance-enhancing drugs or nutritional supplements, burnout, parental misconduct, and the pressure to win have all become considerations requiring attention in what once was an activity organized simply for fun (Brady, 2004; Calfee and Fadale, 2006; Marsh and Daigneault, 1999; Metzl et al., 2001; Wuerth, Lee, and Alfermann, 2004).

An important question, however, is, "How did we arrive at this point in our society with organized youth sport?" Stahura and Apache (2005) offer solid suggestions that "sport is a phenomenon that has firmly embedded itself within our culture, if not our very existence" (p. 4). In many facets of society, we have come to a point of identifying ourselves with some aspect of sport, recreationally and socially. Sport labels and their respective associations have become a part of daily life, all in the name of what some view as a hallowed institution (Stahura and Apache, 2005). As the following discussion suggests, organized youth sport in the United States is a product of many different cultural factors and societal events. In light of these ongoing factors and events, it appears that the vitality of organized youth sport is here to stay.

The History of Youth Sport in the United States

The Late 1800s

The history of youth sport in the United States can be traced back to the late 19th century, a time when industrialization in the United States moved the leaders of our country to encourage children (primarily young boys) to play sports. The idea behind a movement referred to as "Muscular Christianity" advocated early Greek civilization attitudes of balancing the development of the body with the development of the mind and spirit (Wiggins, 1987). Young men were encouraged to be physically active and to develop their bodies through outdoor competitive and recreational play. The theory was that this activity would help instill ideals of group loyalty, national pride, and patriotism in the United States.

The Young Men's Christian Association (YMCA) was one of the first major volunteer-type organizations in the United States to support competitive youth sport programming vigorously. Organized in 1851 by Thomas Sullivan, the YMCA originally promoted Christianity and a mechanism of survival for young men who might otherwise fall prey to a life of ill-repute and/or alcoholism as they embraced life in the city versus that of their former lives on the farm (YMCA, 2008). Luther Halsey Gulick was noted as a pioneer leader for the YMCA organization, establishing a physical training program at the YMCA Training School in Springfield, Massachusetts. Gulick eventually formulated a graduate diploma in physical education (PE), emphasizing courses that included physiological psychology; the history, philosophy, and literature of PE; and anthropometry (Wiggins, 1987).

The Early 1900s

Gulick and his former mentor, G. Stanley Hall, developed a psychology-of-play course that they championed with their work in developing the theory of play. The theory of play and its concepts of preadolescent play mimicked what primitive men and women did millions of years ago to survive in a hostile environment. Running, chasing each other, and hurling objects developed the adolescent's physical and psychic well-being, while team sports played by older children (basketball, football, and baseball) helped foster ideas that emphasized cooperation and moral principles (Wiggins, 1987). Additionally, team sports helped young men develop their perceptions of self-sacrifice, obedience, self-control, and loyalty—desirable traits and characteristics that many feared were disappearing with the modernization of the world.

Gulick's theory of play was tested often in the early 1900s with the formation of New York City's Public School Athletic League (PSAL), an organization that offered every New York City boy an opportunity to participate in organized athletics on one of three different skill levels. These opportunities were available in both internal competitions and competitions between different schools. Sports for females were also included, but those were limited to the competitions within schools and were not available as competitions between schools (Wiggins, 1987).

Gulick's ideas and visions regarding the theory of play were incorporated into other movements toward youth sport during the early years of the twentieth century. By 1910, city playgrounds, along with citywide recreation programs, were developed in various communities around the United States. E.B. DeGroot, a prominent physical educator, was instrumental in developing a number of city parks in the Chicago area. These parks included large playgrounds, in addition to soccer, hockey, football, and swimming pool facilities. A colleague of Gulick and prominent physical educator of this same time in history, Clark Hetherington, established the "Demonstration Play School" at the University of California (Berkeley) in 1913—a school that provided play opportunities for children to develop physically, socially, emotionally, and morally. The school was very successful for some time, but ultimately closed in 1934 because of lack of funds and the Great Depression that occurred in the United States (Wiggins, 1987).

At approximately this same time in history, a few organizations began to follow the leads of Gulick, DeGroot, and Hetherington by establishing a variety of recreational and organized sport activities for children. These organizations were not in any way involved with the public school system, but rather were volunteer organizations, and some had the sponsorships of financially sound businesses that took control of organized youth sport with intentions of maintaining organized youth sports long into the future. The *Los Angeles Times* coordinated the first Junior Pentathlon in 1928; the Catholic Youth Organization initiated a junior tennis program in conjunction with the Southern California Tennis Association; Pop Warner started youth football programming with a four-team league in the city of Philadelphia; and last, but not least, Carl Stotz created Little League Baseball in 1939 (Wiggins, 1987).

The Mid-1900s

During the early 1930s, however, professional educators began discouraging organized youth sport and competitions for elementary and junior high children, arguing that organized sport was over-shadowing academics in the school systems. Additionally, E. D. Mitchell, a prominent physical educator of the time, stated that competitive sport and premature specialization in sport, as well as the potential accompanying notoriety, could be damaging physically and emotionally for children (Mitchell, 1932). This influential statement had an apparent major effect on the availability of youth sport in the educational systems around the country. In fact, until the early 1950s, many education leaders truly believed that rigorous sport competition took away from children's free-play activity, ultimately damaging their normal physical and mental development (Koester, 2002).

Nonetheless, despite the disbanding of organized sport in the public schools at the elementary level, a number of volunteer-organized youth sport groups, with the financial support of a variety of sources, continued to form, to exist, and in some cases, continually grow and thrive. In 1947, the United States Chamber of Commerce became involved with sponsorship of children's sports. A few years later, Biddy Basketball was established with the help of Jay Archer, the director of the Catholic Youth Center (Wiggins, 1987). Pony League Baseball incorporated in 1952, and approximately ten years later, the American Youth Soccer Association would plant its roots in Torrance, California. The Soccer Association for Youth would also be established in Ohio in 1967, the same year that the Junior Olympic Fencing Program was born. Two years later, the National Youth Sports Program (NYSP) was established to give organized sport opportunities to disadvantaged children, ages 10 to 16 years old. This particular organization was originally co-sponsored by the national government Office of Community Services and the National Collegiate Athletic Association (NCAA), and remained sponsored by those organizations until well into the early 1990s (Wiggins, 1987). In July of 1968, the Kennedy Foundation and the Chicago Park District joined forces to inaugurate the first ever International Special Olympics Competitions, hosting approximately 1000 mentally handicapped children from 26 different states and Canada, an event that eventually led all 50 states and Canada to form their own Special Olympic state organizations.

Competitive youth sport increased, both in program availability and in participation, during the middle part of the 20th century, mostly because parents believed the positive aspects of participation far outweighed the negative points. Specifically, parents valued the improved physical fitness, sportsmanship, and overall character development that accompanies youth sports. Adding to the appeal of youth sport involvement was the media coverage and attention given to those successful in professional sports. Parents and young athletes alike began to believe that early-age participation in youth sport might open some of those same doors of professional opportunities and notoriety. Women in the workforce, and the changing lifestyle of adults as a general matter, may have also contributed to the fast-paced growth of youth sports at this time in the US (Wiggins, 1987). More opportunities for leisure activities, especially those involving travel between communities and neighboring states, also helped contribute to expand opportunities for organized sport competition both regionally and nationally.

The Late 1900s

With the increased involvement of children in competitive sport came significant changes regarding gender involvement in sport. For most of the 20th century, competitive youth sport was set up for and played primarily by males. In the 1970s, some important events took place, paving the way for female prominence in sport as we know it today. The 1972 Title IX Educational Amendment became landmark legislation toward ending sexual discrimination in sport, requiring educators and education administrators to offer females of all ages more opportunities in sport. Billie Jean King's increased presence and domination on the women's professional tennis circuit during the early to mid-1970s championed her as a modern-day advocate for woman's rights, giving her the power to demand more prize money for women playing professional tennis. It was, however, the segregation and institutional ban of girls from Little League Baseball, along with the ensuing mid-1970 legal battles, that played a major part in allowing equal opportunities and involvement for females in competitive youth sport (Jennings, 1981).

Originally organized in 1939 in Williamsport, Pennsylvania, by Carl Stotz, Little League Baseball was a baseball program for young boys, ages 8 to12 years old. Often denied the chance to participate in competitive sport because of their size and age, young boys had an opportunity to play organized baseball through this program, which promoted qualities of citizenship, sportsmanship, and manhood. With the birth of the annual Little League World Series in 1947, Little League Baseball was literally established all over the United States. By the 1970s, Little League Baseball boasted approximately 2.5–3 million young participants. For many years, those participants, however, were only boys. In 1973, Little League Baseball was challenged in the courts by the Essex Chapter of the National Organization for Women (NOW) in Hoboken, New Jersey, based upon sexual discrimination against young female players. Specifically, Maria Pepe, a young girl who unsuccessfully attempted to join a Little League Baseball team in Hoboken, sued Little League Baseball based on sexual discrimination. The NOW persuaded the New Jersey Division of Civil Rights to hear a formal complaint on behalf of Miss Pepe and all girls ages 8 to12, who were being similarly denied the opportunity to play Little League Baseball in Hoboken and other areas of the United States (Jennings, 1981).

In March of 1974, the legal battle culminated with a New Jersey Supreme Court ruling that the Little League's National Charter, under which all local leagues organized their youth sport baseball programs, was a "place of public accommodation." The Court therefore determined that not allowing females an equal opportunity to play Little League Baseball was indeed a form of sex discrimination. Based upon the court's decision in the Pepe case, the Little League Baseball organization ordered all of its charter members to allow girls the opportunity to play baseball in their respective communities. Although this order was initially met with some resistance, Little League Baseball eventually became an equal opportunity sport for both boys and girls (Jennings, 1981).

Following the desegregation of Little League Baseball, the growth of competitive organized sport for both boys and girls across the United States was exponential, and with that growth came public awareness and scholarly attention. Professional educators, administrators, and physicians together improved general public awareness about youth sport with an increasing number of professional meetings, symposiums, and professional papers dedicated to the variety of sports available to the young athlete. The American Alliance for Health, Physical Education, Recreation, and Dance (AAHPERD), and the National Association for Physical Education in Higher Education (NAPEHE), and other national organizations improved the public awareness of children's sports by including various youth sport related topics in their respective annual conference events. Throughout the 1970s, numerous papers and books were published to enhance both the professional community's and the general public's knowledge regarding psychological, physiological, sociological, and motor development issues found in youth sport (Wiggins, 1987).

The studies and increased awareness led to more structured and official support for organized youth sport. In 1979, the North American Youth Sport Institute (NAYSI) and the National Council of Youth Sports Directors (NCYSD) were founded to promote and educate those involved with youth sport programming nationwide. Some of the organizations directly involved with the NCYSD included AAU Junior Olympics, American Youth Soccer Organization, Babe Ruth Baseball, the National Federation of State High School Associations, Pop Warner Football, USA Wrestling, and the YMCA (Wiggins, 1987).

Organized in 1981 with similar standards and objectives, the YMCA Youth Sports Training Programs and the National Youth Sports Coaches Association (NYSCA) also developed nationally-recognized programs promoting youth sport coaches training, official coaching certification programming, and research agendas to continually improve the guidelines and standards for youth sport coaches (Wiggins, 1987). Fred Engh, founder of the NYSCA, described that organization's philosophy as seeking to train volunteer coaches to handle the many intricacies of youth sports, including teaching sport-specific skills, dealing with psychological issues involved with youth sport, and providing first aid care and injury prevention guidelines (Quain, 1989).

In 1976, Dr. Rainer Martens, a renowned sports psychologist, founded the American Coaching Effectiveness Program (ACEP) and later expanding to what is known today as the American Sport Education Program (ASEP). The ASEP originally involved a series of summer short courses that emphasized prominent psychological issues in youth sport, sports medicine topics for youth sports, physiological aspects of youth sport, and finally instructional methods for youth sport coaches (Wiggins, 1987). This program has evolved over the years from offering scheduled classroom sessions with certified instructors at a variety of locations around the United States during various months of the year to coordinating online-course opportunities for today's youth sport coaches (American Sport Education Program, 2007).

Since the early 1970s, a number of publications have been written and disseminated praising or condemning competitive youth sport programming for children. These publications include articles in popular literature, research articles, and edited textbooks dealing with a variety of youth sport aspects, including coaching youth sport. The pros and cons of sports specialization; sport-based interventions for preventing alcohol and drug abuse, along with promoting life-long physical activity; facilitating youth sport via parks and recreation leadership and management; childhood and adolescent sports-related overuse injuries; management of sport-related concussion

For most of the 20th century competitive youth sport was set up for and played primarily by males. In the 1970s, some important events took place, paving the way for female prominence in sport as we know it today.

in young athletes; and coaching soccer for dummies merely hints at the wealth of available information (Bach, 2006; Brown and Branta, 1988; Cassas and Cassettari-Wayhs, 2006; Hecimovich, 2004; Martens, 2001; Patel, Shivdasani and Baker, 2005; Silva and Weinberg, 1984; Smoll and Smith, 1978; Spangler and Vinluan, 2006; Strand, 2006; Werch, et al., 2003). Whether one believes organized youth sport represents a key to building character and physical fitness in our children, or a distraction from academic success and free-play activity, one conclusion is inevitable and indisputable: organized youth sport is here to stay.

Formal and informal training programs must continue to be offered for youth sport coaches. Achieving these goals will require a balance of maximizing the positive aspects of organized youth sport while minimizing or, at least, mitigating the potentially negative ramifications of these activities. The implications of continued growth in organized youth sport are sometimes very apparent and clear, but at times, very subtle and dynamic. Apparent and clear implications can be represented by the continued growth in participation in organized youth sport and the obvious need for more resources to support that growth. Subtle yet dynamic implications might involve problems associated with psychological burnout from sport as a result of specialization in sport at a very young age, or problems associated with performance-enhancing drugs that adolescents may consider in light of the top-level competition pressures they face (Hecimovich, 2004; McGufficke, Rowling, and Bailey, 1990; Strand, 2006; Werch et al., 2003). In the end, the goal is for organized youth sport to represent, overall, a positive experience for the participants—a continued challenge for all who might be involved with organized youth sport today and into the future.

References

American Sport Education Program (2007). *ASEP's beginnings*. Retrieved June 18, 2007, from http://www.asep.com/about.cfm

Bach, G. (2006). *Coaching kids soccer for dummies*. Hoboken, NJ: Wiley Pub. Inc.

Barfield, W. R., Kirkendall, D. T., McBryde, A. M. and Padfield, J. A. (2003). Who can coach our youth in sports? *American College of Sports Medicine's Health and Fitness Journal*, 7(5), 10–14.

Brady, F. (2004). Children's organized youth sport: A developmental perspective. *Journal of Physical Education, Recreation, and Dance*, 75(2), 35–41.

Brown, E. W., and Branta, C. F. (1988). *Competitive sports for children and youth: An overview of research and issues*. Champaign, IL: Human Kinetics Publishers.

Calfee, R., and Fadale, P. (2006). Popular ergogenic drugs and supplements in young athletes. *Pediatrics*, 117, 577–589.

Cassas, K. J., and Cassettari-Wayhs, A. (2006). Childhood and adolescent sports-related overuse injuries. *American Family Physician*, 73, 1014–1022.

DiFiori, J. P. (2002). Overuse injuries in young athletes: An overview. *Athletic Therapy Today*, 7(6), 25–29.

Hecimovich, M. (2004). Sport specialization in youth: A literature review. *Journal of American Chiropractic Association*, 41(4), 32–41.

Jennings, S. E. (1981). As American as hot dogs, apple pie and Chevrolet; The desegregation of Little League baseball. *Journal of American Culture*, 4(4), 81–91.

Koester, M. C. (2000). Youth sports: A pediatrician's perspective on coaching and injury prevention. *Journal of Athletic Training*, 35, 466–470.

Koester, M. C. (2002). Adolescent and youth sports medicine: A "growing" concern. *Athletic Therapy Today*, 7(6), 6–12.

Marsh, J. S., and Daigneault, J. P. (1999). The young athlete. *Current Opinion in Pediatrics*, 11(1), 84–92.

Martens, R. (2001). Directing youth sports programs. Champaign, IL: *Human Kinetics Publishers*.

McGufficke, A., Rowling. L, and Bailey, M. (1990). Drug use by adolescent athletes. *Youth Studies Australia*, 9(3), 47–50.

Metzl, J. D., Small, E., Levine, S. R., and Gershel, J. C. (2001). Creatine use among young athletes. *Pediatrics*, 108, 421–425.

Mitchell, E. D. (1932). Trend in athletics in junior high schools. *The Journal of Health and Physical Education* (April), 22.

National Council of Youth Sports. *About NCYS*. Retrieved July 31, 2008, from http://www.ncys.org/about.html

National Youth Sports Safety Foundation. *Recent press releases*. Retrieved July 28, 2008, from http://www.nyssf.org/pressrelease.html

Patel, D. R., Shivdasani, V., and Baker, R. J. (2005). Management of sport-related concussion in young athletes. *Sports Medicine*, 35, 671–684.

Quain, R. J. (1989). An overview of youth coaching certification programs. *Adolescence*, 24, 541–547.

Silva, J. M., and Weinberg, R. S. (1984). *Psychological foundations of sport*. Champaign, IL: Human Kinetics Publishers.

Smoll, F. L., and Smith, R. E. (1978). *Psychological perspectives in youth sports*. New York: Hemisphere Publishing Corp.

Spangler, K., and Vinluan, M. H. (2006). Advocacy update: Facilitating youth sports. *Parks and Recreation*, July, 14–17.

Stahura, K. A., and Apache, R. R. (2005). Classic western understandings on the nature and origin of sport: From ancient Greece to virtual reality. *The Journal of Youth Sports*, 1(1), 4–7.

Strand, B. (2006). An analysis of sport participation and sport specialization. *The Journal of Youth Sports*, 2(1), 16–21.

Werch, C., Moore, M., DiClemente, C. C., Owen, D. M., Jobli, E., and Bledsoe, R. (2003). A sport-based intervention for preventing alcohol use and promoting physical activity among adolescents. *Journal of School Health*, 73, 380–388.

Wiggins, D. K. (1987). A history of organized play and highly competitive sport for American children. *Advances in Pediatric Sport Sciences*, 2, 1–24.

Wuerth, S., Lee, M. J., and Alfermann, D. (2004). Parental involvement and athletes' career in youth sport. *Psychology of Sport and Exercise*, 5, 21–33.

Young Men's Christian Association (2008). *History of the YMCA of the USA*. Retrieved August 24, 2008, from http://wwwspecial.lib.umn.edu/findaid/html/ymca/yusa003 4.phtml.

Gender in School Athletics

By Shelby L. Kinke Smith
Research Starters (EBSCO Publishing), 2008

Gender concerns entered into athletics during the 1970s through a combination of influences. The women's movement brought new attention to gender stereotypes and inequalities; the health and fitness movement encouraged girls and women to develop their physical strengths and abilities; and the passage of Title IX of the Educational Amendments mandated that public schools provide equal resources to male and female athletic programs. Today, more women and girls than ever participate in athletics. However, as budget cuts diminish schools' abilities to fund athletic programs, experts fear that private organizations, which are not subject to Title IX mandates, may fill the void, possibly leading to a resurgence of inequality. Female athletes, coaches, and athletic administrators are encouraged to advocate for women's and girls' sports amongst the wider culture, which may still harbor biases against women.

Overview

Athletic programs are often viewed as important components of the American educational system. These programs are valued for a variety of reasons, some of which include their capacities for developing character, providing opportunities for physical activity, and generating revenue and school pride. But beyond all these benefits, gender-related issues pervade athletics at all levels of participation, from elementary school sports to professional sports.

Gender Ideology

Gender inequities in athletic participation opportunities are rooted in the ideological beliefs and social structures of the dominant American culture. Ideological beliefs describe the system of ideas that characterize an individual or group, whereas a group's social structure is related to the "organization of opportunities and access to resources to take advantage of those opportunities" (Coakley, 2002, p. 253). Beliefs about women's and girl's athletic involvement are greatly informed by the dominant culture's beliefs about femininity (Coakley, 2002). Up until the early 1970s, females were encouraged to participate in graceful, "feminine" sports as opposed to those that required "masculine" traits such as strength, speed, and power (Coakley, 2002). However, since the 1970s countless women have demonstrated their strength, power, and speed by participating in sports like field hockey, lacrosse, and rugby (Coakley, 2002). These women have proved that they are fully able to participate in more physically demanding sports, and, accordingly, ideological beliefs about females and their involvement in athletics have changed.

The term *gender binary* describes the practice of classifying people according to their biological sex, a practice which, critics say, causes gender stereotypes (Coakley, 2002). By constraining men and women to masculine and feminine gender roles, the binary system does not allow space for people who feel or act in ways contrary to their assigned gender roles. Accordingly, these people, like women and girls who participate in "masculine" sports, are marginalized. Ideological beliefs about gender are thus perpetuated as these marginalized athletes receive inequitable opportunities and resources (Coakley, 2002). Sport sociologist, Coakley (2002) noted that, "gender equity cannot be achieved unless people challenge the binary gender classification system and begin to view those in the middle or gray area" (p. 266). In other words, a major cultural shift in ideological beliefs about gender is necessary to move closer to gender equity in athletics. Without an ideological shift, equity and fairness in athletics is not attainable.

Sport Socialization

Socialization is a "complex learning process that involves social development, cognitive processes and cultural beliefs, values, and practices" (Greendorfer, Lewko, and Rosengren, 2002, p. 153). Research suggests that socialization begins at an early age, and can impact whether or not a child will become involved in athletics or physical activity (Greendorfer, Lewko, and Rosengren, 2002).

The socialization process is influenced by cultural ideology and child rearing practices (Greendorfer et al., 2002). Families directly influence their children through a variety of ways including, for example, the types of toys they give them or the style of their bedroom decor. These influences can reproduce cultural messages about gender, such as what activities are gender appropriate, and ideas about masculinity and femininity, and superiority and inferiority (Greendorfer et al., 2002). This process is related to gender role stereotyping, which is defined as "a process in which a child's biological sex frequently determines which activities s/he will and will not be exposed to as well as the way (or manner) in which s/he will experience those activities" (Greendorfer, et al., 2002, p. 154). Research examining parents' influence on their children's motor skills development and participation in athletics and physical activity indicates that gender-based differentiations in parents' treatment of their infants affects the development of infants' motor skills. Also, as a result of socialization and cultural ideologies, there are gender differences in the sports in which boys and girls choose to participate. Most boys tend to participate in male sex-specific sports, whereas 20 percent of girls participate in male sports (Greendorfer et al., 2002).

History

School athletics participation opportunities for girls have been increasing since the early 1970s, before which these opportunities were virtually non-existent (Coakley, 2002). Athletic opportunities for girls and women came in the forms of new teams and activities for females; however, these opportunities were not always accompanied by sufficient funding or funding that was equal to boys' and men's athletic programs (Coakley, 2002). This inequality was rectified in 1972 with the passage of the now thirty-five-year-old Title IX of the Educational Amendments, which also led to an increase in female sports participation (Coakley, 2002). This legislation declared that "no person in the United States shall, on the basis of sex, be excluded from participation in, be denied the benefits of, or be subjected to discrimination under any educational program or activity receiving federal financial assistance" (Coakley, 2002). Title IX, as it is commonly known, required federally funded educational programs to follow certain mandates in order to create equal athletic opportunities for girls and women. The enforcement of Title IX was delayed five years as the existing sport establishment was resistant to sharing resources with programs for females (Coakley, 2002). As evidenced in the NFHS 2006–2007 participation survey results, Title IX has been a successful contributor to the creation of new athletic participation opportunities for women and girls. However, inequities still exist in the United States and at the international level (Coakley, 2002).

The women's rights movement (or women's lib movement) of the later tweintieth century has also been a factor in the development of new athletic participation opportunities for girls and women. Supporters of the movement believed that females are "enhanced as human beings when they develop their intellectual and physical abilities" (Coakley, 2002, p. 237). Over the years, this movement has encouraged women to pursue opportunities to be involved in athletics and physical education (Coakley, 2002). The women's rights movement is also linked with an increase in the number of women who pursue professional teaching certification in physical education and thus the number of female physical education teachers in the public school system.

The health and fitness movement has also impacted the number of opportunities for females to participate in athletics (Coakley, 2002). This movement upset the traditional feminine ideal which cast women into stereotyped gender roles and limited them to "feminine" sports like dancing, figure skating, and swimming. By touting the health benefits of physical activity, it has encouraged women and girls to seek out opportunities to engage in athletics and develop physical strength and competence, thus causing a shift in the feminine ideal (Coakley, 2002). The movement and its acceptance have coincided with an increase in the amount of media coverage of female sport and athletes (Coakley, 2002). The coverage of these sporting events sends the message that athletics are for women as well as men, perpetuating increased athletic participation among females.

Applications

Opportunities for Participation
The annual National Federation of State High School Associations Participation Survey obtains data on participation rates from all of its member schools in the

United States. The most recent Participation Survey results indicated that a record high number of girls participated in high school athletics during the 2006–2007 school year (NFHS, 2007). During this year, 7,342,910 students participated in school athletics, of which 3,021,807 were female. These results represent more than thirty years of legal, political, and social conflicts that have sought to gain equal and fair opportunities for girls and women to participate in athletics. Several factors have contributed to increased levels of female participation in athletics, some of which are Title IX, the women's rights movement, the health and fitness movement, and the increased media coverage of female sports (Coakley, 2002).

Gender Inequities

Despite the increase in types of opportunities for females, the financial resources afforded to female athletes and their programs are not at the same level as those afforded to male athletes and their programs (Coakley, 2002). Inequities in athletic programs associated with schools, community centers, and private programs can occur through unequal

- Access to facilities
- Quality of facilities
- Availability of scholarships[*]
- Program operating expenses
- Provision and maintenance of equipment and supplies
- Recruiting budgets[*]
- Scheduling of games and practice times
- Travel and per diem expenses
- Opportunities to receive academic tutoring[*]
- Numbers of coaches assigned to teams
- Salaries for administrators, coaches, trainers and other staff
- Provision of medical and training services and facilities
- Publicity for individuals, teams, and events

Viewpoints

Future Growth in Participation

While sport participation rates for girls and women have continually increased, sport sociologist Coakley (2002) suggests using caution when predicting future participation rates of women and girls in athletics for several reasons. Title IX was the impetus for an increase in athletic programs offered at the school level, yet some school districts may have to cut their athletic programs due to budget constraints. Budget cutbacks have, in some cases, led to the privatization of athletic programs.

---

[*] Applies primarily to American colleges and universities (Coakley, 2002, p. 253).

Unlike public school programs, these private programs are not responsible for meeting Title IX mandates. If school-age athletic programs are shifted to the private sector, these private organizations may or may not choose to provide equitable athletic programs for girls and women. This trend could lead to stagnant future growth in the number of females participating in athletics. Coakley (2002) also notes the resistance from the status quo as being a barrier to future increases in female participation. Coakley (2002) states, "[T]hose

> *Budget cutbacks have, in some cases, led to the privatization of athletic programs. Unlike public school programs, these private programs are not responsible for meeting Title IX mandates.*

who benefit from the status quo often resist government legislation that mandates change" (p. 247).

Another barrier to continued growth is the backlash from groups and individuals who resent changes that favor women who are more likely to challenge the gender ideologies (Coakley, 2002). The specific content of gender ideologies vary from culture to culture, but all "influence how we think of ourselves and others, how we relate to others and how social life is organized at all levels, from families to societies" (Coakley, 2002, p. 263). A challenge to American gender ideologies may change the status quo and create power shifts even in the realm of athletics.

Despite the increases in female participation in sports over the last three decades, there is still an underrepresentation of women in decision-making positions within sport administration and coaching roles (Coakley, 2002). With a lack of women in positions of power, the future of athletic opportunities for women and girls could be at risk as sports for females are often trivialized (primarily at the collegiate, amateur, and professional levels) by individuals who believe that sports are for males.

The final barrier or cause for tentative prediction of future participation rates is homophobia and its concomitant tendency of labeling female athletes as lesbians (Coakley, 2002). Coakley (2002) suggested that "parents may steer children away from sports that they believe attract lesbians and away from teams or programs where lesbians are believed to play or coach" (p. 249). Similarly, heterosexual women may hesitate to participate in athletics or be defensive about their participation because of the threat of being labeled a lesbian (Coakley, 2002).

Equitable Funding and Resources

Title IX has helped to decrease the gap between the resources provided for female programs and those offered to male programs, yet inequities still exist in athletic programs. Title IX and the changing views of female sports have also led to inequities in the coaching and administration of female athletics. As programs for females have become more important and prevalent in American sport culture, the number of women in coaching or administrative roles has decreased drastically (Coakley, 2002). In 1972, 90 percent of women's collegiate athletic programs were administered by women; however, by 2002 only 18 percent of women's programs were administered by women, and 19 percent had no female administrators (Coakley, 2002). Coakley (2002) offers several causes of women's underrepresentation in coaching and administrative positions within sport (p. 255):

- Men use their established connections to help them during the job search and hiring process, whereas women tend not to have the same professional connections and networks.

- The subjective criteria used by search committees may often leave women looking less qualified than the male applicants.

- Support systems and professional development opportunities are limited for women seeking a career in athletic coaching and administration.

- Women may carry the perception that athletic programs have corporate cultures that do not allow much space for individuals who see and think about sports differently than men.

- Sport organizations are seldom organized to be sensitive to the family responsibilities of coaches and administrators.

- Sexual harassment is more likely to be anticipated and experienced by women than by men.

Proponents of athletic equality still face challenges from individuals who support equity in theory, but who are not willing to sacrifice their privileges to effect equality (Coakley, 2002). The Women's Sports Foundation serves as an advocate for women and girls in athletics. The Women's Sports Foundation administration suggests several strategies for sport groups or administrators seeking organizational equality. These strategies focus on public relations, political lobbying, pressure, education, and advocacy (Lopiano, 1991, as cited by Coakley, 2002). These strategies encourage individuals to:

- Confront any discriminatory practices that occur within their organizations;

- Serve as advocates for fair and open employment practices;

- Keep track of gender equity data from their organizations and have independent groups issue a gender equity report card every year to local media outlets;

- Spread awareness and educate others about recognizing discrimination;

- Refuse to support policies that could negatively impact women's and girls' sports participation;

- Promote women's athletics as programs capable of producing revenue;

- Recruit women into coaching, provide professional development opportunities for young, female professionals, and utilize women's hiring networks when conducting hiring searches; and

- Focus on developing a supportive climate for women, and establish policies to eliminate sexual harassment (Lopiano, 1991, as cited by Coakley, 2002).

Conclusion

Gender, Sport Participation, and Academic Performance

Though research has been conducted to examine the relationship between high school sport participation and educational outcomes (including academic performance), so the data has been inconclusive (Miller, Melnick, Barnes, Farrell, and Sabo, 2005). Several variables have been examined including gender, race, athletic identity, and participation status (Miller et al., 2005). Specific to gender, findings have suggested that female athletes have the highest grade point averages (Miller et al., 2005). In a discussion of this finding, Miller and her colleagues (2005) cited the developmental perspective that through participating in sport, athletes have the opportunity to develop skills, habits, and values that are transferable to the academic realm because sport integrates these students in the network of peers and adults that provides incentives for the student to remain in school, and achieve academic success and commitment.

Scholastic athletic programs provide students with opportunities to engage in school-related extra-curricular activities. While these programs should be appropriately equitable and in compliance with Title IX, there are still inequities in how programs are viewed, managed, and coached. Cultural beliefs and gender ideologies about the importance and types of programs for girls often underlie decisions about the types of programs offered students, what program needs may or may not be, and who should be coaching a team. A major cultural shift is needed to effect large gains toward equity and fairness in sports programs. Without a cultural shift, the basic mandates of Title IX will be met with a minimal emphasis on continued growth, opportunity, and support for everyone involved in athletics.

Bibliography

Coakley, J. *Sport in Society: Issues and Controversies*. 8th ed. Boston: McGraw, 2004. Print.

Greendorfer, S. L., Lewko, J. H., and Rosengren, K. S. "Family and Gender-Based Influences in Sport Socialization of Children and Adolescents." *Children and Youth and Sport: A Biopsychological Perspective*. Ed. F.L. Smoll and R.E. Smith. Dubuque: Brown, 2002. Print.

Miller, K. E., Melnick, M. J., Barnes, G. M., Farrell, M. P., and Sabo, D. "Untangling the Links Among Athletic Involvement, Gender, Race, and Adolescent Outcomes." *Sociology of Sport Journal* 22.2 (2005): 1780–93. EBSCO Academic Search Complete. Web. 16 October 2007. http://search.ebscohost.com/login.aspx?direct=true&db=a9h&AN=17323502&site=ehost-live.

National Federation of State High School Associations. *High School Sports Participation Increases Again; Girls Exceed Three Million for the First Time*. NFHS.

2007. Web. 7 October 2007. http://www.nfhs.org/web/2007/09/high%5fschool%5f sports%5fparticipation.aspx.

Theberge, N. *Higher Goals; Women's Ice Hockey and the Politics of Gender.* Albany: SUNY P, 2000. Print.

Whannel, G. *Media Sport Stars: Masculinities and Moralities.* London: Routledge, 2002. Print.

Youth Sports Can Be Expensive, but They Aren't Played by Just the Wealthy

By Dave Barber
Bangor Daily News, May 9, 2012

Baxter Cole, the young son of Charles Cole of Bangor, repeatedly told his father he wanted to play youth hockey.

The cost of such an undertaking can be daunting for youth sports that involve a lot of potentially expensive equipment.

"To be honest, we stayed away from it for a couple of years because of the financial obligation," Charles Cole said.

Baxter kept asking, though, and last fall Cole relented.

"I try to give kids all the opportunity to try whatever they're interested in," said Cole, who grew up playing hockey in Bangor in the 1970s. "His friends were playing, so he wanted to play."

Cole registered Baxter, now 8, in Bangor Youth Hockey's mites program for children ages 6 to 8 years old.

What Cole found was that there are a number of ways that youth sports groups help parents cover or reduce their costs.

And parents find ways to help each other through carpooling to tournaments and getting together to swap equipment that has the potential to be expensive.

"Baxter's skates, he's probably the third person to use them," said Cole. "We'll probably pass them on to someone else. That saves a lot."

Cole added, "It's not just the wealthy few who are playing hockey."

A mother of four, Lee'Ann Wells of Bangor knew she wanted to involve her children in activities outside the home.

Wells and her now ex-husband started their sons DeAndre, now 14, and Dillan, 10, and daughters Isabella, 12, and Julia, 6, in gymnastics at 18 months.

After a couple of years, they were old enough to look into other sports.

"On military bases, you can start playing team sports at 4 years old," she said.

The Wellses are both soccer enthusiasts, so it was natural to steer the kids that way, she said.

Since then, DeAndre has also started studying mixed martial arts, Isabella has picked up horseback riding and piano and Julia is also a swimmer. Only Dillan is just playing soccer.

Costs Can Be Daunting

When the Wells family arrived in Bangor four years ago, the children started joining Bangor Soccer Club, a nonprofit recreational organization for children from age 4 through eighth grade.

The cost for the six-week Bangor Soccer Club spring program is $40 for residents and $45 for nonresidents.

A set of travel programs divided according to age and ability is conducted by Blackbear United Football Club, based in Bangor. Some Bangor Soccer Club participants, including the Wellses, gravitate toward Blackbear United for the higher level of competition.

A full Blackbear program such as High School Academy is $225 per eight-week session. When a child registers for all three sessions, the cost drops to $600.

The top Blackbear program, Premier, is $775 for the session, which started its season December 6 and runs through June 14.

"We didn't even consider travel soccer. We thought it was way too expensive," Wells said.

Cole said his re-introduction to hockey was "a bit of an eye-opener."

"The [cost of the] uniform, the price of skates, then you add in the cost of travel, hotel stays and food," said Cole.

The total ice hockey equipment that families are responsible for consists of skates, a helmet with face cage, shin guards, elbow pads, gloves, hockey pants, shoulder pads and jock shorts plus the bag to carry it all and a stick.

Local sporting goods retailers are sensitive to families' initial shock. Gunn's Sport Shop in Brewer offers a package to youngsters in Learn-to-Skate programs. If they or their parents buy any five of those items, including the bag, they qualify for a 25 percent discount.

"It's $225 [tax included] for the whole package," said Mike Merritt, manager of Gunn's.

Gunn's carries mostly entry-level to mid-level new equipment, according to Merritt. And they might be able to order equipment they don't regularly carry. Gunn's also sells some used equipment on consignment, and allows old skates to be traded in toward new ones.

Cole found that football, which Baxter also plays, doesn't cost as much as hockey.

"The majority of the equipment is owned by Bangor Youth Football," said Cole. The family is responsible for the cleats, a mouthguard and other personal gear.

And the fee for Baxter to play flag football was $30. Full-contact football is $75. His hockey registration was $300 with another $250 for the Mighty Mites travel program.

For Little League baseball, costs are on a par with football.

Travel Adds to the Burden

Traveling is a major cost in sports such as soccer, ice hockey and basketball, with weekend trips for in-state matches as well as in-state and out-of-state tournaments.

"You're easily talking on a trip to, say, Kents Hill, it's $40 to $50 for gas, probably, and by the time the day's over, it's close to $75 to $100," said Cole.

That's one of the shorter trips. And it's not just once.

"That's every other weekend," said Cole. "It adds up over the course of a season."

Other hockey trips can be more far flung, including Presque Isle, Canada, and Massachusetts.

"Through the year, you continually get advice from parents where to eat, where to get the cheapest gas and the best hotel for the price," said Cole.

Paying for It All

Youth organizations offer supplemental funding opportunities as a way of reducing costs and increasing participation.

Scott Bussiere, fundraising coordinator for the former Auburn Youth Hockey (it's merging with Lewiston Area Youth Hockey League for next season), said calendars have been their biggest moneymaker.

Half of the $10 sale price for each calendar goes to the association and half goes toward the player's assessment, said Bussiere. Their annual fee for mites is $650; for squirts (ages 9–10), peewees (11–12) and bantams (13–14), it's $700.

"Parents know if they sell 100 [calendars], they get $500 back off their assessment," he said.

They can also win prizes donated by local businesses.

The Maine Coast Skaters Association out of Rockport has the Hat Trick Auction Dinner as its big fundraiser, which it puts on with the Camden Hills Windjammers' high school team and the Midcoast Ice Cats. That dinner raised more than $130,000 in its first six years and now has an annual goal of $30,000.

Cole is excited by his son's fundraising opportunities.

"I think [Baxter] paid off his entire Mighty Mites bill through selling wreaths," said Cole.

Scholarships are often available, also, and many, if not all, youth sports groups offer some form of financial aid.

Wells also volunteers at Blackbear United for partial payment of her bill and referees, too.

"[Cost] is an issue, but we work it out," Wells said.

Is It Worth It?

Wells guesses that the cost for her kids' participation in soccer runs $1,500–$1,700 a year.

> *Traveling is a major cost in sports such as soccer, ice hockey and basketball, with weekend trips for in-state matches as well as in-state and out-of-state tournaments. "You're easily talking on a trip to, say, Kents Hill, it's $40 to $50 for gas, probably, and by the time the day's over, it's close to $75 to $100," said Cole.*

"That's uniforms, shoes. … And that's not including any volunteer work I may do," she said.

When her children want something extra, they have to do a chore over and above what they already do.

Cole said of his family's expenses, not including what Baxter earned through fundraising, "It's easily over $1,000 and that's being pretty thrifty."

It's a lot, but then they look at what they get for their money.

"[Baxter] needs that outlet, that physical activity," said Cole.

Wells sees other benefits as well.

"I love that they know they're not going to get something for free," she said. "It's good life lessons all the way around."

Youth Olympic Games: From Vision to Success

By Ng Ser Miang
Sports Journal, April 1, 2011

Introduction

When Pierre de Coubertin revived the Olympic Games in 1894, he sought to do more than just create a modern sporting competition. He founded the Olympic Movement as an education movement, believing that sport would contribute to the harmonious and well-balanced development of the body, mind and character, and helped create a more peaceful and better world. It is the convergence of sport, culture and education that defines the concept of Olympism and the modern Olympic Movement. It is therefore my pleasure and privilege to share with you the Youth Olympic Games, a new creation that truly epitomizes the spirit of the modern Olympic Movement.

The Youth Olympic Games (YOG) is the brainchild of Dr. Jacque Rogge, the President of the International Olympic Committee (IOC). The vision and the concept of the YOG were deliberated at great length by the IOC Executive Board and the IOC members. The 119th IOC Session held in Guatemala in 2007 unanimously approved the creation of the YOG.

Vision

It is the vision of the IOC that the YOG will inspire the youths of the world to take part in sports and adopt and live the Olympic Values of Excellence, Friendship and Respect.

IOC President Jacque Rogge envisaged that the YOG, and I quote, "...is the flagship of the IOC's determination to reach out to young people. These games will not only be about competition. They will also be the platform through which youngsters will learn about the Olympic values and the benefits of sport, and will share their experiences with other communities around the globe."

The Concept

The concept of the YOG called for the participation of the world's top young athletes in Games with equal emphasis on sports, culture and education. For the Summer Youth Olympic Games, 3,600 athletes would compete in 26 Olympic sports, stay together for a full 12 days and take part in culture and education programs created especially for them. The host city would make use of existing sports facilities and accommodation. The standard and service level would be different from that of the standard Olympic Games.

The Inaugural Games

The Inaugural Games attracted a lot of interests from around the world. On Sept. 3, 2007, the IOC announced that 11 cities,[1] including Singapore, had indicated their intention to bid for the first YOG.

In November 2007, after the preliminary evaluation of the IOC, the competition was narrowed down to five cities—Singapore, Turin, Moscow, Bangkok and Athens—from nine cities. In January 2008, this was further reduced to Singapore and Moscow, following a video conference between the cities and the IOC Evaluation Commission.

On February 21, 2008, the IOC President declared Singapore as the winning city to host the inaugural YOG in 2010. Singapore beat Moscow by 53 to 44 votes.

Co-constructing the Inaugural Games

Singapore had just about two and half years to organize the Inaugural Games. The Singapore Youth Olympic Games Organizing Committee (SYOGOC) had worked hand in glove with the IOC, the 26 International Sports Federations, 205 National Olympic Committees and different stakeholders to co-construct this very first Games. In particular, it was a special challenge in designing the Culture and Education program, which was the defining element of these Games.

SYOGOC's mission was to create an inspiring and memorable experience for all participants, while establishing an enduring legacy for Singapore and the Olympic movement.

In the two and a half years leading up to the YOG, and during the YOG, Singapore implemented a series of programs[2] with integrated sports and educational and cultural elements to connect the young people with the Olympic values and one another. SYOGOC saw this engagement important before, during and after the Games.

YOG participants experienced Singapore 2010's programs in four ways:

1. Learning through workshops, forums, and events and taking part in various projects;

2. Contributing to causes and communities to appreciate how the Olympic values can help improve the lives of others;

3. Interacting through competition that is friendly and mutually respectful, living in the Youth Olympic Village, encountering new cultures, sports and communities and making new friends; and

4. Celebrating together the diversity of the Olympic Movement, in which many cultures are united through their common adherence to the Olympic values of excellence, friendship and respect.

Olympic Education

As an important legacy of the YOG, the Ministry of Education in Singapore and the Singapore Olympic Academy produced and launched the Olympic Education Resource Package in December 2008 for all the schools in Singapore. Henceforth, Olympic education became entrenched in Singapore's education system.

Journey of the Youth Olympic Flame

For these very first Games, the IOC Executive Board had given approval for the Flame of the YOG to travel across the five continents, stopping at one continent where athletes and young people of the continent will gather for a celebration and herald the arrival of the Youth Olympic Games. To me, it was an important proposal of SYOGOC to promote YOG and the Games in Singapore. Hundreds of thousands of youth and people around the world participated in the Journey of the Youth Olympic Flame and there were many magical moments.

> *"You will learn the difference between winning and being a champion. To win, you merely have to cross the finish line first. To be a champion, you have to inspire admiration for your character, as well as for your physical talent."*

Sizzling Performances during the Games

Through the 12 days of the Youth Olympic Games in Singapore, from Aug. 14 to 26, 2010, we witnessed sizzling sports performances from the young athletes, not only in their events, but also in mixed team events comprising boys and girls of mixed nationalities within the teams. The bold call for the Games to go beyond sports did not in any way dilute the quality of the sporting competition. In fact, in some instances the Games have brought to the fore some of the world's biggest young stars, many of whom are expected to achieve even greater marks in sport in the future. Despite the competition, the athletes embraced the Olympic ideals of Excellence, Friendship and Respect. As an athlete from Trinidad put it, and I quote, "At the starting line everyone wished each other good luck; it was like one big family."

The sport competition also taught the athletes valuable lessons, which they will remember for life, as an athlete from Gabon, Jessica Oyane, said: "Through this competition, I have seen my weaknesses and what I need to improve. I will work harder to show the people of Gabon that I am doing my best, and make them proud."

Culture and Education Program

For the first time in Olympic history, all athletes remained for the entire period of the Games where an extensive range of activities was organized for them to live together, and learn and understand one another through the Culture and Education Program (CEP). The CEP focused on 5 key themes of Olympism: Skills Development, Well-Being, Healthy Lifestyle, Social Responsibility and Expression.

Singapore 2010 produced the world's first batch of Young Olympians influenced with the belief that sport is not just about winning, but being a champion in life.

As Dr. Jacque Rogge, IOC President put it, and I quote, "You will learn the difference between winning and being a champion. To win, you merely have to cross the finish line first. To be a champion, you have to inspire admiration for your character, as well as for your physical talent."

Making History

The IOC President has said that the Inaugural YOG was a huge success and beyond his highest expectations. The Young Olympians, the National Olympic Committees and the International Federations were all extremely happy and satisfied with the Games. Young people from around the world were actively involved in making the Games a great success whether working in the Singapore Youth Olympic Games Organizing Committee, as Chef De Mission, as coaches or team officials, as contributors to the Culture and Education Program, or as Young Ambassadors or simply as spectators. There were many innovations and new ideas in sports, such as the 3-on-3 basketball, mixed and continental teams that went beyond sport competitions to promote Olympic Values and understanding. The Young Olympians competed head-on against one another in their sport and came together as teammates and friends in the CEP, discussing issues critical to them, such as the fight against doping, health and the environment.

These are the significant successes for sport, the Organizing Committee and the IOC.

This is just the beginning. This YOG will be an inspiration for generations to come. Connected through sports and by bonds of friendship, these young people will help to build a more peaceful and harmonious world. We are all part of this legacy, by living the Olympic values in our lives.

References

1. The 10 other cities were Algiers (Algeria), Athens (Greece), Bangkok (Thailand), Belgrade (Serbia), Debrecen (Hungary), Guatemala City (Guatemala), Kulau Lumper (Malaysia), Moscow (Russian Federation), Poznan (Poland) and Turin (Italy).
2. These programs fall within five groups: Pre-Games Engagement Program (involving twinning of all Singapore schools to some 200 National Olympic Committees); Sports Program (featuring all 26 Summer Olympic sports); Culture and Education Program (special modules designed for the young athletes in the areas of Sports Issues, Global Issues, World Culture, Community Involvement, Adventure); Youth Olympic Village (with lively exhibition and performance spaces for the young athletes); and New Media (wide use of new media platforms to promote connectivity among the youth of the world before, during and after the YOG.

2
Gender and Title IX

Moravian's Brittany Onesto and Kyleigh McGovern of Liberty fight for the ball in a high school lacrosse match.

Title IX, Women, and Sports

Part of a package of federal legislation known as the Education Amendments of 1972, Title IX is a law that requires gender equality in any education program that receives federal funding. Though the law applies to many different types of programs, including career education, education for pregnant and parenting students, standardized testing, math and science, and technical education, the most famous result of Title IX was the promotion of gender equality in educational athletic programs. Over more than forty years of implementation, Title IX has been one of the most controversial legislative issues in sports, and many critics still feel that Title IX restrictions cause unnecessary reductions in funding for male athletics. Despite objections, the program has been successful in increasing educational and athletic opportunities for female students.

Origins of Title IX

The 1964 law known as Title VII, part of the Civil Rights Act, prohibits discrimination in employment based on race, gender, or religious beliefs. In its original form, Title VII did not mention "sex" or "gender," and it was not until the National Organization for Women pressured President Lyndon B. Johnson to issue an executive order in 1967 that gender discrimination was expressly prohibited in hiring practices.

Even though Title VII addressed discrimination in the workplace, women still faced discrimination within educational institutions, which continued to utilize discriminatory policies to determine admission, access to certain educational programs, and the allocation of resources. Women's rights activists felt that a separate law was needed to extend the protections guaranteed under Title VII to American educational institutions.

In 1970, US representatives Edith Green and Patsy Mink worked with women's rights activist Bernice Sandler, who had filed several lawsuits against the US Department of Education citing violations of Title VII within American universities, to draft a version of a bill that would require educational institutions to abide by Title VII standards. Indiana senator Birch Bayh, who was also involved in a number of other antidiscrimination legislative efforts, became the primary Senate sponsor of the bill that became known as Title IX, which expressly forbids sex and gender discrimination in any university program that received federal funding. Senator Bayh introduced the bill to the Senate in February 1972.

Title IX was signed into law in June 1972 and was not considered particularly controversial. The wording of Title IX is generalized, and there was no specific mention of athletics, though the funding of athletic programs became the most controversial aspect of the law. It was only after Title IX was adopted that controversy emerged regarding the implementation of the law and its potential effects on funding for athletic programs, which were at the time focused on male athletes. Despite being famous for its effects on women's athletics, Title IX has also been important in increasing science and mathematics education for women and in protecting the rights of pregnant students to pursue educational goals.

Challenges in Implementation

As collegiate sports organizations began to realize the potential implications of Title IX, there were legislative efforts proposed to protect the existing funding structure for athletic programs. The first major challenge to the law was proposed by Senator John Tower, who wanted to create an exemption for athletic programs that produced revenue. The proposed Tower Amendment was rejected in Congress, and the Javits Amendment, proposed by Senator Jacob Javits, was adopted in its place, calling for reasonable consideration in regulations to be given to each sport. Under Title IX, federally funded organizations were not required to provide "equal" funding to athletic programs for men and women, but rather to provide equality in opportunity and in the quality of educational options offered to both sexes.

In 1979, the Department of Health, Education, and Welfare finalized the requirements for Title IX compliance in collegiate institutions and introduced three primary methods by which a university could comply with the standards of the law, a system that became known as the "three-prong test." According to this system, an institution was seen as complying with Title IX if it could demonstrate any one of the following: that it was providing athletic participation opportunities that were equal for both genders, according to undergraduate enrollment demographics; that there was a continual expansion of athletic programs for the underrepresented sex; or that it was fully accommodating the interests and abilities of the underrepresented sex.

After oversight of Title IX was transferred to the Office for Civil Rights (OCR) in 1980, there was a considerable lack of aggressive enforcement. In 1984, the Supreme Court ruled in the case of *Grove City College v. Bell* that Title IX did not apply generally to entire educational institutions but only to programs that were directly tied to federal funds. Women's athletics organizations objected to this ruling, arguing that educational institutions would then adjust their athletic programs so as to avoid needing to provide substantially equal funding for women's sports. A coalition of women's rights activists and congressional leaders passed the Civil Rights Restoration Act of 1988, overriding a presidential veto from Ronald Reagan; the act specifically outlawed gender discrimination in any institution, if any part of the institution received federal funding.

One of the last major changes to Title IX regulations came after the Supreme Court case of *Franklin v. Gwinnett County Public Schools*, in which the Court ruled that litigants were allowed to seek monetary damages from schools that failed to meet Title IX requirements, despite previous local and appellate court rulings that Title IX did not specify such. Title IX supporters cite the 1992 ruling in *Franklin v. Gwinnett County* as an important step, providing potentially damaging monetary consequences for institutions that failed to adhere to the law.

Another major step associated with implementation of Title IX came with an amendment to the Elementary and Secondary Education Act of 1994, which required universities and high schools to release all information regarding their spending on athletic programs. Prior to this amendment, colleges and high schools were not required to release this information; thus, it was difficult for women's rights organizations to determine precisely how each institution was attempting to address Title IX funding requirements.

Success and Importance of Title IX

Prior to Title IX, few athletic opportunities were available to women in educational institutions, and women were not often able to obtain scholarship assistance based on athletic merit. In 1972, according to the Department of Health, Education, and Welfare, there were 31,852 women participating in collegiate athletics (as compared to 170,526 male athletes). This figure includes women who attended women-only universities and those involved in cheerleading and other activities that were then considered traditional female athletics. Since the implementation of Title IX, women's and girls' athletics participation has shown marked growth each decade. For instance, according to the National Federation of State High School Associations, in 2010, there were more than 3.2 million women involved in high school athletic programs (as compared to 295,000 in 1972). According to the National Collegiate Athletic Association (NCAA), women have also increased their representation in collegiate athletics, from 74,000 in 1982 to more than 193,000 in 2011.

In addition to attracting more women to sports, Title IX provisions have increased the variety of athletic programs available to women. While women were generally filtered into a small number of athletic programs in the 1970s—such as dancing, cheerleading, softball, and soccer—women's baseball, basketball, hockey, and other sports have received significant support as a result of Title IX regulation. The provisions of Title IX that call for "equal quality" have resulted in an overall increase in the quality of women's athletics facilities, whereas pre-1972 investigations revealed that high schools and colleges invested far less in the training staff, equipment, and environmental facilities offered to female athletes.

According to the 2008 study "Women in Intercollegiate Sport," the five most frequently offered women's sports in the collegiate environment were basketball (more than 98.8 percent of schools offer women's basketball teams), volleyball (95.7), soccer (92.0), cross-country (90.8), and softball (89.2). There has also been an increase in the percentage of athletic scholarships given to women, though female athletes still receive far fewer scholarship opportunities than male athletes. Some studies have indicated that the increase in women's athletics have had peripheral benefits on the educational and health statuses of American women, resulting in lower obesity rates in the high school and college populations, increased educational attainment overall, and reduced college dropout rates among women.

During a 2012 speech to commemorate the fortieth anniversary of Title IX, President Barack Obama described the historic legislation as an important step in gender equality in the United States and emphasized the importance of the continued effort to promote equality in educational and athletic benefits. President Obama also remarked that he shared the belief that the psychological and sociological benefits of Title IX expanded beyond allowing equality in sports participation to helping inculcate in generations of young women in the United States the idea that they are free to pursue achievement in any field.

Continued Inequities in the Twenty-First Century

Estimates indicate that female high school athletes are offered approximately 1.3 million fewer opportunities than their male counterparts. At the collegiate level, women have sixty thousand fewer opportunities to become involved in athletics. While women make up more than 53 percent of the population at NCAA schools, only 43 percent of athletes are women; also, female sports programs receive a disproportionately smaller share of athletics revenues than male programs do. For instance, it has been estimated that women's athletic programs receive only 41.4 percent of the funding for head coaches and peripheral staff and receive only 36 percent of recruiting funds. While some argue that women simply have lower levels of interest in athletics participation, studies indicate that female sports programs receive proportionately lower levels of funding even if adjusted to account for differing levels of interest.

A number of journalists and women's athletics advocates have also called attention to the fact that Title IX developments have led to a decline in women coaches and athletic directors as more women have become involved in student athletics. In 1972, more than 90 percent of women's sports coaches were women, whereas only 43 percent of women's sports coaches were women in 2012. Some argue that, as funding has increased for women's athletics, the male-dominated sporting community has promoted a greater number of male coaches in pursuit of this funding rather than supporting the training and hiring of female coaching staff.

Title IX Controversies

The most significant controversy surrounding Title IX regards the three-prong system of compliance, which some critics believe is prejudiced against male athletes. According to this argument, forcing educational institutions to engage in proportional spending reduces the funding that would otherwise be available to male athletes and causes some institutions to reduce the number of sports offered to the male population. Some critics of Title IX argue that males have a higher interest in sports than women do and should therefore receive a greater proportion of athletics funding without suffering from Title IX regulations and potential penalties.

In 2005, with the approval of then-president George W. Bush, the "Additional Clarification of Intercollegiate Athletics Policy" was added to the official OCR policy on Title IX regulations. According to the "additional clarifications," the burden was placed on female athletes and female athletics organizations to demonstrate the desire and need for further funding for female athletic programs. Critics of Title IX supported this policy change because they believed it addressed the issue of "differing interest" between the sexes and allowed institutions to defend placing greater emphasis on male athletics than on female sports.

In 2010, the Obama administration directed the OCR to remove the additional clarification policy, thereby forcing institutions to prove compliance by returning to equal opportunities for all students. That same year, the US Commission on Civil Rights recommended altering the existing three-prong system by increasing efforts to gauge athletic interest among both male and female populations through web and direct surveys of students; the results of these measurements would be used to determine whether a university or high school was taking appropriate steps to address Title IX requirements.

Despite the widely held belief that Title IX enforcement has caused a reduction in athletic opportunities for male athletes, studies of high school, college, and university athletic departments indicate that athletic opportunities for both sexes have increased since the passage of Title IX, as has the diversity of athletic opportunities across gender lines. In addition, objections to the three-prong system are often erroneously based on the belief that the OCR requires a "gender quota" from schools that wish to receive federal funding. Though schools must increase their focus on maintaining equality of opportunity, there are no specific quotas required for Title IX compliance. Issues regarding different levels of interest are currently unclear, and it is hoped that better survey systems may help to address some of the most common criticisms of the Title IX system.

40 Years Later, Title IX Is Still Fighting Perception It Hurt Men's Sports

By Gloria Goodale
Christian Science Monitor, June 23, 2012

Mention Title IX and most people think of its impact on college athletic programs, primarily, say coaches, because it is blamed for cuts in men's sports. Supporters say that's a bum rap.

Say "Title IX"—the landmark gender equality legislation marking its 40th anniversary June 23—and most folks these days will respond, "sports."

While this "little statute"—one small provision in an omnibus education bill—actually targets parity across the entire education landscape, for most people it has become inextricably linked with its impact on school athletic programs.

That's largely because, say many coaches and athletic directors who have weathered these years, Title IX has often been blamed for cuts in men's programs. But, supporters say, that is a bum rap.

"There are many myths and preconceptions about Title IX that hinder its effectiveness," says Metropolitan State College's Joan McDermott, in Denver, a rare female athletic director at the higher education level and a veteran of the battles over changes required by the law.

"That's because when a men's sport gets dropped, most people say, it's because of Title IX when that's just not true," she says. "It's because of budget choices by the administration, so that's an ongoing rap that Title IX gets."

The Office for Civil Rights of the US Department of Education has guidelines for compliance with Title IX, the main one of which requires sports participation that is proportional to the gender balance in the school's population. But according to the American Sports Council (ASC) in Washington, a nonprofit coalition of coaches, parents, and athletes, Title IX hurts men's sports, in part due to this requirement.

"When schools have too few female athletes (i.e., the percentage of females enrolled exceed the percentage of athletes), they're presumed noncompliant. They're then forced to create the illusion of substantial proportionality by denying men the opportunity to participate," writes ASC advisory board member Karen Owoc, on the nonprofit's website.

This means, she continues, that many women's teams have not been helped, "but rather, men have been hurt."

The Fairness in Sports Foundation site catalogues a long list of men's programs that have been cut, it states, due to Title IX requirements.

The numbers however, tell a different story. Regarding collegiate sports, Title IX focuses on access and participation. In a list of FAQ's on its website seeking to refute allegations that Title IX has hurt men's athletics, the NCAA points out that since the law's inception, both male and female participation in college sports have increased.

Just between 2002 and 2011, the NCAA says, the number of men in college sports increased by 38,482 between 2002 and 2011. During that same period, the number of females went up by less, some 32,662.

The NCAA also points out that nonrevenue men's sports are often cut to provide more funds for the two big revenue sports, football and basketball. In 2006, for instance, Rutgers University dropped men's tennis, a team with a budget of approximately $175,000. The National Women's Law Center points out that Rutgers spent about $175,000 in the same year on hotel rooms for the football team—for home games.

The biggest ongoing misconception about Title IX is that it's a law against men, says Robert Schneider, author of the textbook, *Ethics of Sport and Athletics: Theories, Issues, and Practice*. In fact, he says via e-mail from Turkey, where he is presenting a paper on Title IX at a conference, "it's a law that requires universities to make choices as to the sports they will offer for men and women in a way that allows for equal participation by both men and women.

The law itself, notes Professor Schneider, who teaches sport management at The College at Brockport in New York, "receives an 'A.' Enforcement of the law receives a 'C.' And depending on the university, following the letter and spirit of the law ranges from an 'A' to an 'F.'" Some universities adhere completely to it, he notes, while "others make every effort to circumvent it."

From its inception, opponents such as the late Sen. Jesse Helms, sought to eliminate it. Title IX has fought off attempts to weaken it in the courts, in Congress, and in the executive branch, says Erin Buzuvis, professor of law at Western New England University in Springfield, Massachusetts, and co-founder of The Title IX Blog.

"It endures a constant barrage of misinformation promoting the myth that Title IX's gains have come at the expense of men," she notes via e-mail. For instance, though men's athletic opportunities have, like women's, steadily increased over the last 40 years, many blame Title IX for the fact that some schools and colleges choose to concentrate men's athletic opportunities in the large-roster sport of football rather than offer men a more diverse array of opportunities.

Those who have labored in the trenches from the law's inception say it has been worth the fight.

"We used Title IX as a way to push for what we deserved," says Vicki Staton, the former Washington & Jefferson College head women's basketball and volleyball coach, who coached from 1975 to 2003.

In 1975, she was one of the few coaches in western Pennsylvania recruiting at a time when local high schools did not provide for women to play sports. "There were many nights when I would think to myself 'What am I doing this for?' "

She says she once asked a local sports reporter, "'Why don't you cover our team?' and his response was 'C'mon, it's women's sports.'" Ten years later, she says, "his daughter attended my youth basketball camp."

"It's been a long process, she says, "but we have always just been fighting for a chance to participate and showcase the athletic skills young women possess. Without Title IX, I don't think that would have ever been possible."

> *In 1975, [Staton] was one of the few coaches in western Pennsylvania recruiting at a time when local high schools did not provide for women to play sports.*

Education about the law is the ball that was dropped from the start, says Ellen J. Staurowsky, a professor of Sport Management at Drexel University in Philadelphia, who co-authored a 2010–11 study of some 1,100 coaches and athletic directors to determine their knowledge of Title IX.

This was the first study of its kind, she points out, and notes that "we found that there was very little actual grasp of the specific requirements of the law." One of the most important requirements—a Title IX coordinator at every school to facilitate programs for every constituency—"was simply never done," she says, adding, "and so the kind of mass education that was supposed to happen around Title IX never took place."

It is not enough for the DOE's Office for Civil Rights to say schools do not have to cut men's sports to be in compliance with the law, she says, adding, "while that is true, that is not sufficient to get people to believe otherwise."

The proof is in the numbers, she says.

In a typical elite Division I school, some 80 percent of all sports funds go to two men's sports, football and basketball. On the other hand, she notes that at a typical Division 3 school, 70 percent of money for men's sports goes to a wide array, with only 30 percent spent on those two sports.

"Those are administration decisions, not Title IX," she says, so the sooner "we begin to have a more accurate discussion about Title IX, the healthier it will be for the next generation."

Cheer Factor

By Sean Gregory
Time, April 1, 2012

On a Friday night in February, 2,000 fans start filing into the University of Oregon's Matthew Knight Arena for a cheerleading contest. But if you are expecting pom-poms and megaphone yells, this is not your event. These are female athletes, not sideline supporters. At least that's what they want the NCAA to acknowledge, and there are legal implications for all college athletic programs. The new event is called *acro*, as in acrobatics and tumbling, and even if it has roots in traditional rah-rah cheerleading, its organizers have rebranded it to shield it from stereotypes like makeup and bare midriffs. Acro teams keep the more athletic aspects of cheerleading—the tosses, the pyramids—and ditch the go-team-go stuff. The cheers are for them, not by them.

Three schools—the University of Oregon, Azusa Pacific University and Quinnipiac University—are here to compete head to head to head. Judges score the event and pick a winner after the acro teams complete a series of gymnastics-like twists, tucks and dismounts.

With its dedicated teams, competitive format and de-emphasis of traditional measures of cheerleading success, acrobatics and tumbling, which is finishing just its second season on the college level, can comfortably call itself a women's sport. Still, acro exists on the fringe of college athletics: the three schools at the Oregon meet account for half the nation's college acro teams.

The fledgling sport's size, however, belies its importance, given that acro has reignited the debate about equal access to college athletic teams decreed by Title IX, the landmark gender-equity law celebrating its 40th anniversary this June. If acrobatics and tumbling and another new sport with roots in cheerleading called stunt can be recognized under Title IX, these new forms of competitive cheer may explode as a college sport.

Since 1972, Title IX has spawned great progress for women's athletics. Still, women don't enjoy equal access to athletic opportunities: 252,946 men competed in NCAA sports on all levels in 2011, compared with 191,131 women. If cash-crunched athletic departments want to create additional opportunities for women, acro and stunt would seem to be an easy choice. All you really need is a mat.

It won't be quite that easy, given that acro and stunt can't agree on a set of rules and the courts have not fully endorsed them as Title IX sports. To make the push for Title IX recognition, Oregon joined forces with five other schools, renamed competitive cheer "acrobatics and tumbling" and aligned itself with USA

Even if acro survives any Title IX challenges, some women's-sports leaders aren't rooting for competitive cheer's success. Call it acrobatics, call it tumbling, call it stunt—it still started with pom-poms and glorifying male athletes from the sidelines. You can't simply rename it and pretend that women have been getting equal opportunity. "It's very difficult to belie history," says Missy Park, founder of the Title Nine women's-sportswear company.

Gymnastics. The governing body for cheerleading, USA Cheer, created stunt and has signed up 22 schools.

Acro is clearly more formalized. In the six acro schools, the sport is run out of the athletic department as a varsity sport. Acro is a full-time obligation. At this point, most stunt athletes are sideline cheerleaders who compete, on average, in just three regular-season stunt events. (ESPN occasionally televises a more traditional competitive-cheer event that involves the rah-rah routines.) "We're sideline cheerleaders first, competitive cheerleaders second," says Kristen Pirie, a cheerleader and stunt athlete at Georgia Southern University. In competition, one major difference between the two cheer versions is that stunt teams perform side by side, while acro teams perform sequentially.

In order to be granted "emerging sport" status, however, the two rivals have been asked by the NCAA to file a joint proposal. The emerging-sport stamp from the NCAA virtually assures schools that they can count acro and stunt toward Title IX compliance. Such NCAA recognition will help the sport expand. Right now, athletic departments have little incentive to create teams that may not count toward their Title IX requirements, especially for a type of sport that lost a Title IX lawsuit just two years ago.

But acro and stunt are far from united. "I think stunt is a shoddy imitation of what we created," says Felecia Mulkey, the Oregon acro coach and a former gymnast. While acro tries to downplay the sport's ties to cheerleading—"No, no, thank you," one of the Oregon athletes responded at an acro practice when asked whether she ever picked up pom-poms on the sidelines—stunt embraces them.

To acro, stunt's ties to USA Cheer are another sticking point. The board president of USA Cheer, Jeff Webb, is also founder and CEO of Varsity Brands, a $200 million company that sells cheerleading equipment and apparel and regulates and administers cheerleading events across the country. Is USA Cheer ultimately concerned with developing college athletes or with cheerleading for the bottom line of Varsity Brands? USA Cheer defends stunt's structure. "No one has brought that up as a problem other than them," says USA Cheer executive director Bill Seely, referring to acro's leaders.

The groups have also taken very different approaches to Title IX. USA Cheer admits that stunt is far from ready for Title IX recognition, since it's mostly an extra-curricular activity for traditional sideline cheerleaders. Oregon and three other acro schools have counted their athletes toward Title IX. Acro's decision to move on Title IX makes strategic sense. The sooner schools see that acro passes Title IX muster, the quicker they will field teams. Still, these schools are putting themselves at some Title IX risk.

Even if acro survives any Title IX challenges, some women's-sports leaders aren't rooting for competitive cheer's success. Call it acrobatics, call it tumbling, call it stunt—it still started with pom-poms and glorifying male athletes from the side-lines. You can't simply rename it and pretend that women have been getting equal opportunity. "It's very difficult to belie history," says Missy Park, founder of the Title Nine women's-sportswear company.

Erin Buzuvis, a professor at Western New England College School of Law and co-founder of the Title IX Blog, offers a counterargument: Acro's and stunt's start in cheerleading is empowering. To Buzuvis, taking an activity that marginalized women and turning it into a sport that displays female competitiveness, physicality and grace is a feminist victory. "Liberal feminism—the idea that what the men get women get too—is a great start for equality," says Buzuvis, who outlined her case in an excellent 2011 *Boston College Law Review* article. "But in the end, it falls short of being fully transformative. The true measure of equality comes when we choose the definition of the [sport] itself."

And Oregon is a great example of the transformation. At this Friday-night meet in Eugene, the crowd shrieks as the Ducks take the mat for the final event of the night, the team routine. The music starts, and 24 women begin to flip, tumble, and jump in near perfect synchrony. Toward the end, they all zigzag across the mat, jumping and flipping in different directions like carp in a lake. It feels like the most spirited halftime show you'll never see, and at the end, the women come together and let out their only cheer of the night, a "Go, Ducks!" to punctuate their effort.

The crowd again goes berserk, then quiets as the judges tally the final scores. At last, the numbers flash: the Ducks have clinched a win. "O! O! O! O!" the crowd and the team chant. "So it's not swimming," says one Oregon acro athlete, Megan Bamford, when asked to make the case for acceptance of her sport. "So what? Tra-dition shouldn't matter. It's cool to try something new. Because then we're making history."

A Sporting Chance

By Elinor Nauen
America, October 20, 2008

Title IX and the Seismic Shift in Women's Sports

Imagine: if only the boys at your school could play on the football, track, wrestling, basketball and baseball teams, and the girls had...synchronized swimming. Or imagine a coach saying, "There's a place for women's athletics: after 7 p.m. and before 6 a.m." Or a judge remarking, as he legally barred girls from competing on a boys' high school cross-country team even though there was no girls' team: "Athletic competition builds character in our boys. We do not need that kind of character in our girls." Imagine that people believed women runners would be unable to bear children, would grow a mustache or wanted to be men.

Actually, you do not have to imagine any of this. These are true examples from the world before 1972. Marj Snyder, chief program officer of the Women's Sports Foundation, remembers those days. She also remembers two boys being admitted to a college that had rejected her, even though her test scores and grades were better. But they had team experience, an option that did not exist for her. As Dolly Brumfield White, who played in the 1940s All-American Girls Professional Baseball League, recalls: "We weren't allowed in the weight room—it was as bad as going to a pool hall."

Then as now, sports were a microcosm of society. The lack of teams, facilities and encouragement went hand in hand with narrower opportunities in other areas; women became teachers and nurses, not principals and doctors. Without coaches or practice times and subject to being teased or hassled when they tried or even wanted to play sports, is it any wonder that so many girls did not see themselves as strong, vigorous, talented, capable beings?

Then Things Changed

What jumpstarted a seismic shift in American life was a law Congress passed in 1972 known as Title IX. Its text read: "No person in the United States shall, on the basis of sex, be excluded from participation in, be denied the benefits of, or be subjected to discrimination under any educational program or activity receiving federal financial assistance." In essence, Title IX prohibits any and every institution that receives government money from practicing gender discrimination. That was and is nearly all of them.

The statistics illustrate an important part of the transformation since the law went into effect. In 1971, fewer than 300,000 high school girls participated in athletics. Today that number is close to three million, with almost half of all female high school students on a team. In 1972 about 16,000 young women participated in college athletics, a number that has grown to over 180,000. The number of women's teams per campus has increased from an average of 2.5 before 1972 to 8.5 in 2006.

"Title IX built a base for sports that led to the 1999 World Cup and women's professional basketball—so many things that go beyond the traditional women's sports of figure skating, tennis and golf," notes Snyder of the Women's Sports Foundation. "Once schools realized they had to open their doors to women and let them onto the playing fields, they added sports like softball, track, field hockey and soccer, sports with high participation numbers." The Summer Olympics have also witnessed a sharp increase in the number of women athletes that began two decades ago. In 1972, 1,058 (or 16 percent) of 7,123 athletes in total were women. In the 2008 games in China, that number rose to 4,746 (or 42 percent) of the total of 11,196 athletes.

The Benefits

Numbers are only part of the story, of course. Consider the benefits to the athletes. "We've always said sports are opportunities for boys and men to benefit from fun, to build character and confidence, to become physically fit and healthy. And to network—your teammates are your future colleagues," says Snyder. "Lots of evidence demonstrates that girls also benefit. Girls who participate in sports have less osteoporosis, less obesity and better heart health. Psychologically, they have a better body image, higher self-confidence and self-esteem, and they do better in business. They are less likely to get pregnant, more likely to delay sexual activity till later, more likely to have fewer sexual partners and less likely to use drugs and smoke." Snyder concludes: "If you don't play on a team, where do you learn risk-taking in a safe environment? Now girls have access to that training ground."

An analysis from the Department of Education backs this up. Its 1997 report *Title IX: 25 Years of Progress* noted that "the critical values learned from sports participation—including teamwork, standards, leadership,

Despite what some critics claim, Title IX does not require any college to eliminate men's teams in order to be compliant. Adding women's opportunities is not supposed to be done by taking them away from men, but by expanding them for everybody. In fact, last year more college participation opportunities were added for men than for women. Schools drop or add sports for many reasons, not only because of Title IX. Money is a key factor.

discipline, self-sacrifice and pride in accomplishment—are being brought to the work-place as women enter employment in greater numbers, and at higher levels than ever before. For example, 80 percent of female managers of Fortune 500 companies have a sports background."

Note too that Title IX was not meant to apply exclusively to sports but was also intended to combat quotas that kept women out of law, medical, and engineering programs. It has worked there too. Before Title IX, more than a quarter of men but less than a fifth of women completed college; that gap has disappeared. Five times as many women receive medical degrees now as 35 years ago, six times as many earn law degrees and almost twice as many are awarded doctoral degrees.

By Title IX's 25th anniversary in 1997, Richard W. Riley, the US Secretary of Education, could say that "America is a more equal, more educated and more pros-perous nation because of the far-reaching effects of this legislation.... What strikes me the most about the progress that has been achieved since Title IX was passed in 1972 is that there has been a sea change in our expectations of what women can achieve. More important, women have shown skeptics again and again that females are fully capable of being involved as successful and active participants in every realm of American life."

Many coaches are well aware of this. Bruce Rasmussen graduated from college in 1971 and began teaching in a small town in southern Iowa. "I was low on the totem pole, so when the women's coach left, I took that on," he recalls. "What I found was that the girls were much more receptive to coaching. The boys thought they knew it before they knew it, but the girls were appreciative of any commitment and attention. It was 'we *get* to practice' versus 'we *have* to practice.' It was an eye-opener." Now director of athletics at Creighton University in Omaha, Rasmussen says: "I see our female athletes have embraced and grown and learned from values such as attention to detail, playing a role on a team and discipline just as much as males, if not more. For years people believed in the value of athletics for what men can achieve. If we believe athletics has a value beyond wins and losses, then that value is there for female athletes as much as male. There are benefits at home, on the job—everywhere."

Jean Hastings Ardell, author of *Breaking into Baseball: Women and the National Pastime*, puts it this way: "Title IX blew apart the old limitations for half the popula-tion of this country."

Enforcement and Challenges

Not surprisingly, implementing such sweeping legislation caused plenty of confu-sion, foot-dragging and challenges. Courts have upheld Title IX at every turn, in cases of school athletics and also in regard to sexual harassment, standardized tests, pregnant students and much more. In 1997 a Supreme Court ruling sent a clear message that just offering women's sports was not enough. Educational institutions had to provide facilities, equipment, practice and game times, as well as encouragement.

"I don't think the men who wrote the law envisioned that this is how it would turn out," Snyder says. One of the three ways the law is enforced is by proportionality—you must demonstrate that sports programs are offered to men and women in percentages equivalent to their enrollment. "The men probably thought they would always have a big advantage, because in 1972 only 35 percent of college undergrads were women. Today, it's 57 percent." (Compliance is also gauged by whether opportunities for women are increasing and whether the school satisfies the athletic interests and abilities of its female students. Schools need to meet only one of the three criteria.)

Despite what some critics claim, Title IX does not require any college to eliminate men's teams in order to be compliant. Adding women's opportunities is not supposed to be done by taking them away from men, but by expanding them for everybody. In fact, last year more college participation opportunities were added for men than for women. Schools drop or add sports for many reasons, not only because of Title IX. Money is a key factor. The cost of insurance, equipment, facilities or team travel may determine what can be offered.

Rasmussen came to Creighton as the women's basketball coach in 1980. "We had a team but there were no scholarships, no budget, no assistance," he recalls. "Now there's a full complement of coaches, we're fully funded the same as the men, we play a national schedule, and we get just as much priority in workout times." Creighton is currently building a $40 million facility for women's basketball and volleyball.

Before Title IX, only a handful of women got athletic scholarships. Donna de Varona may have won two gold medals in the 1964 Olympics, but that did not mean she could garner a college swimming scholarship. Today, college women receive about 42 percent of college athletic scholarship dollars. Much less is spent on women's operating expenses, recruiting costs and head coaching salaries, according to the 2000-01 Gender Equality Study. Full equality still lies ahead.

Tim Wiles, director of research for the Baseball Hall of Fame, served on the Title IX Compliance Committee at the University of Northern Iowa when he was librarian there in 1994. When the committee circulated a draft report, he says he was visited by one assistant athletic director who "tried to pressure us to write something different. This was 22 years after IX passed, and they still didn't know what to do with it. They still were trying to keep the status quo."

"I was born in 1964," Wiles added. "There were girls in Little League and Biddy Basketball but there was no prohibition against denigrating the skills or participation of females in sports. It was very socially acceptable to consider women participants second-class. It was expected that if you were a boy you'd get better times and fields. I'm sorry to say I was one of those kids who had the general idea that sports were for boys and 'you girls should go away and do your own thing.' No one would go to a girls' game in high school."

How that has changed! One anecdote from Marj Snyder illustrates the shift in attitude. "When my sister was coaching her older daughter in basketball, she took both girls to high school basketball games and taped women's basketball. One day her five-year-old daughter asked, 'Do boys play basketball too?'"

"If there's something you want to do, you should have the opportunity. Thank goodness, we mostly have the opportunities today. That's what Title IX did: It put pressure on schools to offer facilities and opportunities for girls," concludes Dolly White, who played, then taught and coached from the 1940s through the 1990s. "How do you know what you can do until you try?"

What About Women's Schools?

Although single-sex schools are not bound by the provisions of Title IX, they have been greatly affected. "Title IX was and is a great, great piece of legislation to protect women's rights," says Patricia McGuire, who is in her 20th year as president of Trinity College, a women's school in Washington, D.C. But, she adds, Title IX is "one of the forces that contributed to decline in enrollment in women's colleges." Before Title IX, only women's colleges had gyms readily available to women. Title IX equalized resources, "but because we were a single-sex college, we didn't have to equalize our facilities."

Eventually, McGuire says, "We saw it was hurting us—it was an excuse not to keep up. A college that says it stands for women's rights and advancements can't take a pass. We have to do the same as big universities to give equal opportunities." In Trinity's case, that meant building its Center for Women and Girls in Sports, which opened in 2002—the first new building on campus in 40 years.

"Whether we like it or not, sports in higher education drives perceptions of institutional liveliness and attractiveness," McGuire adds. "Being able to offer high-class sports has turned our enrollment around. Women expect to have that and Title IX created that expectation."

Title IX at 40: Examining Mysteries, Myths, and Misinformation Surrounding the Historic Federal Law

By Mary Jo Kane
*President's Council on Physical Fitness and
Sports Research Digest,* September 1, 2012

"No person in the United States shall, on the basis of sex, be excluded from participation in, be denied the benefits of, or be subjected to discrimination under any education program or activity receiving federal financial assistance"—United States Congress, June 23, 1972

These 37 words, which make up the federal law known as Title IX, forever changed the landscape of women's sports as well as the lives of millions of girls and women, both on and off the playing fields. We have just honored and celebrated the 40th anniversary of this groundbreaking piece of civil rights legislation. All across the country, in ways large and small, the social, psychological, and physical benefits that occurred in the wake of Title IX have been well documented.[1-4] But in spite of its overwhelming success, many of the important issues surrounding Title IX—from its historic beginnings to its impact on changing (and challenging) gender roles—remain shrouded in mystery and misinformation for far too many Americans. The purpose of this article is to highlight these issues and to shed light on the pervasive and harmful myths and stereotypes that continue to define Title IX 40 years after its passage. My hope is that by doing so, I can dispel the misinformation embedded in these myths, and increase public awareness about the beyond-our-wildest-dreams consequences, some intended and some not, that resulted from this unprecedented moment in women's sports.

Historic Beginnings—The Father of Title IX

Birch Bayh, the former senator from Indiana, is often referred to as the "father of Title IX" because he co-authored and sponsored the bill in the Senate (Patsy Mink [D-Hawaii] was also a fierce advocate for Title IX and is seen as vital to the law's passage). Against a background of social change and upheaval in the 1970s, Bayh said he went into public service to "make a difference in people's lives," and he was particularly committed to issues of gender equality. Bayh credits the influence and inspiration of women in his life—especially his maternal grandmother and his first wife—for making him keenly aware of such injustice.[5] As a young boy, he lived with his grandmother, Kate Hollingsworth, after his mother died and his father was deployed in the armed services. Even though his grandmother worked as hard as any man, Bayh realized that under the law at the time, she could not have inherited the family farm. Bayh's wife, Marvella, also experienced gender discrimination. She was a straight-A student in high school, as well as class president, but was denied admission to the University of Virginia because until 1970, state law barred women from attending. So when Bayh had the opportunity to support a federal law designed to prohibit gender discrimination within an educational setting, he was more than ready: "I think Title IX has [made a real difference]. And I'm proud to have been a part of it."[5]

The Mystery of Title IX

For the past 25 years, I've been engaged in teaching and conducting research in the social sciences. Two of my bread-and-butter courses—Sport & Society and Sport & Gender—have always included a major section on Title IX. Before I present the material, I ask my students to tell me what they know about the law. Even today, 40 years after passage, Title IX remains a mystery to the vast majority of my students, both male and female. It is particularly amazing to me, not to mention highly ironic, that those who have benefited most from the law, meaning female scholarship athletes, routinely respond with two basic observations: (1) it has something to do with making sure women get the same athletic opportunities as men; and (2) it's also the law that forces schools to drop men's sports. I emphasize these observations not as a criticism, but simply to point out that even though Title IX has fundamentally altered the landscape of women's sports, public knowledge and awareness about one of the most successful pieces of civil rights legislation in our nation remains deeply rooted, as the title of this manuscript suggests, in mysteries, myths, and misinformation.

With this as background, I begin my lecture with a personal touch. I tell my students that as a young girl who grew up in the 1950s and 1960s in the state of Illinois, I was the neighborhood "tomboy" who loved playing sports, but who also, as a pre-Title IX athlete, didn't have the opportunity to participate in any competitive, formal way. I also point out that it didn't matter how good or dedicated I was because there were simply no teams, let alone scholarships, available to me. Upon hearing my story, many of them look at me as if I had just landed from Mars. This type of reaction is a direct result of Title IX's success: Young women today grow up with a sense of entitlement to playing sports, even at the most elite levels of competition, and in most cases no longer hope for, but actually expect, a scholarship. It is a reaction that others who share their pre-Title IX stories also encounter. Judith Sweet, a pioneering athletic administrator and former president of the National Collegiate Athletic Association (NCAA), says that when she tells female athletes about her lack of opportunities compared to what is available to them today, "all I get are blank stares."[6]

Why Title IX Matters

Before Title IX was passed in 1972, advocates of women's sports were at the mercy—or goodwill—of athletic administrators. Perhaps not surprisingly, many of these administrators had attitudes about females engaging in athletic competition that ranged from noblesse oblige (a fund-raising breakfast here, a hand-me-down uniform there), to one of outright resistance and hostility. Far too many also believed that women's sports would be a drain on men's sports, at best, or would inevitably gut non-revenue sports, at worst. Title IX leveled the playing field for those who believed that young women deserved the same opportunities to participate in—and benefit from—a sports experience.[7,8] Now, instead of receiving a cold shoulder or an occasional meager handout, parents and supporters of athletically gifted females could (and did) sue for equal treatment under the law. And because Title IX is a federal law, athletic directors (ADs) were given a mandate to invest in women's sports all over the country, from the most respected universities within prestigious intercollegiate athletic conferences to little-known high schools in rural communities.

Though women's sports have yet to achieve parity 40 years after the law's passage, there have been some remarkable gains. According to the Women's Sports Foundation, approximately 300,000 young women played high school sports in the early 1970s but in 2011, that number had skyrocketed to just over three million.[1] At the intercollegiate level nationwide, approximately 30,000 women played competitive sports, but today it's close to 200,000.[9] And finally, before Title IX, scholarships for sportswomen were virtually unheard of, but in 2012, close to 43 percent of all college athletes who receive scholarships are female (J. Sweet, written communication, January 26, 2012). After decades of critics asserting that "females aren't that interested in—let alone very good at—playing sports," and that "no one would ever watch anyway," every March, the NCAA women's basketball Final Four breaks attendance and viewership records.[10] In addition, U.S. women routinely dominate in a variety of sports at the Olympic level. For example, during the 2012 Summer Games in London, female athletes captured 66 percent of all gold medals won by the American team.[11] Interest in U.S. women's sports was unprecedented: 4.4 million watched the gold medal women's soccer match between Japan and the United States, the most-watched event in the history of the newly launched NBC Sports Network.[12] At the professional level, sports leagues such as the Women's National Basketball Association (WNBA) provide career opportunities for highly gifted athletes beyond the college level. In short, Title IX "built them a ball field" and they have come—and excelled—in overwhelming numbers.

Challenges Related to Title IX Enforcement—Three Compliance Option

It is one thing to pass a law. It is quite another to enforce it, particularly when the law itself challenges, both structurally and ideologically, notions of power, prestige, and untold resources. Under such circumstances, resistance—and even backlash—inevitably occurs.[13,14] In the case of Title IX, such resistance took place most frequently in the world of sports, even though athletics was not a major consideration when the law was being written. As you may have noticed, the words "sport" or "athletics" do not appear anywhere in the statute. But as Carpenter and Acosta[6] point out, enforcement of Title IX within the athletic realm has received more attention from the legislative, judicial, and executive branches than any other area of the law's jurisdiction. They highlight two reasons why this has been the case: "First, athletics involves a mainly sex-segregated construct [unlike law, sociology, or literature] and thus, discrimination is readily apparent. Second, athletics involves a historically male-centered domain, and opening the door to new participants means having to share resources previously thought to be for males alone" (p. 65). One early and obvious example of such sports-related gender imbalance, not to mention injustice, involved student fees. For decades, college and university athletic budgets were funded primarily from student fees. Female undergraduates were required to pay the same amount as their male counterparts, yet nationwide, budgets for women's sports represented only 2 percent of the overall athletic budget.[15] Another example of gender inequity during the pre–Title IX era comes from a letter to the editor of the *Minneapolis Star Tribune*: "In 1970, the Minneapolis school district spent more money on boys' hockey sticks than on the entire girls' athletic budget."[16] It is safe to say that similar scenarios existed in almost every university and school district throughout the country.

The federal institution charged with enforcing Title IX is the Office of Civil Rights (OCR) housed within the Department of Education. Over the years, OCR developed what is called the "three-prong test." In order to be in compliance, a school needs to meet only one of the three prongs. They are as follows: (1) provide participation opportunities substantially proportionate—the "proportionality prong"—to the ratio of females to males in the undergraduate population; (2) demonstrate a history and continuing practice of program expansion; and (3) meet the interests and abilities of the underrepresented group, which in the vast majority of cases refers to females. Not surprisingly, it has been very difficult to rely on prongs two and three because there is no standard, uniformly accepted way to accurately measure what is meant by, for example, "demonstrating a history of program expansion." Three sports in five years? Four sports in seven? Similarly, how does one measure "meeting the interests and abilities" of athletic females? Face-to-face interviews? Surveys or petitions? In contrast, the proportionality prong is much easier to measure: Calculate the percentage of female versus male students enrolled at the institution in question and compare that ratio to the percentage of participation opportunities available to female athletes. Though the first prong is easiest to measure, it is also the most controversial. Critics say that proportionality relies on a "quota system" that uses a numbers game based on roster management to determine participation opportunities.[17,18,19] They further argue that these so-called "participation quotas" pressure schools to drop men's nonrevenue sports such as wrestling and gymnastics. Why? Because when fewer male athletes participate—due to eliminating a sport—you have less need to add a women's sport to increase their numbers in ways that are proportional to the number of males who are participating at any given institution.

On the surface, the concern over proportionality as a way to measure compliance seems reasonable, and appears to provide a case for opponents of Title IX who claim that universities are forced to drop men's sports in order to comply with the law. But which sports are dropped, and that includes women's as well as men's, has far more to do with the large roster sizes and expenditures in collegiate football in particular, than anything related to Title IX. I say this because athletic directors typically have three options when it comes to complying with the law. The first option is to add a women's sport, though to do so requires a significant financial investment. Even the smallest of sports such as golf, with only two coaches and six scholarships, could mean a financial commitment between $600,000 and $800,000 of recurring money for a sport that does not generate revenue that exceeds expenses. The second option is to drop a men's nonrevenue sport and save between $600,000 and $800,000 of recurring money for a sport that will also never break even, let alone turn a profit.[20] What athletic director wouldn't want to recoup such additional monies on a yearly basis that could then be used to offset the ever-escalating expenditures needed to fund today's college sports programs? The key point here is that when a university meets compliance requirements by deciding to eliminate a men's sport, Title IX has often been blamed for these decisions.

The third option is to rein in spending habits related to larger team sports such as men's football, the details of which I will outline in the section below on "football pays for everybody." But for now, it is important to note that when athletic directors try, for example, to curtail the recruiting budget of the football coach, they are far more vulnerable to pushback from influential boosters, alumni, and a large fan base than when they decide to drop men's tennis. Under such circumstances, it is easy to see why ADs have typically chosen option number two and state that "Title IX made me do it" versus taking on football, which is a particularly popular and power-ful sport in the world of college athletics. But as supporters of Title IX emphasize, there is nothing in the law—either the letter or the spirit—that requires an educa-tional institution to increase opportunities for females by decreasing those for their male counterparts. Unfortunately, in the pressure-cooker reality of big-time college sports, Title IX has far too often been a convenient scapegoat.[21] Indeed, Keating's research provides an in-depth analysis of how the distribution of scholarships allot-ted by the NCAA—versus Title IX—puts pressure on schools to drop men's sports.

None of this is to suggest that dropping a men's sport is done in a hasty, cavalier manner. Athletic directors who make such agonizing decisions must face current and former players and coaches, their families, and fan base, and defend what many will consider assaults on, and even the deaths of, proud traditions.

Nevertheless, it is important to note that these decisions are made at the local level rather than mandated by the government at the federal level. And whether it is deliberate or not, what frequently happens in the aftermath of dropping a sport is that women's sports get pitted against men's, we get distracted from taking a closer and critical look at funding decisions in men's major sports, and the impression is created that it was Title IX, and Title IX alone, that left university administrators and regents or trustees with no other options.

The Dueling Narratives of Title IX

Over the past 20 years, two major narratives have emerged regarding the critical discourse surrounding Title IX. One narrative—advanced by opponents of Title IX—is that it is a well-intentioned but unfairly enforced law that forces schools to drop men's nonrevenue sports and thus needs to be overhauled.[22] The other, or counter-narrative, comes from supporters of Title IX who, as mentioned, argue that neither the letter nor spirit of the law requires educational institutions to decrease opportunities for men so that sportswomen can achieve gender equity. They also point out that, ironically, football is both the problem and the solution when it comes to addressing many of the concerns associated with Title IX.[23] The opponents' master narrative can be broken down into four major interrelated arguments. Proponents of Title IX have answered each argument with counter-arguments of their own. In the section below, I outline in detail each of these major arguments as well as their corresponding counter-arguments, respectively. In doing so, I attempt to highlight the myths, mysteries, and misinformation associated with Title IX.

Opponents' Argument #1: Women's Sports Don't Pay for Themselves

At the heart of this argument is the idea that because the vast majority of women's sports don't support themselves financially, they become an enormous federally mandated drain on the overall athletic budget. Proponents of Title IX have countered this assertion by making two essential points. First, when was it decided that educational institutions, supported by tax dollars, should offer only those extracurricular activities that pay for themselves? If that's the case, does this mean that a school should eliminate their marching band or cheerleading squad? What about student government or debate teams? Second, if this becomes the new policy, then almost all sports, including the overwhelming majority of football teams, will need to be eliminated. In the latter instance, recent data indicate that only 11.6 percent (14/120) of Division I football programs actually made a profit.[24] The reasons for this are myriad and are addressed below under opponents' third major argument.

Opponents' Argument #2: Title IX Is a "Quota System" That Forces Schools to Drop Men's Sports

Though this issue has been addressed in great detail above, it is the most deeply embedded—not to mention the most powerful and pervasive—argument against Title IX and thus needs further analysis. Proponents of the law reply to this argument by stating that, as is often the case with Title IX, all roads lead to football.[17] One key to understanding how this sport in particular, as opposed to Title IX, puts financial pressures on athletic budgets is to make a roster comparison between the National Football League (NFL) and NCAA Division I football programs. The average size of a big-time college football team is 117[25] with 85 full scholarships; the roster size of all NFL teams is 53. If the gold standard in the industry, meaning the NFL, only requires a work force of 53, why do college teams need over twice that many players as well as an inordinate number of scholarships? A related issue has to do with the size of a team's travel squad. Most Division I schools travel to an away game with a squad size of between 60 and 70.[17] When a team plays away from home they begin at a competitive disadvantage, so why compound that disadvantage by going up against a team with over 100 players? I suggest the answer has far more to do with saving money than with actually believing a team of 60 players is insufficient against a team of 117. The essential point here is that college football teams do not need such a large roster size in order to be truly competitive. It should be noted, however, that a policy to reduce roster size (as well as the number of scholarships) would need to come from the NCAA as a nationwide mandate because without it, individual schools and/or athletic conferences may feel they will be unfairly disadvantaged if they reduce the size of their roster but others do not.

What does all of this have to do with argument number two? First, supporters of Title IX argue that the real quota system in college athletics is the 85 scholarships allotted to football. Second, if we were to reduce the size of the team and the number of scholarships to, say, 70 and 50, respectively, the savings that would occur on an annual basis would go a long way toward adding a women's sport without dropping a men's. Andrew Zimbalist, an economics professor at Smith College, has estimated that "if football scholarships were cut to 60, the average college would probably save over $1 million annually" (p. 118).[25] Making such reductions would also alleviate some of the participation pressures that are tied to the proportionality prong of Title IX: Because fewer males would be participating overall, there would be less need to add more participation opportunities for females.

Opponents' Argument #3: Football Pays for Everybody in Athletics

This particular argument contains one of the most damaging myths surrounding Title IX. Steeped in misinformation that is so widespread, so much a part of the common-sense wisdom of big-time college sports, and so rarely challenged in our all-pervasive sports media that it is simply stated as an obvious fact with no need for further discussion. And how can this not be the case? We see with our own eyes filled-to-capacity football stadiums, are exposed to 24/7 media coverage, and hear about college football programs that garner millions of dollars for their respective academic institutions. For example, the SEC's latest television contracts over a 15-year time period with ESPN ($2.25 billion) and CBS ($825 million) reflect the enormous sums of money surrounding intercollegiate football.[26] No one would argue that college football programs are revenue-generating machines. However, there is another side to the financial ledger that is routinely ignored by the law's critics. As I have argued elsewhere, when it comes to football, we must make a distinction between revenue-producing versus profit-generating financial outcomes.[17] According to Weiner and Suggs,[27] it is simply a myth that college football (and men's basketball) not only cover their own expenses, but fully support all other sports: In

2007–08 alone, 93 out of 119 athletic departments at the Division I level ran a deficit, with losses averaging just under $10 million.

There are a number of reasons why football, in spite of its capacity to generate millions of dollars, is, in reality, a significant drain on athletic budgets in the majority of cases.[28] First, football is an incredibly expensive sport to operate and maintain, ranging from equipment costs to stadium upkeep. Second, the salaries of head football coaches continue to escalate far out of proportion to any other university employee, including the president. Finally, as we have discussed, college football has a disproportionately large work force, meaning, in most cases, a squad size of 117 or more.

Because football teams are much larger than those in any other sport and, as a general rule, are given the highest priority within an athletic department, they typically require an enormous infrastructure whereby numerous employees' primary responsibility is to focus their efforts on this particular sport. Supporters of Title IX thus make the case that if you reduced the size of the football team by one-third, you would also reduce the over-sized infrastructure devoted to its care and maintenance. In sum, if intercollegiate football programs were downsized by even a third, the number of individuals needed to support the program would also be reduced proportionately and the annual savings would be significant. Clearly, under this scenario schools would recoup millions of currently invested dollars. But there is an additional reason that underscores the need to reduce the size of college football teams—doing so would not harm athletic departments' revenues. For example, having a smaller roster would not impact the amount of money a school receives from television contracts or conference revenue-sharing agreements. Schools would also continue to capture significant sums of money from merchandising and sports apparel associated with their respective teams. And it is hard to imagine that individuals and families would stop attending games—or cancel their season tickets—to protest smaller squad sizes. The critical point here is that downsizing not only the football team, but the massive infrastructure that surrounds it, means that expenses would be significantly reduced but the institution's income would remain stable or possibly even increase.

Supporters of Title IX are well aware of (and sensitive to) the argument that significantly downsizing football programs would, in reality, cost a number of people their jobs. But when intercollegiate athletic directors claim there is no money in the budget to add a women's team, or that by doing so they would be forced to drop a men's team, it is simply unacceptable to ignore our hands-off policy toward football—where ever-escalating expenditures continue to put pressure on already strained or even maxed-out budgets—because of the myth that football supports the entire athletic department.

Opponents' Argument #4: Big-Time College Sports as an Economic Model Is a Fact of Life in the 21st Century

When critics of Title IX hear the counter-arguments advanced above by the law's supporters, they often respond by saying that even if the never-ending race to the top does play a role in eliminating some men's sports, we have nevertheless entered into a "new world order" where the notion of amateur athletics is outdated and a profit versus loss mentality (and reality) rules the day. In short, if you want to make money, you need to invest money. Given the state of today's sports culture, it is hard to argue with such an assessment, but if this is indeed the new economic model, proponents of Title IX are right on point when they raise the following issues: Name a CEO who would keep his or her job by maintaining a work force that is over twice the size of your major competitor, meaning the number of players

The spirit behind Title IX, as well as the intent of those who fought so hard to make it a reality, was that a "rise in female sports participation would automatically translate to increased leadership opportunities for women in sport." Forty years after the passage of Title IX, nothing could be further from the truth.

on an NFL roster. And how would this same CEO justify the excesses—and unnecessary expenditures—associated with college sports, such as allowing the men's basketball and football teams (and their numerous staff members) to spend the night in a hotel before every home game, a practice that is widespread throughout the country? Recruiting budgets and operating expenses continue to escalate, and we have already discussed the salaries of head coaches in college football, though there are many more examples that could easily be highlighted.

Title IX advocates point out that there is little effort to curb these types of expenses, while monumental efforts go into building new facilities, securing high-powered coaches, and raising even more money from wealthy donors, often with strings attached. In this for-profit economic model, few seem to be held accountable to the bottom line. Though it's certainly the case that coaches will be fired if they don't win, football programs can (and do) go for decades without a winning record, let alone a bowl appearance. But it is rarely the case, especially at the NCAA Division I level, that there is ever any serious thought given to actually eliminating the "product" under such circumstances, something that would occur in a profit-loss business model outside of college sports. If we were truly operating in a profit-loss world, there would be little resistance to, for example, the notion of downsizing where obvious and enormous savings would be captured on an annual basis. Excessive expenditures would be reined in and after-the-fact profits—versus revenues generated—would make up the bottom line.

Earlier in this article I pointed out that even though supporters of Title IX were highly critical of the way in which football is allowed to operate, they are also aware that if football did actually downsize, and curbed many of its unnecessary expenditures, the sport could, ironically, end up being Title IX's best friend. I say this because under the right circumstances, football is the only sport that can generate enough revenue—and actual profit—to support all sports, including women's. There is another "under the right circumstances" element that would also create an environment where gender equity could be realized for women's sports without harming men's. Rather than rely on their "economic fact of life" argument and their "golden goose" claims, opponents of Title IX could actually do the unthinkable—join forces with the law's supporters and make the case that budget pressures tied to big-time college football, not Title IX, are the real reasons why men's nonrevenue sports are eliminated. So why don't these "right circumstances" ever take place? I suggest it is for the same reasons that athletic directors choose to drop a men's sport rather than confront football. Critics realize that it is far easier (not to mention safer) to blame Title IX rather than risk the wrath of one of the most powerful institutions on the planet.

Unintended Consequences of Title IX

The spirit behind Title IX, as well as the intent of those who fought so hard to make it a reality, was that a "rise in female sports participation would automatically translate to increased leadership opportunities for women in sport."[29] Forty years after the passage of Title IX, nothing could be further from the truth. In fact, when it comes to females occupying positions of leadership in intercollegiate athletics—even in their own sports—we have turned back the clock in a rather dramatic fashion. Prior to Title IX, over 90 percent of all head coaching positions in women's sports were occupied by females; today that number is just 43 percent.[30] When it comes to the position of athletic director, a highly visible and powerful occupation, women are even more marginalized: At the NCAA Division I level—which represents the most prestigious and influential athletic conferences—only five out of 120 ADs are women, yet prior to Title IX, more than 90 percent of all athletic directors in women's college sports were female.[30]

The great irony here is that Title IX has been under constant assault for hurting men's sports. But when it comes to occupational employment, it's been an incredible boon to men because they now enjoy two career tracks—both men's and women's sports. It should be noted that women have not made similar inroads into men's athletics. They represent only 2 percent of all head coaching positions of men's collegiate teams, and rarely in a team sport such as football, basketball, or hockey.[30] I suggest it is no coincidence that we rarely (if ever) hear about this unintended outcome, meaning when it comes to employment opportunities, Title IX has been far more beneficial for men than for women.

The Impact of Title IX at 40 Years and Counting

As we look back over four decades, it's important to assess what Title IX has meant to our society in general and women's sports in particular. I will highlight three interrelated issues that have, in fundamental ways, changed the landscape not only in women's sports, but as a recent issue of *Sports Illustrated* honoring the 40th anniversary of Title IX makes clear, forever changed the role of women in society. First, as a direct result of Title IX, there is unprecedented participation by young girls and women at all levels of sport involvement, from recreational to professional. This, in turn, leads to the second issue—for the first time in our history there is a critical mass of females involved in sport and physical activity. Throughout our history, women have always engaged in sports, even at the highest competitive levels, from Babe Didrikson Zaharias to Althea Gibson to Billie Jean King. What is different today is that even though these sportswomen were pioneers—and made an impact beyond measure—they were considered path breakers not just because they were exceptional athletes, but because they were so few in number. As Harvard scholar Rosabeth Moss Kanter has argued in a different context, reaching critical mass reflects a "tipping point" in society, creating a more balanced gender ratio whereby the population in question (in this case, female athletes) moves beyond the status of outlier, at worst, or token presence, at best.[31] Having reached critical mass leads directly to the final issue regarding the impact of Title IX. As mentioned earlier, young women today grow up with a sense of entitlement when it comes to participating in sports. It is simply assumed that if the talent and desire are there, an opportunity will be forthcoming. In this way there has indeed been fundamental change—we have moved from a pre–Title IX era that questioned the very nature of women's sports participation, to a 21st century belief system where it is no longer a contradiction in terms to be a female and an athlete.

A sense of entitlement extends to parents as well, and they have become some of the fiercest defenders of Title IX. Much has been written about "dads with daughters" and how those who fought hardest to ensure a young girl's right to play was, in many cases, her father. As Donna Lopiano, the retired CEO of the Women's Sports Foundation, points out, "[Dads] understood how much sport gave their children. Dad was the one who took his daughter into the backyard to play catch" (pp. 65–6).[32] This is not meant to minimize the importance of moms in understanding the impact of sport on their daughters, nor their support for Title IX. But as Messner's[33] research indicates, due to sexism and the "old boys" network, mothers are often marginalized within the sports world and are therefore, on average, less engaged in a more formal sense (e.g., as coaches) than are fathers.[34]

Conclusion

Though we have come a very long way, 40 years after the passage of Title IX, we still have miles to go before we reach parity. I say this because the majority of educational institutions are still not in compliance with the law, particularly in smaller, rural communities at the high school level.[35] With respect to high school participation rates, young girls have 1.3 million fewer opportunities than do their male counterparts.[1] Women's sports also lag behind men's at the NCAA intercollegiate level: In Division I alone, women receive just 36 percent of the recruiting budgets and 39 percent of the operating budgets. Finally, also at the Division I level, the median total institutional salary expenditures for head coaches of men's sports is approximately $916,000, compared to a median of $646,000 for head coaches of women's sports.[36]

Even with these less-than-optimistic statistics, when one measures progress by using Title IX as a basis of comparison, the glass is not only half full for women's sports, its cup runneth over. In a recent article in *Athletic Management Magazine* devoted to the 40th anniversary of Title IX, Jim Fiore, the AD at Stony Brook University, speaks for many when he says, "I truly hope that Title IX is never forgotten… rather, simply unnecessary."[37] For me, the key to understanding what Title IX really means is simply this: In one generation, we have gone from young girls hoping there is a team to young girls hoping they make the team. Because of those 37 words, there is a universe of difference in that measure of hope. So Happy Anniversary, Title IX. We as a nation are now—and forever—in your debt.

References

1. Anderson K. "Nine for IX." *Sports Illustrated* 2012; 116(19): 49.
2. Sabo D. "The gender gap in youth sports: Too many urban girls are being left behind." *J Phys Education, Recreation & Dance* (JOPERD) 2009; 80(8): 35–37, 40.
3. Weiss MR, Wiese-Bjornstal DM. "Promoting positive youth development through physical activity." *Res Digest* 2009; 10(3).
4. Fitness is fun: The Official Newsletter of the President's Challenge. *President's Challenge*. March, 2012. Available at https://www. presidentschallenge.org/newsletter/march-2012.html. Accessed May 31, 2012.
5. Isaacson M. "Birch Bayh: A senator who changed lives." *espnW*. May 3, 2012. Available at http://espn.go.com/espnw/title-ix/ 7883692/birch-bayh-senator-changed-lives. Accessed May 31, 2012.
6. Carpenter LJ, "Acosta RV." *Title IX*. Champaign, IL: Human Kinetics; 2005.
7. Brake DL. *Getting in the game: Title IX and the women's sports revolution*. New York: New York University Press; 2010.
8. Suggs W. *A place on the team: The triumph and tragedy of Title IX*. Princeton, NJ: Princeton University Press; 2005.
9. National Collegiate Athletic Association. "Student-athlete participation— 1981-82—2010-11 NCAA sports sponsorship and participation rates report." *NCAA Publications*. October, 2011. Available at http://ncaapublications.com/ p-4243-student-athlete- participation-1981-82-2010-11-ncaa-sports-sponsorship-andparticipation-rates-report.aspx. Accessed May 31, 2012.
10. Bibel S. "NCAA women's basketball overnight rating up over last year." *TVbytheNumbers*. April 4, 2012. Available at http:// tvbythenumbers.zap2it. com/2012/04/04/ncaa-womens-basketballovernight-rating-up-over-last-year/127494/. Accessed June 2, 2012.
11. Eldred S. "2012 Olympics: Year of U.S. women." *Discovery News*. August 13, 2012. Available at http://news.discovery.com/adventure/ us-women-olympics-london-120813.html. Accessed August 14, 2012.
12. @NBCSportsPR. "4.35 million watch Team U.S.A-Japan gold medal soccer match on @NBCSN. Most-watched event in the history of NBC Sports

Network #Olympics." Available at https://twitter.com/ NBCSportsPR/status/234012042556755968. Posted August 10, 2012.

13. Coakley J. *Sports in society: Issues and controversies*. Boston: McGraw Hill; 2007.

14. LaVoi NM, Kane MJ. "Sport sociology for sport management." In: Pedersen P, Thibault L, Quarterman J, eds. *Contemporary Sport Management*. 4th ed. Champaign, IL: Human Kinetics; 2011: 373–391.

15. National Women's Law Center. "The battle for gender equity in athletics in colleges and universities." *National Women's Law Center*. August 25, 2011. Available at http://www.nwlc.org/resource/ battle-gender-equity-athletics-colleges-and-universities. Accessed June 2, 2012.

16. Pauly S. Letters from readers. *Star Tribune*. September 2, 1999. Available at http://www.highbeam.com/doc/1G1-87011214.html. Accessed May 31, 2012.

17. Kane MJ. "We have passed this way before: A response to 'Dollar dilemmas during the Downturn—A financial crossroads for college sports.'" *J Intercollegiate Sport* 2010; 3: 135–146.

18. Thomas K. "Suit filed arguing Title IX uses quotas." *New York Times*. July 21, 2011. Available at http://www.nytimes.com/2011/07/22/ sports/group-files-suit-claiming-title-ix-uses-quotas.html. Accessed August 7, 2012.

19. Hogshead-Makar N. "A critique of tilting the playing field: Schools, sports, sex and Title IX." In: Hogshead-Makar N, Zimbalist A, eds. *Equal play: Title IX and social change*. Philadelphia: Temple University Press; 2007: 218–238.

20. U.S. Department of Education. "Equity in Athletics Data Analysis Cutting Tool [Web-based data set]." *U.S. Department of Education*. Available at http://ope.ed.gov/athletics/index.aspx. Accessed August 1, 2012.

21. Keating P. "The silent enemy of men's sports". *espnW*. May 23, 2012. Available at http://w.espn.go.com/espnw/title-ix/7959799/ the-silent-enemy-men-sports. Accessed June 2, 2012.

22. Fagan K, Cyphers L. "Five myths about Title IX." *espnW*. April 30, 2012. Available at http://espn.go.com/espnw/title-ix/ 7729603/five-myths-title-ix. Accessed August 7, 2012.

23. Kane MJ. "Title IX at 40: Changing the landscape in women's sports." Paper presented at: The Minnesota Federal Bar Association; March 2012. Minneapolis Club, Minneapolis, MN.

24. Grasgreen A. "Divisive reforms." *Inside Higher Ed*. January 12, 2012. Available at http://www.insidehighered.com/news/2012/01/12/ ncaa-convention-educators-question-academic-reformmeasures#ixzz1jkDos9mU. Accessed June 2, 2012.

25. Zimbalist A. "Dollar dilemmas during the downturn: A financial crossroads for college sports." *J Intercollegiate Sport* 2010; 3: 111–124.

26. Mandel S. "TV deals for major conferences." *SI.com*. July 24, 2009. Available at http://sportsillustrated.cnn.com/2009/writers/stewart_ mandel/07/24/tv-deals/index.html. Accessed June 2, 2012.

27. Weiner J, Suggs W. "College sports 101: A primer on money, athletics, and higher education in the 21st century." *Knight Commission on Intercollegiate*

Athletics. October, 2009. Available at http://www.knightcommission.org/index. php?option=com_ content&view=article&id=344&Itemid=84. Accessed June 2, 2012.

28. Svare B. "Life's not just a football game." *Times Union.* August 1, 2012. Available at http://www.timesunion.com/default/article/ Life-s-not-just-a-football-game-3755600.php. Accessed August 4, 2012.

29. Cooky C, LaVoi NM. "Playing but losing: Women's sports after Title IX." *Contexts* 2012; 11(1): 42.

30. Acosta RV, Carpenter LJ. "Women in intercollegiate sport: A longitudinal, national study: 35-year update, 1977–2012. 2012." *Women in Sport / Title IX Home Page.* Available at http://acostacarpenter.org/AcostaCarpenter2012.pdf. Accessed June 2, 2012.

31. Kanter RM. "Some effects of proportions on group life: Skewed sex ratios and responses to token women." *Am J Sociol* 1977; 82(5): 965–991.

32. Wolff A. "Father figures." *Sports Illustrated* 2012; 116(19): 65–66.

33. Messner M. *It's all for the kids: Gender, families, and youth sports.* Berkeley, CA: University of California Press; 2009.

34. Kane MJ, LaVoi NM. The 2007 *Tucker Center research report: Developing physically active girls: An evidence-based multidisciplinary approach.* Minneapolis, MN: The Tucker Center for Research on Girls & Women in Sport; 2007.

35. Whitacre K. "Title IX: Work left to do." *Athletic Management.* May 31, 2012. Available at http://www.athleticmanagement. com/2012/05/31/title_ix_work_ left_to_do/index.php. Accessed June 2, 2012.

36. National Collegiate Athletic Association. "NCAA gender-equity report, 2004–2010." *National Collegiate Athletic Association.* January, 2012. Available at http://www.ncaapublications.com/ productdownloads/GEQS10.pdf. Accessed June 2, 2012.

37. Fiore J. "Title IX: Work left to do." *Athletic Management.* May 31, 2012. Available at http://www.athleticmanagement. com/2012/05/31/title_ix_work_left_ to_do/index.php. Accessed June 2, 2012.

3
The Big Business of Collegiate Sports

Alabama running back Eddie Lacy (42) breaks a long touchdown run during the first half of the Alabama vs. Georgia SEC Championship NCAA football game in 2012.

The Money Game in College Sports

The debate over collegiate athletics has a long history and involves issues that are both obvious and nuanced. On one hand, there are measurable developmental and educational benefits to those who participate in collegiate athletics, and the industry helps to provide education to thousands who would otherwise have difficulty affording a college education. On the other hand, as critics argue, the collegiate sports industry exploits students, encourages corporate corruption of the higher-education system, and draws funding and focus away from academics and education.

While collegiate athletics is a multibillion-dollar industry in and of itself, it is also the training ground through which athletes matriculate into professional sports, another of the nation's largest and most profitable commercial industries. Given the billions of dollars tied into the industry, any attempt to change the system faces intense opposition unless the proposed changes do not threaten existing financial structures. Despite this difficulty, there are individuals both within the industry and without attempting to reform the collegiate system so that college athletics will be protected in perpetuity while shedding the practices and policies that pose a threat to both students and the academic focus of the higher-education system.

A Brief History of Collegiate Sports

Since antiquity, athletic competitions have been considered an important part of education, training the body as well as the mind to face the challenges of adult life. However, American colleges and universities did not offer organized athletic competitions until the mid-nineteenth century. The first organized college sports club in the United States was the Yale University Boating Club, founded in 1843; a similar club at Harvard started the following year. In 1852, the Yale Rowing Club and the Harvard Rowing Club had their first organized competition, which was the beginning of the intercollegiate sporting industry.

Other colleges and universities followed by introducing both competitive sports and organized physical fitness classes into their curricula. The first intercollegiate baseball game was held in 1859 between Williams and Amherst Colleges; baseball was followed by American football, which began with intercollegiate competitions among the schools that have come to be known as the "Big Three"—Harvard, Princeton and Yale—in 1872. Track and field, tennis, ice hockey, gymnastics, and basketball followed before the beginning of the twentieth century, and the intercollegiate athletic competitions became a significant focus for American colleges and universities. Before the turn of the century, some American universities and colleges were already investing more per year in athletics programs than in any of their academic departments.

From the beginning, funding for college athletics programs was often provided by alumni, who contributed funds as a way of expressing support for their alma mater. For many, supporting or following their college athletic teams is about far more than a choice of entertainment; it represents a broader sense of history, lineage, and identity, similar to the way that many fans feel about city or state teams in professional sports. The sense of personal connection to and pride in the success of an athletic team, as a symbol of one's identity and heritage, was the most important reason for the rapid growth of college athletics in the United States.

Colleges and universities attempted to capitalize on fan interest by promoting collegiate competitions and selling tickets to spectators. The development of radio and television increased the potential for revenues and led to exponential growth in the economics of collegiate sports. As competition increased, athletic success rapidly became a matter of funding, thus setting up an economic battle for athletic superiority that has lasted into the twenty-first century.

In the 1920s, as the US government became concerned over the alarming number of injuries that occurred each year as a result of contact sports such as football and boxing, the National Collegiate Athletic Association (NCAA) was established to set basic safety and educational guidelines for collegiate athletics. The overall goals of this organization was to prevent the growing economic incentive for aggressive recruitment to place the institutions or their students at risk.

Spending on Collegiate Athletics

One of the most controversial issues in the realm of collegiate sports is the rising cost of maintaining athletic programs in relation to the overall increase in college costs and tuition rates. A January 2013 report from the American Institutes for Research indicated, among other findings, that colleges and universities spend between three and six times as much on each college athlete as on a nonathlete student. This discrepancy is largely the result of the rising cost of scholarships (in comparison to tuition), coach and support-staff salaries, and the demand for new facilities. In addition, the report indicated that this trend is likely to intensify, as spending for athletics is increasing at twice the rate of spending for other academic programs.

It is often argued that athletic programs provide marketing and advertising benefits for a university that are difficult to quantify in terms of economic value. Collegiate football is the leading subset of the college sports industry and generates more annual revenues than any other athletics program. Out of the more than 800 collegiate football teams in the United States, the 119 teams of the NCAA Division I Football Bowl Subdivision (FBS) are the most successful programs in the nation. Studies indicate that, when an FBS school has a successful season, it experiences a moderate increase in applications for a one-to-two-year period following the season. However, economic analysis indicates that this increased enrollment does not significantly increase overall profitability.

Supporters of college athletics argue that sports programs provide significant economic advantages to colleges and universities, but economic analysis indicates that few schools benefit financially from their sports programs and most spend far more than they earn in an effort to compete in the industry. However, less than 40 percent of college and university athletic programs break even in terms of funding, and less than 25 percent of those institutions that are able to cover their expenses earn funds in excess of what they spend each year. The remaining 60 percent of American colleges and universities fund their collegiate athletics departments through "allocated funding" derived from student tuition, government subsidies, and institutional donations that are not specifically given for use to fund sports programs.

Exploitation or Opportunity?

In the twenty-first century, supporters of collegiate athletics often tout the role of athletics programs in helping underprivileged individuals who are athletically gifted obtain a college education. The first sports scholarship in the United States was offered in the 1960s, and since that time, thousands of students have earned their way through college by participating in college sports programs.

Because student athletes are recruited for their athletic skills and not necessarily their academic merits, there has been a tendency for universities to downplay academic achievement in student athletes. In an effort to combat this trend, the NCAA has attempted to restructure the student-athlete educational model, providing more academic assistance to athletes and requiring academic achievement for students who want to remain involved in the athletics program. Since 2003, the NCAA has conducted its own measurements of Graduation Success Rate (GSR) to measure the progress of student athletes relative to the general student population.

Traditionally, student athletes have performed poorly in comparison to the general population, but the NCAA has reported marked improvements, indicating that student athletes graduate at similar levels or, in some isolated sections of the population, higher rates than general students. Currently, the NCAA estimates a 79-percent graduation rate for student athletes as a whole, though the figures drop to as low as 44 percent among student athletes at some of the most prominent football- and basketball-focused institutions. Some critics have pointed out that the NCAA figures can be misleading because they do not subtract points from their calculation for students who transfer to other institutions, while the Department of Education does subtract points for transfers when calculating overall GSR statistics.

Additionally, more detailed examinations of GSR statistics indicate a significant difference between the success rates for black and white students. Black student athletes graduate at a lower rate and are less likely than white students to find work in lucrative sectors of private industry if they fail, for whatever reason, to achieve success in professional sports. A 2013 report from Kansas State University examining the experiences of student athletes indicated that black athletes were more likely to feel they received little guidance in choosing a major and were also less likely to feel they were encouraged to pursue academic success outside athletic participation.

In addition, the benefits of academic scholarships are dependent on performance and physical fitness. Recipients of athletic scholarships who fail to perform to the expectations of the program or who sustain an injury may lose their academic assistance. Many of these individuals may be unable to pay to continue their college education without assistance. There are more than twelve thousand injuries to college athletes reported each year, and more than 30 percent of college athletes experience some form of injury that requires medical attention during their college careers. In the case where an injury derails a student's college athletic career and requires continued medical treatments, colleges generally cover only a portion of the costs of initial treatment and do not guarantee to compensate players or their families for extended medical care.

Amateurs or Professionals

Collegiate athletes are not permitted to receive a salary for their participation in college sports competitions. There are some critics who believe that providing salaries for players may be one of the best ways to address many of the financial and exploitative issues that plague the industry. Because players are not recruited with the promise of salaries, there is a perception that amateur sports are free from the corporate corruption and commercialism of the professional sports industry. Some believe that providing salaries to players would lead to an increase in these negative qualities within the industry. Others argue that student athletes are currently rewarded with tuition assistance and the opportunity to receive an education, representing a form of compensation that is both fair and ultimately more beneficial than simple monetary compensation.

Those who support the idea of paying salaries to college athletes have argued that corporations and business interests already play a dominant role in the college sports industry and that the numerous cases of corruption revealed over the years indicate that college sports has not been spared the deleterious effects of commercialization. Further, the billions of dollars generated by the industry benefit corporations, investors, and the coaches and support staff who manage and promote the industry but not the athletes whose effort and risk of physical injury are the real basis of college sports. Some argue that it is a basic inequity to allow young students to endure the struggles of attempting to maintain a successful sports career while attending classes without providing them with some portion of the revenues their skills and effort make possible. Salaries for players might also help to ease the plight of those whose college careers are cut short by injury or who suffer from persistent medical issues after their careers end.

No Single Solution

In essence, college sports is a multibillion-dollar industry both because it is an indispensable part of professional sports industry recruitment and because it is associated with so many intimate concepts of community and identity. From the rowing clubs of Harvard and Yale to the major collegiate football programs of the twenty-first century, collegiate athletics has been a source of both pride and shame for American society. It represents both the heritage of the higher education system and the failure to contain one of the largest recreational industries within a system whose ultimate purpose was intended to be educational advancement, rather than entertainment promotion. In terms of identity, recognition, advertising, and institutional pride, universities benefit from investing in the success of their collegiate athletics. From a perspective of financial spending, academic priority, and protecting student welfare, the system is often detrimental. As each issue affecting the industry comes in and out of the spotlight, there is recognition among many of the researchers and columnists who study the industry that resolving these complex problems will require changes on many levels. Ultimately, solving these problems may require adopting controversial changes that will call into question the foundations of college athletics.

How Television Changed College Football—
and How It Will Again

By Andy Staples
Sports Illustrated, August 6, 2012

They had taken their fight for liberation all the way to the Supreme Court and won. So why, less than five months after the nation's highest court had ruled in *NCAA vs. the University of Oklahoma Board of Regents* that the NCAA's restrictive football television package violated federal antitrust laws, did almost everyone in the college football business feel they had lost? Consider the following paragraph from an October 15, 1984, *Sports Illustrated* story on a dip in college football ratings despite a spike in college football telecasts.

The glut is pernicious, not propitious. Unless the CFA and Big Ten and Pac-10 kiss and make up and legally curtail the number of games on TV—a dubious prospect, considering the Supreme Court ruling and the bitterness between them—the colleges will be left with a depressed marketplace," wrote William Taaffe in a piece that bore the headline *Too Much of a Good Thing*. "There will be no money to prop up non-revenue sports such as swimming and wrestling. The big network paydays will be over, assuming the networks remain in college football at all. As Nebraska athletic director Bob Devaney says, 'I don't see any great resurgence in the next year or so. I'm not predicting colleges will go broke—but it isn't going to be the bonanza it was.'

Whoops.

Twenty-eight years later, viewers and television networks have proven every prediction in that passage laughably wrong. While the stripping of rights from the NCAA caused an immediate drop in prices, that dip didn't last. Rights fees rose, and television revenue has turned college football into a multibillion-dollar business. More college football on television didn't create fan apathy as the sport's leaders feared in the mid-'80s. Quite the contrary. While fans continue to flock to games in person, even more plop down on their sofas for Saturday football orgies that begin at noon on the East Coast and last into the wee hours of Sunday morning. (This, after watching mid-week MACtion and games on Thursday and Friday nights.) In the splintered cable universe, college football has proven a reliable ratings-grabber and brand-builder.

That success has driven rights fees to heights the Bob Devaneys of 1984 never dreamed possible. College football television revenue pays for the scholarships of athletes in non-revenue sports and builds bigger and fancier stadiums. It also has inspired a rash of conference-hopping that began a few years after the Supreme Court ruling and hasn't stopped. (It has not, however, changed the fact that the student-athlete labor force is allowed by the NCAA to receive only tuition, books, room and board.) Television has changed college football—and all of college athletics, for that matter—for better and for worse, and despite a host of new distribution methods already in use and on the horizon, television's influence doesn't appear in danger of eroding anytime soon.

In 1984, *The Associated Press* estimated that all the college football rights agreements in the newly deregulated landscape would generate $43.6 million. That was down from the $69.7 million paid for the entire NCAA package for the 1983 season. To put that in perspective, ESPN will pay a reported $80 million to broadcast the Rose Bowl on January 1, 2015. Adjusted for inflation, those 1984 deals would be worth $90.3 million. So 30 years after the Supreme Court ruling, *one game* will be worth almost as much as an entire season of college football was immediately after the decision. According to some experts, college football remains a relative bargain compared to the NFL, meaning the earnings ceiling remains even higher.

So what happened? The answer is complicated. Technology changed. Viewing habits changed. The model for financial success in television changed. Media companies broke apart and then reconsolidated. Ditto for college conferences. This confluence of events resulted in unprecedented financial growth.

"It's not just limited to college sports," said Chris Bevilacqua, an early true believer in the value of college sports who co-founded CSTV, later helped design the Pac-12's landmark media rights deal as a consultant and recently helped negotiate the Rose Bowl's upcoming 12-year deal with ESPN. "It's sports in general. College sports, because it's such a fragmented offering, was so undervalued compared to other live sports."

College administrators didn't simply wake up a few years ago and realize the tremendous sums to be made from football on television. First, the market had to adjust. Neal Pilson, the former CBS Sports chief who now runs a consulting firm, notes that immediately after the ruling in 1984, his network was one of three potential major buyers in the market for college football. ESPN was still in its infant stage and couldn't offer big money. Besides, the prevailing attitude held that if you couldn't get your games on a broadcast network, you were nobody.

"The leverage changed," Pilson said of the court ruling. "Up to that point, the NCAA was the only seller of college football. There was one seller, and two or three buyers. When that ruling came down, there were multiple sellers. The rights fees dropped 50 percent."

The sellers weren't as fragmented as they are now. The College Football Association was a group of 63 schools that negotiated television rights as a bloc. Its leader, Chuck Neinas, spearheaded the effort to rip the football television rights away from the NCAA and give them to the schools. "That was going to get done, whether we did it or not," said Neinas, who recently returned to his consulting business after a stint as the interim commissioner of the Big 12. "The NCAA control features stymied the development of college football. Opening it up to television obviously has promoted the sport. I think everyone has basically benefitted from it. Now, I never anticipated the television revenues that are there now."

It took the breakup of the CFA for schools to truly realize the power they had. The deal Notre Dame signed with NBC in 1990—the network began broadcasting Fighting Irish home games in 1991, and still does—was the first major blow to the CFA's power, and it touched off a wave of realignment. Knowing the CFA wouldn't last much longer, independents and schools in weakened conferences quickly moved to shore up their affiliations. Penn State joined the Big Ten. Arkansas and South Carolina joined the SEC. Florida State joined the ACC. Miami joined the Big East.

Two deals signed by Pilson's CBS unit eventually crushed the CFA and ushered in the modern era of college football on television. In December 1993, the NFL awarded the rights for NFC games to upstart Fox, stripping CBS of one of its most reliable sports properties. CBS moved quickly to secure other rights. In February 1994, CBS announced deals with the SEC and Big East to broadcast football games, effectively destroying the CFA. The same free market CFA members had sought to exploit when fighting the NCAA had ultimately broken up the alliance because of one fundamental principle: Some conferences were more valuable TV properties than others. When the CFA broke up, it was every conference (and independent) for itself.

The SEC on CBS deal, which took effect during the 1996 season and initially paid the conference a reported $17 million per year for five years, became the envy of college sports for the next 10 years. Pilson explained that after losing the NFL, his team sought brands that delivered steady audiences with little change year-over-year. Alabama, Auburn and Georgia were—and still are—those kind of brands. Though Pilson was forced out shortly after CBS and the SEC agreed to the deal, his successors placed a bet that viewers nationwide would want to watch the SEC schools despite conventional wisdom that suggested no one in California would want to watch Alabama play Auburn. For the first five years of the deal, the biggest SEC games went out to a nationwide audience. In 1998, CBS signed a deal that guaranteed *all* SEC games broadcast on CBS would go to every affiliate beginning in 2001. While ABC continued to split national telecasts between two or three games, the SEC enjoyed a nationwide broadcast all its own. "It seemed like a risk at the time," Pilson said. "But it was really a safe bet. ... We probably didn't anticipate the strength of the SEC nationwide." In 2011, the SEC on CBS package turned in the highest ratings of any college football package in America for the third consecutive year, averaging a 4.2 share and nine million viewers.

While CBS harnessed the strength of the SEC beginning in the late '90s, ESPN continued to use almost every conference to help turn itself into the most powerful—and bankable—brand in sports. ESPN executives realized long before anyone else the spell college football (and basketball) cast on viewers, and as the profit model in television shifted, that realization gave ESPN the upper hand against its broadcast rivals. In its infancy, ESPN needed content, and after the Supreme Court decision, college football was among the cheapest major properties available. So the network began scooping up rights and broadcasting games on a single feed to a national audience. While the ratings wouldn't challenge anything on a broadcast network for years, they proved the profitability of college football.

Burke Magnus, ESPN's senior vice president for college sports programming, said ESPN's early leaders tapped into something their fellow network executives needed years to find. "I think we understood how deep the well was before anybody else," said Magnus, who was an unpaid intern at CBS Sports when the landmark SEC and Big East deals were signed in 1994. "No. 2, I think we figured out that despite it really being an affiliation of regional entities, it stitched together into a national proposition."

While the broadcast networks continue to make most of their money from advertising, ESPN and other cable networks have two major revenue sources: subscriber fees and, to a lesser extent, advertising. Each cable or satellite provider charges subscribers a fee for each channel, but those fees aren't broken down on the bill. So while the smaller audiences for college football on ESPN didn't command the same ad rates, they did allow ESPN to gradually raise the fee it charges carriers for its signal. The fierce loyalty of college football fans was especially effective in helping ESPN hit the mother lode of subscriber fees. As the extended recent spat between Dish Network and AMC has shown, viewers aren't calling in droves to cancel their service if they miss scripted shows—even shows as excellent as *Mad Men* and *Breaking Bad*. But if viewers think they might miss their favorite college football team's game, they'll threaten to cancel their cable service and install a satellite dish or cancel their dish service and hook up their cable. The same applies for fans of the professional leagues, and ESPN executives realized that by stockpiling rights for games viewers felt they couldn't live without, they could strong-arm carriers into paying inflated subscriber fees which would then be passed along to customers.

Pilson, whose job as a consultant requires him to negotiate with ESPN and other networks, knows exactly how much value that strategy created. "They are now getting over $5 a sub, every month, times 100 million," Pilson said. In other words, just from ESPN—not the company's other channels, which command much smaller but not-insignificant subscriber fees—the network rakes in about $500 million per month ($6 billion per year) before the first ad is sold. Meanwhile, industry sources estimate the next-highest subscriber fee for a channel is in the $1.40 range. With a big assist from college football, ESPN has more than lapped the field in the cable industry. "History would show that we've built businesses off these rights. New businesses," Magnus said. "That's part of the justification for some of these deals where you scratch your head and say, 'Boy that's a lot of money.' But it allows us to build new businesses. Whether it's ESPN to ESPN2, ESPN2 to ESPNU, ESPNU to ESPN3 and now WatchESPN and our mobile products. College content has been, in many ways, the spinal cord of each of those."

ESPN's influence also has changed the culture of the sport. Even today, college coaches use televised games as a major part of their recruiting pitches. But while a coach in 2012 argues about the prestige of the network carrying the games, coaches in the '80s and '90s bragged if their team's games were televised at all. In the stone age of the NCAA television deal, the narrator of Clemson's 1981 recruiting video boasted about a recent three-year span: "During these years," the narrator boomed, "Clemson's exposure reached an all-time high as it appeared on television 12 times—one of the highest exposure rates in the country." Now, Clemson fans would riot if they could only watch their team play on TV four times per season.

"We've sort of reset expectations from a fan perspective," Magnus said. "Well, I don't think we can take all the credit. But now, the expectations are such that it's almost a birthright. Now, you'll see your team wherever you may live. Now it's not just the big games. It's all the games."

Because rights to games provide the bulk of ESPN's leverage with cable and satellite carriers, it has a tremendous incentive to ensure it doesn't lose those rights to another network. But since the SEC on CBS deal proved how valuable college football can be to a network, ESPN has faced fierce competition for rights in recent years. When Fox outbid ESPN for BCS games from 2007–10, ESPN executives learned they would have to pay more. Meanwhile, consultants such as Bevilacqua, Pilson, Chuck Gerber and Dean Jordan (the latter two are advising various BCS conferences on the rights deal for the recently created playoff) advised their clients that ESPN and the broadcast networks could afford the higher fees by better educating their clients about what their rights were worth. That, along with a paradigm shift created by the Big Ten, has caused the market to reset itself twice in the past six years and sparked a wave of realignment even more disruptive than the early-'90s shakeup.

On a Mount Rushmore of executives who helped television change college football, Neinas certainly deserves a spot. But so does Big Ten commissioner Jim Delany. Outraged in 2004 by what he considered a lowball offer from ESPN for his league's rights, Delany promised to create a Big Ten–only channel that would show games and allow the league's schools to keep a larger percentage of the revenue by cutting out the network middleman. (For all the gory details, take a moment and read Teddy Greenstein's excellent 2011 story about the negotiations and savor Delany's re-gifting ruthlessness.) Delany wound up selling the Big Ten's best football games to ESPN/ABC, but he made good on his promise by partnering with Fox to form the Big Ten Network.

At first, the Big Ten struggled to convince cable companies to grant the network the desired level of carriage. After Appalachian State beat Michigan in the first game the network broadcast on September 1, 2007, and as the network proved its broadcasting chops, cable companies slowly began coming around. Now, industry sources estimate the BTN gets more than $1 per subscriber every month within the Big Ten's geographic footprint. The revenue is split between the Big Ten and Fox, which owns 51 percent of the network. By 2009, the network was profitable and generated an additional $7 million per school per year. That per-school revenue number has increased despite the addition of Nebraska—the lucky school that won the right to join the Big Ten after the success of the network convinced Delany and the league's presidents that the conference should expand.

With the Big Ten raking in cash from its own network, the nation's other financially dominant conference needed to keep pace. The SEC explored the idea of a conference network, but it was a risky proposition given its smaller population base. Instead, in 2008, the SEC continued its relationship with CBS and sold the rest of its football and basketball games to ESPN. The result? A pair of fifteen-year deals worth a reported $2.85 billion that would begin with the 2009 football season. The contracts, signed amid one of the nation's worst financial crises, proved how valuable college football was to the networks. It seemed the SEC had dominated as thoroughly in the meeting room as it did on the football field. But a year later, another league would hire a commissioner who would—with the help of television executives—shake up college athletics again.

When Larry Scott came to the Pac-10 from the Women's Tennis Association in 2009, he didn't worry about slaughtering sacred cows. He explored every avenue to increase his league's profile and revenue. He had his work cut out for him. Scott replaced Tom Hansen, whose attitudes toward television seem to have been formed when he ran the NCAA's football television package. The Pac-10, despite dominating some of the nation's largest media markets, lagged far behind in television revenue. "We were fifth," Scott said. "And we were a distant fifth."

Before Scott took his league's rights to market in 2011, he tried to reshape the league itself. After studying various models and discussing them with his presidents and with people in television, Scott decided a 16-school league would provide the most desirable media rights deal. In June 2010, the Pac-10 was only days away from adding Texas, Texas A&M, Texas Tech, Oklahoma, Oklahoma State and Colorado when Texas backed away from the table after a change of heart about relinquishing all media rights to the league. Scott believed his plan would only work if all the schools turned over their rights and agreed to share media revenue equally. Television also drove the Longhorns' decision to walk away from the deal, because the Big 12 would allow Texas to partner with ESPN to form The Longhorn Network. Meanwhile, then-commissioner Dan Beebe convinced ESPN and Fox to pay the same amount for a 10-school league as they had for a 12-school league. Only Colorado went to the Pac-10, and everyone else stayed in the Big 12. The Pac-10 quickly scooped up Utah to give itself a 12th member, which allowed the league to stage a championship game and make more television money.

In the stone age of the NCAA television deal, the narrator of Clemson's 1981 recruiting video boasted about a recent three-year span: "During these years," the narrator boomed, "Clemson's exposure reached an all-time high as it appeared on television 12 times— one of the highest exposure rates in the country." Now, Clemson fans would riot if they could only watch their team play on TV four times per season.

With the league's membership set and the conference rebranded as the Pac-12, Scott and Bevilacqua set about selling it to television executives. They also had to sell their vision for a new kind of rights deal to their presidents. One of the Power-Point slides Bevilacqua showed the presidents was a flow chart illustrating how money moves in a standard media rights deal. The entity providing the product—either a sports league or an entertainment production company—sells its product to a network. The network then sells at a higher price to a cable/satellite company, which then sells that product at an even higher price to viewers. Bevilacqua then showed the presidents a slide that illustrated how much ESPN stood to make off its new deal with the SEC. While $2 billion over 15 years sounded like an awful lot of money, Bevilacqua showed how the network could use SEC rights to drive ESPNU and ESPN3 toward full distribution. In the parlance of ESPN's Magnus, the SEC rights would be the spinal cord providing the nerve impulses to help grow those businesses—and make ESPN a tidy profit relative to its initial investment.

Scott and Bevilacqua convinced presidents to hedge their bet on a network plan by selling some of the league's games the traditional way. The difference? They would ask for a significantly higher price per game. In 2010, ESPN paid $1.1 billion per year for 18 NFL *Monday Night Football* games. That number will rise to $1.9 billion in 2013. At the same time, ESPN paid less than $1 billion for rights to about 400 college football games and about 1,500 college basketball games. (Part of this disparity stems from the fact that the NFL charges ESPN a steep premium to use a wide array of highlights from other games that ESPN then turns into shoulder programming that creates additional value, but even after taking that into account, the cost-per-viewer gulf remains huge.) At the same time, other major bidders had entered the market. Comcast and NBC had recently merged, and that company sought content for NBC, Versus (later rebranded NBC Sports Network) and all of Comcast's regional sports networks. Meanwhile, Turner Sports had recently made a huge investment to broadcast the NCAA men's basketball tournament and was exploring other college content. Unlike when the SEC made its deal, the Pac-12 had more hungry customers. Scott knew he was asking for a lot, but all they could say was no.

"After a couple of them got up off the floor when told what our expectations were—on top of the fact that we planned to withhold certain rights to launch our own network—ultimately we structured a great deal with ESPN and Fox," Scott said. That deal would pay the league just less than $3 billion over 12 years beginning with the 2012 football season. Even the average fan could see the Pac-12 deal outpaced every other league's deal, but the reason it sent shockwaves through the college athletics business was the amount of inventory the league sold to reach that amount. ESPN and Fox bought 44 football games and 68 men's basketball games a year. By contrast, ESPN and CBS will televise or sublicense 99 SEC football games in the 2012 season.

Bevilacqua and Scott then studied the various network models. The Big Ten Network had changed the game, and they looked into a similar arrangement. "We had four or five conversations with entities that would be equity partners like the

Big Ten Network model," Scott said. "They wanted at least a 50 percent share, and in return they would provide financial backing and distribution and marketing muscle." At the same time, a more radical idea emerged. Why not produce the product, sell it directly to the cable and satellite companies and keep all the money? This was Delany's Big Ten Network plan taken one step further. Instead of sharing network profits with an equity partner as the Big Ten does with Fox, the Pac-12 would keep all the money generated by its network. "We thought that long-term that we should be in the business ourselves," Scott said. "For the schools, we would be masters of our own destiny."

The downside to such a plan is risk. In a more traditional deal, ESPN or CBS or Fox takes all the risk, while the league can safely budget a set dollar figure every fiscal year. That figure may not rise beyond the agreed-upon amount, but it won't fall, either. There is no such guarantee when a league goes into the media business by itself, and that is precisely what Pac-12 leaders were discussing. "What you're really talking about," Bevilacqua said, "is building your own media company."

That media company, The Pac-12 Networks, will launch August 15. It has a built-in inventory of 35 football games and 120 men's basketball games as well as hundreds of contests in the non-marquee sports. For this, the league will keep 100 percent of the profits and take 100 percent of the risk. Scott has hedged that risk as well. Before the Pac-12 even announced the networks, it inked a deal with a consortium of cable companies that account for almost half of the cable or satellite subscribers in America. In return, the league promised those cable companies to split the networks into seven localized feeds to appeal to fans in specific markets. "The whole idea is super-serving your fan base," Scott said. "Fans in LA want more USC and UCLA than fans in Oregon, who want more Oregon and Oregon State." The league remains in negotiations with DirecTV to reach that company's 19.9 million subscribers, but it will launch with adequate carriage even if that deal doesn't get done immediately. (To make it happen faster, the league has cribbed one of the classic network carriage campaigns and adapted it for the Twitter age; now, various Pac-12 luminaries close their tweets with the #IWantPac12Networks hashtag.)

The Pac-12's deal set the realignment machine in motion again. The ACC took Pittsburgh and Syracuse from the Big East and has since reworked its ESPN deal to reflect its larger membership. The Big East later embarked on a quest to collect schools from every corner of the country, and that league hopes its patchwork of schools will draw a decent media rights deal when it begins negotiations this fall.

Meanwhile, those in the SEC don't like being second—or third—place in anything, and commissioner Mike Slive was not about to settle for a deal that didn't pay the SEC like the nation's best college football conference. But he had a problem. He had already sold his football and basketball inventory to ESPN and CBS. There was nothing left to sell—unless the league suddenly created additional inventory by adding additional schools. But who? In the summer of 2011, television issues continued to make the members of one league unhappy and willing to explore other opportunities.

The Longhorn Network, the reason Texas backed away from the Pac-10, stood poised to destroy the Big 12. Texas A&M officials, who had flirted with the SEC in 2010, bristled at the notion of a 24/7 propaganda tool for a conference rival—especially after Longhorn Network executive Dave Brown went on a radio show and essentially said the network would televise the high school games of Texas recruiting targets. Oklahoma and Oklahoma State put out feelers to the Pac-12. Missouri, which had been rebuffed in its attempt to join the Big Ten, continued to look elsewhere.

The Oklahoma schools didn't want to go to the SEC, but a healthy portion of Texas A&M's power base had been ready to go there in 2010. By 2011, few wanted to remain in the Big 12. By joining the SEC, the Aggies could rebrand themselves. By taking Texas A&M, the SEC could add the Lone Star State's massive population (25.7 million) to its geographic footprint. By adding millions more cable and satellite subscribers, the SEC could justify launching its own network. Later, when it came time to add a 14th school, SEC leaders took Missouri. Clemson or Florida State might have made more geographic sense, but they wouldn't have opened any new television markets for the league. Missouri did. The SEC couldn't tear up its contracts with ESPN and CBS, but adding so much earning power did give the league leverage to renegotiate.

Last month, Slive essentially confirmed at SEC Media Days that the league is working on a network. "We now call it Project SEC," Slive said. "Our objective long-term is to work with our television partner to provide fans with greater access to favored teams, more opportunities to watch rivals, and more insight into who we are: a conference of 14 great universities." Because ESPN already owns the bulk of the SEC's rights, the SEC Network would have to be a partnership with ESPN. When it begins will depend on how the league and network want to handle existing over-the-air syndication deals for football games, for which two years remain. ESPN could buy out the final year and launch the SEC Network in 2013, or it could allow them to expire and launch in 2014. How much money will Project SEC make for the league?

"We were pleased to set the market back then," Slive told SI.com's Stewart Mandel during a podcast last month. "We have aspirations of resetting the market. ... You can't see me smiling, but we have every expectation to reset the market."

While ESPN keeps coming up in regard to realignment, Magnus bristles at the notion that ESPN was the man behind the curtain moving schools from conference to conference. "The misunderstanding that is out there is that we were the architects behind this or that we cared to influence it," Magnus said. "I can say this with very, very personal knowledge and experience. If I could change the clock back to November of 2008 with a snap of my fingers, I would do that in a second. We were better off as a company." Magnus is correct. Before the most recent wave of realignment began, ESPN paid far less for college rights and made a higher profit margin off those rights. Few companies would pull strings to significantly increase their overhead. "Change happens," Magnus said. "If you fight change, you're going to lose."

So what comes next? In this most recent round of deals, network executives wisely bought rights to a wide variety of distribution methods. They know fans now expect the ability to watch games on televisions, gaming systems, smartphones and tablets, and they have locked up rights that allow them to offer games everywhere. ESPN has been at the forefront of the TV Everywhere movement, beginning with ESPN3.com and continuing with the WatchESPN app for smartphones and tablets. Turner and CBS, meanwhile, made the NCAA basketball tournament completely portable this year. As the hit-or-miss streaming on NBC's website has shown during the Olympics, the rest of the industry is chasing college sports up the curve. "It's the most important thing," ESPN's Magnus said. "The reason we're able to do deals of that length with college conferences is that they're willing to sell us the rights to exploit the content across all technologies whether we know of them now or whether they come halfway through the term."

Money and technology remain the wild cards. The NFL rakes in such huge sums because it is a single seller. It is the only entity selling elite professional football. There are five sellers (ACC, Big Ten, Big 12, Pac-12, SEC) of elite college football. That holds prices down somewhat. Will those leagues someday merge and sell their media rights as a single entity for an even more astronomical sum? They did it as the BCS for postseason games, and they'll do it again with the playoff. If they ever chose to pool regular-season rights, they'd be the CFA all over again. The Pac-12's Scott sees significant barriers to that, but with college sports still undervalued relative to their earning potential, anything is possible. "It would be no small undertaking," Scott said. "But I've said for some time that I do see—over time—you'll see further consolidation of conferences or more consolidation for how rights are sold. As there is more sophistication in the college space, you realize that value for schools is left on the table because of fragmentation. I think markets tend to correct."

Of course, one or two key technological advances could blow up the existing market and create an entirely new one. That's why networks and leagues have signed such long-term deals recently. They want to protect the universe they've created in case outside factors shift the paradigm again. "The only thing that is holding the [television distribution] industry—in my opinion—is live sports," Bevilacqua said. "Once that HD stream becomes so good that it comes into your 60-inch, Internet-enabled Apple television, then you're in a whole new world."

Share the Wealth

By Harry Edwards
Chronicle of Higher Education, December 1, 2011

The utterly unconscionable situation that exists in big-time revenue-producing col-legiate athletics today is reminiscent of the environment that existed more than 40 years ago, which prompted the "revolt of the black athlete" in the late 1960s. That reform effort drew sustenance from the black-power movement and changed the plantation structure of big-time intercollegiate sports, altering its landscape for all time. Now we are at another such pivotal moment, and it is crucial that the NCAA recognize it—and act swiftly on it.

As it exists today, the collegiate athletics arms race is both increasingly unman-ageable and ultimately unsustainable. It is characterized by problems associated with recruitment violations, illegal payments, and academic-eligibility issues; mul-timillion-dollar contracts for head coaches and expanded coaching staffs in football and basketball; the continuing expansion of conferences; and the grossly expanding athletics budgets and facility debt-service obligations, resulting in financial burdens upon students' tuition and fees and colleges' general-fund resources.

Of even more concern is the fiscal trajectory of "superconference" athletic-de-partment budgets. According to a 2010 report released by the Knight Commission on Intercollegiate Athletics, by the year 2020, "top collegiate athletic programs are expected to have overall budgets exceeding $250-million, athletic budgets serving an average of only 600 students."

Here is what has to happen now:

1. Athletic departments must wean themselves from the pressures, constraints, and uncertainties of their colleges' general-fund re-sources and gain increased support from outside corporate spon-sors. In other words, we could well be watching the "X-Oil Cor-poration" California Bears playing the "Y-Sports Drink" Oregon Ducks. In fact, the Ducks already have corporate sponsorship, as evidenced by the athletic department's multimillion-dollar rela-tionship with Nike. It's no secret—and it shouldn't have to be. If you can't be right, you can at least be honest. Aggressively solicit-ing and expanding corporate sponsorship of collegiate athletics would allow colleges to be both right and honest, while enjoying a sustainable flow of revenue without overburdening the general fund.

2. Big-time collegiate football and basketball programs must share the wealth with the athletes who produce the wealth. How can colleges tell these young men and women that they are amateurs while the campus bookstore sells their names and faces on T-shirts? How is it that the coaches are driving Mercedes while the players who do the hard work don't get paid? In October, the Division I Board of Directors changed the rules to allow conferences to provide up to $2,000 to players for miscellaneous living expenses, but that just kicks the can down the road. For one thing, it's not mandatory. This could result only in the creation of even greater imbalances in the athletics arms race, because some colleges that can better afford it will choose to provide such support, while other, less-profitable programs will not. Reasonably sufficient allowances for living expenses should be mandatory for all Division I grant-in-aid athletes on an individual-need basis.

3. The NCAA should start a conversation that includes labor lawyers, academics, athletic directors, college presidents, senior athletes who have gone through the system, experts who understand the agency system, and people who understand pro sports. This group should work out a system in which athletes could be represented by and paid by agents, who would take the risk of signing up those athletes in whom they want to invest. The students might receive advances, loans, or some other designated financial support from agents who are vetted by, registered with, and subject to accounting oversight by the NCAA and the conferences, colleges, and athletic departments involved. The exact character of such arrangements would need to be worked out, but the result would be a more equitable system, which would bring into the sunlight what is sometimes happening under the table right now.

This is the time for action. The culture of sports mirrors the larger societal culture in this country, and the movements that create change in each are intertwined. The civil-rights movement led to greater participation by African-Americans in sports at the college and professional levels, the black-power movement led to increasing numbers of black coaches, and the promotion of Title IX of the Education Amendments of 1972 by the women's-liberation movement led to greater equity for women's sports programs.

If the Occupy movement continues to gain resonance on campuses across the country, as earlier movements did, its effect on collegiate sports will not be far behind. That's what the line of history tells us. And if the NCAA does not get ahead of the curve and take advantage of the opportunity to shape the future of collegiate sports in this historical moment, it will find itself increasingly reduced to irrelevance—or worse.

How the SEC Became the Richest Conference in College Sports

By Victor Luckerson
Time, January 7, 2012

If any team has a reason to hold a grudge tonight as the Alabama Crimson Tide and the Notre Dame Fighting Irish battle for college football's national championship, it's probably the Georgia Bulldogs. Georgia came within 5 yards of upsetting the Tide in the Southeastern Conference (SEC) championship and earning a shot at the national title. It was a tough win for 'Bama to pull out and a tougher loss for Georgia to accept—Bulldogs quarterback Aaron Murray has said the loss will likely haunt him forever.

But nine days after the game, University of Georgia president Michael Adams already decided whom he'd be rooting for in the title game. "The pain is still there, but I'll be pulling for Alabama," Adams says. "I'm an SEC person."

That's a common sentiment in the South, where chants of "S-E-C!" often ring out in the stadiums of some of the country's most successful sports programs. But for the people in control of the Southeastern Conference—the university presidents, athletic directors and conference leadership—supporting the SEC is about much more than Southern pride. It's about protecting what has quickly grown into a billion-dollar enterprise that still has plenty of room left to grow.

Back in 2004, when the SEC's clout was so small that an undefeated Auburn Tigers team was left out of the national championship in favor of Oklahoma and Southern California, the athletic departments of the 12 SEC schools pulled in about $620 million, according to data collected by the Department of Education. By 2011 that number had ballooned to almost $1.1 billion, and the SEC had reached parity with the Big Ten to become one of the most valuable athletic conferences in college sports.

The fuel driving this economic engine has been winning of an unprecedented nature. If Alabama defeats Notre Dame on Monday, the SEC will claim its seventh consecutive national championship in football and its eighth in 10 years. The victories have catapulted what was once a regional brand with passionate local fan bases all the way into the national spotlight, and the schools are reaping the benefits. "I don't think there's any doubt that everybody [in the SEC] today is better funded, better recruited, better coached, better supported than we were a decade ago," Adams says. "It shows in the final [Bowl Championship Series] rankings where six of the top 10 schools were SEC schools."

Monetizing a Passionate Fan Base

The money that flows into college athletics comes from a myriad of sources, and SEC schools have been able to capitalize on most of them. With many of its schools located in small towns hundreds of miles from professional sports teams, the conference has led all of college football in ticket sales since 1998, with average attendance topping 75,000 per game in 2011. Half of the top 10 earners in merchandise and licensing revenue in 2011 came from the SEC, according to the Collegiate Licensing Company. Athletic boosters, a big component of a major college-sports budget, are especially prominent in the South, with six SEC athletic departments receiving more than $25 million in contributions and donations in 2011, according to data gathered by ESPN. "It's probably the best conference in the country right now in terms of potential for making money," says Dan Fulks, a research consultant for the NCAA.

While SEC fans are big game attendees, they're even bigger TV viewers. This year's SEC Championship between Alabama and Georgia earned 16.2 million viewers, triple the next most watched championship game, according to data provided by Nielsen. Last year the November matchup between the undefeated Alabama and LSU teams drew more than 20 million viewers, the most since 1989 for a regular-season college-football game on CBS. And despite the ongoing carousel of SEC teams in the national championship, the game has continued to pull in consistently huge viewership, with many predicting that this year's Alabama–Notre Dame matchup could set a ratings record. "There's a lot of interest in us whether you're for us or against us," says conference commissioner Mike Slive. "One of the reasons we're a significant television attraction is that our fans are interested not only in the game in which their institution is competing, but they're also interested in other SEC games."

Such impressive ratings are the reason the conference is well positioned in its current TV contract renegotiations with CBS and ESPN. Slive says the SEC set the bar for college athletics TV deals in 2008 when it negotiated contracts with the two networks worth over $3 billion in total over 15 years. Now he's getting an early opportunity to demand even more cash because newcomers Missouri and Texas A&M have vastly expanded the conference's media market. Experts predict that the new SEC deal will be the biggest one ever in college sports.

Texas A&M president R. Bowen Loftin readily admits that one of the main reasons his school bolted from the Big 12 after 15 years was money. In the SEC, revenue from bowl appearances and TV contracts are split evenly, while Big 12 payouts were based on the number of television appearances a team made until 2011. "We wanted to enhance the economic value to Texas A&M," Loftin says. "As TV contracts are renegotiated, as other revenue streams come online, we believe we'll see a rapid growth of revenue to all the schools in the SEC." Already, he says, licensing revenue has increased 26 percent year-over-year, and donations to the athletics department have risen sharply.

Trapped in an Arms Race

Now flush with cash, SEC schools find that spending heavily is the only way to stay competitive. "If you're going to compete in the Southeastern Conference, that means you have to have very competitive facilities, playing venues, workout spaces, coaches' offices, indoor training facilities," Adams says. "There clearly has been somewhat of an arms race the last 10 or 15 years."

Nowhere is the monetary competition clearer than in the salaries of coaches, which have shot up more than 70 percent across all major Football Bowl Subdivision colleges since 2006, according to *USA Today*. Alabama's Nick Saban is now the nation's highest-paid coach at almost $5.5 million per year, while SEC schools LSU, Auburn and South Carolina were also part of a small handful of institutions that paid their coaches more than $3 million in 2012.

"The money drives what's available to pay these coaches," says University of Florida president Bernie Machen, whose Florida Gators pay football head coach Will Muschamp about $2.5 million per year. "It's basically a market-driven phenomenon that we're sort of stuck in."

Facilities have also seen rapid improvements in recent years. A 2010 expansion brought Alabama's football-stadium capacity above 100,000, and LSU is planning an expansion that will bring its stadium near that number in 2014. The money flows into other sports programs as well, including an upgraded $4 million gymnastics practice facility at Florida, a $7 million dormitory for the Kentucky basketball team and a $35 million baseball stadium at South Carolina. Those investments are also paying dividends, with SEC teams claiming national titles in eight sports besides football in 2012.

But the gridiron remains the economic engine powering Southern athletics. "Football provides 75 percent of our budget here at Auburn," says athletic director Jay Jacobs. "Without the revenue from football, we wouldn't be able to operate very many sports."

There are drawbacks to participating in a conference that's so competitive physically and financially. Expensive buyouts of underperforming coaches have become common in the SEC, with six of the league's 14 schools spending a total of $26.5 million to pay coaches to leave in the past two years, according to *USA Today*. Tennessee's athletic department posted a $4 million deficit for the fiscal year back in August, largely because of expensive buyouts of former football, basketball, and baseball coaches. And despite a cleaner record than in years past, SEC football programs have still been subject to penalties in four cases of major infractions against NCAA rules since the championship streak began in 2007. "There is the issue of bigger and better and more, but I think institutions have to be very cognizant of what their limits are and what their resources can demand," Slive says.

This year, the SEC has not shown its signature imperviousness during postseason play. Northwestern defeated Mississippi State for its first bowl victory in over 60 years, LSU was foiled by Clemson, and Florida's surprising loss to Louisville was the biggest upset in BCS bowl history. A Notre Dame victory over Alabama could do a lot to undermine the image of otherworldly dominance the SEC has spent years building. So the Crimson Tide plays not only to earn a third championship in four years but also to preserve a brand that has become the gold standard for one of America's most popular sports. Even Jacobs, the athletic director at bitter in-state rival Auburn, acknowledges that a 'Bama win would benefit the conference as a whole. Winning begets money, which begets more winning. With a frenzied regional fan base, a national audience that's

> *Such impressive ratings are the reason the conference is well positioned in its current TV contract renegotiations with CBS and ESPN. Slive says the SEC set the bar for college athletics TV deals in 2008 when it negotiated contracts with the two networks worth over $3 billion in total over 15 years.*

yet to change the channel and two new teams that extend the conference's reach into the Midwest, the SEC may just be getting warmed up financially.

"Some people sit back and rest on their laurels when they're successful, but they've been investing back into their product," says Tom Regan, a professor in the department of sport-and-entertainment management at the University of South Carolina. "That's good business."

Women's Basketball Matures, but Not Without Growing Pains

By Libby Sander

Chronicle of Higher Education, December 9, 2011

When the women's basketball teams from Texas A&M and Notre Dame squared off for the national title in April, the game capped a three-week NCAA tournament that drew the highest television ratings since ESPN began airing the event more than 15 years ago.

The sport's rise hasn't happened by accident. Colleges are pouring money into women's basketball, and while that investment hasn't resulted in profits, the television exposure alone—ESPN and other networks will broadcast some 1,000 games this season—is giving more colleges a gateway to hundreds of thousands of viewers. But the on-air interest hasn't always translated to the campus, where many programs struggle to fill arena seats.

Those empty seats are one of several challenges facing the sport. To continue to thrive on the air, universities have to step up their marketing of women's hoops, says Carol Stiff, ESPN's vice president for programming and acquisitions.

"I'm just concerned that when we do have a game on television, that we maximize the look of the game to make sure there's energy in the building and great crowds," she says. With so many options on TV and Internet streaming, "if you come upon a game and the crowd's not there, the perception is [that] this isn't worth watching."

It's a perception that many officials are eager to fight. Solving the marketing puzzle will require colleges to figure out how to reach more fans who also love the men's game—and how to appeal to new followers.

Colleges must tackle that challenge amid changing times for the sport. As salaries and investment in the game grow, colleges are ratcheting up their expectations of coaches. Pressure to win has also heated up the recruiting scene, and with it growing concerns that coaches are now more inclined to bend or break NCAA rules to land top recruits.

All are familiar complaints to followers of men's basketball, which grapples with more-extreme versions of those problems. Indeed, as women's basketball grows more visible, it invites more comparisons with its popular but troubled counterpart for men—and some coaches, though enthused by the overall growth, fret that women's basketball is being forced down a road that increasingly runs parallel to the men's game. (In a small but significant move, some point out, even the three-point line in the women's game was moved back one foot this year, to match the men's.)

It leaves coaches puzzling over a question whose answer carries increasing weight as investment in the sport grows: Must women's basketball be a mirror image of men's basketball? Or can it thrive on its own?

Brenda Frese, head coach at the University of Maryland at College Park, sees a distinction. "We should be creating our own path," says Ms. Frese, who coached the Terrapins to the national championship in 2006. "Let's learn from the mistakes that the men have already made."

Big Investments, Big Goals

For years, the familiar orange uniforms of the University of Tennessee and the dark-blue ones of the University of Connecticut have been the choice of nearly all the top female players. Those famed programs have combined to win 15 of the last 25 national titles. In the world of women's basketball, the teams' head coaches—Pat and Geno—require no surnames.

But even the most impressive dynasties come to an end, or at least make room for new rulers. The two juggernauts still dominate—three weeks into the season, they were both ranked in the top 10—but parity is increasing, and it has opened the door to other serious contenders.

One of them is Ms. Frese's team at Maryland. Players here enjoy a wealth of amenities to propel them through a winning season. They practice and compete in a sparkling arena, work out in a new weight room all their own, and are nearly outnumbered by a small army of coaches and support staff charged with everything from replacing the players' busted shoes to monitoring how many classes they take. There's even a performance coach who quizzes the players each day to make sure they've eaten breakfast.

But nothing makes clear that the Terps—and women's basketball—are on the move so much as the head coach's employment contract. It is proof in writing that big universities see women's basketball as an increasingly visible component of their athletic programs: In 2010, Ms. Frese brought in nearly $1 million, making her the third-highest-compensated state employee.

In all, Maryland spent nearly $2.6 million last year on women's basketball. Revenues came in at just under $900,000, resulting in a deficit of $1.7 million. That exceeded the budget shortfall most big programs are willing to

According to NCAA surveys of current and former women's basketball players, some say they distrust their head coaches' integrity. Players' performance in the classroom lags, too: On the whole, women's basketball players do not fare as well academically as female athletes in other sports, according to NCAA studies. And many athletes have complained about spending nearly 40 hours a week on basketball-related activities—nearly double what is allowed under NCAA rules.

stomach for the sport: In 2010, the NCAA estimated that median losses totaled $1.2 million for women's basketball programs in the Football Bowl Subdivision.

Overall, women's basketball teams at 53 public universities in the six largest athletic conferences tallied operating losses in the 2010 fiscal year of nearly $110 million, according to a recent Bloomberg analysis. (Men's basketball teams at those institutions posted operating profits of $240 million.)

Yet colleges are sinking money into women's hoops for a reason. And it's increasingly the same reason they invest in the men's game.

"If you can find a way to get to the NCAA basketball tournament, the exposure it provides for your institution has such an unbelievable impact," says Jim Paquette, assistant vice president and athletic director at Loyola University Maryland, where expenditures last year on women's basketball, at $1.2 million, accounted for roughly a quarter of all money spent on the university's nine women's teams.

Last year Mr. Paquette's Greyhounds got a taste of something similar: They went to the Women's National Invitation Tournament and hosted the University of Virginia on their Baltimore campus. For a small institution, Mr. Paquette says, the game was a big deal, packing the modest basketball arena and creating an excitement on the campus he says he's rarely seen.

A Marketing Challenge

Despite the enhanced resources, growth and prosperity in women's basketball are hardly equitable—and even at flourishing programs like Maryland's, there are occasions when it's clear that women's basketball still has a long way to go.

Nothing illustrates that better than the Terps' season opener last month against Loyola.

Thirty minutes before tipoff, the Comcast Center, where 17,950 people make a full house, was a sea of empty red seats. Only a few dozen spectators milled about, far outnumbered by support staff, ushers, and the pep band.

The Greyhounds, who compete in the Metro Atlantic Athletic Conference, struggled from the start. With its taller, stronger, and flashier players, Maryland quickly assumed a double-digit lead, and held it for the entire game. Obvious enthusiasm over squaring off against a nationally ranked team couldn't help Loyola convert adrenaline into extra points. The final score left little room for interpretation: 84–46, Maryland.

Lopsided score aside, the game provided what fans of women's basketball love to see: crisp passes, aggressive drives to the basket, and—from the Maryland players, at least—a smothering defense. Along the sideline, Ms. Frese's twin sons, who were born during the 2008 season, bounced along to hip-hop music blaring from the loudspeakers during a timeout.

The contest was more than a glaring example of the slow growth of parity in women's basketball. It exposed a marketing challenge that continues to vex officials at Maryland and beyond.

The Terps usually draw a healthy crowd of spectators to their home games: Last season they averaged 5,161 fans and drew more than 10,000 people for a contest here against their conference rival, Duke University. But there were thousands of empty seats against Loyola. Attendance peaked at 2,271.

In many ways, Maryland faces an easier task in reaching out to fans. With a national title under their belt, the Terps have already made a name for themselves. The men's program, meantime, has deep roots at the institution. And metropolitan Washington is a basketball-loving region. Still, the season-high attendance record against Duke filled only about half the seats in the Comcast Center. The sparse crowd that showed up at the Loyola game skewed toward older fans of retirement age and young families.

At Loyola, marketing for women's basketball takes a different tack. Officials there focus promotions for women's basketball on families and youth groups. "If you close your eyes, you can tell if you're at a women's game or a men's game. You can tell from the pitch of the voices," Mr. Paquette says. The screams of young girls fill the small arena.

Sluggish ticket sales, particularly during the opening rounds of the NCAA tournament, have broader implications for the sport, too, especially as it captures the attention of TV suitors. Although the women's Final Four has sold out for 17 of the 30 years of its history, institutions that host games during the opening rounds of the tournament still struggle to fill all the seats despite efforts to play up the games.

Nonetheless, TV networks have been quick to ramp up their coverage of women's basketball even as the sport grapples with ticket sales. In 1996, the first year that ESPN broadcast the women's tournament, it aired 24 games. This season, it will air more than 300.

Sue Donohoe remembers how it used to be more than a decade ago.

"We were lucky if there were a couple hundred ball games on TV," says Ms. Donohoe, who has just stepped down from her post as an NCAA vice president, charged with helping women's basketball grow. This year, more than a thousand games will be shown across various platforms. She depends on a 26-page master TV schedule to guide her through the season.

Finding Balance

The big money many elite programs are pouring into women's basketball is a source of pride for coaches, some of whom have been with the game since its humble origins. But the heightened exposure also has some of them concerned about the impact of increased attention to their sport—particularly in recruiting.

"In the cave-woman era of women's basketball, no one cared. Why would you cheat if nobody cares?" says Tara VanDerveer, the longtime head coach at Stanford University. "But as there's more money put into it, there's more pressure to win. There's more visibility."

Ms. VanDerveer is co-chair of the Women's Basketball Coaches Association's ethics committee, formed a couple years ago to address increasing concerns about coaches' behavior. The NCAA is paying more attention, too: Its enforcement division has increased staffing for women's basketball.

According to NCAA surveys of current and former women's basketball players, some say they distrust their head coaches' integrity. Players' performance in the classroom lags, too: On the whole, women's basketball players do not fare as well academically as female athletes in other sports, according to NCAA studies. And many athletes have complained about spending nearly 40 hours a week on basketball-related activities—nearly double what is allowed under NCAA rules.

None of this has escaped the notice of Jody Conradt, who began her coaching career in 1969 and has been protective of the game ever since. "It's a two-sided coin," says Ms. Conradt, the longtime former coach at the University of Texas at Austin. "We're interested in building a sport with a fan base of people who care and watch. But on the other hand, all of that attention brings with it the things that aren't necessarily so attractive. The real trick is, how do we balance all that?"

In finding the answers, some officials are trying to pinpoint how it is that the final rounds of the NCAA tournament have proved to be so wildly successful while regular-season ticket sales tend to be far more modest.

Are there lessons to be learned from the opening rounds of the NCAA tournament, where sales have been unpredictable and officials still puzzle over how to solve it? It's a question that lingers for Kathy Meehan, associate vice president for athletics at St. John's University, in New York, who serves on the NCAA committee charged with managing and drumming up support for the three-week event.

"We've been stagnant in our fans and attendance," she says. "With all the time and investment we've put into it, we still haven't hit the mark. We're butting our heads against a great men's game, and there's only so much time that people have to go and watch an event."

And then there is the timing of the tournament. Some think the marquee event for women's basketball is overshadowed by the men's tournament, which takes place at the same time. Over the next few months, the NCAA will explore whether to slide back the women's championship to eliminate, or minimize, the overlap.

There are obstacles to that plan. ESPN might not favor such a move. Ms. Stiff, for one, says the network feels confident that the current scheduling allows the spotlight to shine brightly on the women's games. And March is a magical month for college basketball—not a bad time to be wedded to the men's tournament.

Still, there are some advocates of the sport who clearly feel that some middle ground is necessary.

"I think it's a disservice to the game to always compare it to the men's game," says Ms. Donohoe, formerly of the NCAA. "This game has grown enough that it has merit enough to stand on its own."

The tournament is still months away. But here at Maryland, where the Terps raced into the top 10 after winning their first several games, Ms. Frese is plotting her team's path to March and beyond. Her staff is already evaluating prospective players who are now sophomores in high school. She tunes out the headlines, she says, and focuses only on her team.

Lately, though, there have been reminders of just how favored her program is. The athletic department here is reeling from a decision last month to make major cuts in its programs. Expenses were spiraling upward, and without action the budget shortfall was projected to reach nearly $9 million within two years.

To save money, eight of the university's 27 teams will be discontinued next year. Women's basketball wasn't on the list.

Victory is sweet: Conseco Fieldhouse, in Indianapolis, erupted when Texas A&M beat Notre Dame in the NCAA women's basketball championship last year, but that enthusiasm has yet to be felt on campuses, where marketing the women's game, and filling the seats, have proved challenging.

"We should be creating our own path," says Brenda Frese, head coach of the University of Maryland's Terps. "Let's learn from the mistakes that the men have already made." So far, even successful programs like hers (which won the NCAA title in 2006) are not turning a profit.

Game On! Why Rupert Murdoch Wants to Tackle ESPN

By Sam Gustin
Time, March 6, 2013

In a word: money.

For months, News Corp., the media giant conglomerate run by billionaire mogul Rupert Murdoch, has been preparing to launch a new national Fox sports network. On Tuesday, Murdoch finally stepped into the batter's box. Fox Sports 1, as the company is calling it, presents a direct challenge to ESPN, which dominates cable sports and is one of the most lucrative cable channels on television.

Murdoch's move is just the latest indication that live sporting events have become one of the hottest areas of the media business.

The debut of Fox Sports 1 is not a surprise. Last month, News Corp. COO and trusted Murdoch deputy Chase Carey, called the network's launch "the world's worst-kept secret." Fox's challenge to ESPN, which is majority-owned by Disney, comes amid an increasingly crowded playing field. Both CBS and Comcast-owned NBC have launched national sports networks. So have the major professional sports leagues and many of the most powerful college conferences.

This August, Fox Sports 1 will become available in 90 million homes across the country, according to company officials, who unveiled the new channel at an event in New York on Tuesday. The network, which is replacing the company's Speed motor sports channel, will broadcast Major League Baseball games, college basketball and football, World Cup soccer, and NASCAR racing, among other sports. Fox Sports 1 will also feature the return of legendary talk-show host Regis Philbin, who has been hired to host a 5 p.m. afternoon show. Veteran football broadcaster Terry Bradshaw will also join the network.

It's not hard to understand why Murdoch is moving aggressively onto ESPN's turf—he's been planning this play for years. Americans love to watch live sports, which is why advertisers devote so much effort into developing ads for the Super Bowl, which is considered to be the advertising showcase of the year.

"ESPN, quite frankly, is a machine," Fox Sports executive vice president Bill Wanger said in comments cited by the *Associated Press*. "They have very consistent ratings, obviously huge revenue. We're coming in trying to take on the establishment. It's no different than Fox News or Fox Broadcasting back in the '80s. We're going to have to scratch and claw our way all the way to the top."

Murdoch is the underdog here, but he has defied the odds before, as with the introduction of the wildly successful FOX broadcast network and Fox News Channel, which dominates the cable news ratings. "We would remind those who think ESPN's incumbency is insurmountable that Fox has succeeded as the insurgent in two other significant cases: broadcast, with the launch of FOX in the mid-80s, and cable news, with the launch of Fox News Channel in the mid-90s," RBC analyst David Bank wrote in a research note cited by Reuters.

> *It's not hard to understand why Murdoch is moving aggressively onto ESPN's turf—he's been planning this play for years. Americans love to watch live sports, which is why advertisers devote so much effort into developing ads for the Super Bowl, which is considered to be the advertising showcase of the year.*

ESPN, which generates $6 billion in revenue every year, commands $5.15 per month for each subscriber from the major cable television companies, the highest subscription fee of any cable channel. By comparison, Fox Sports North, among the most lucrative of the Fox regional sports channels, only generates $3.68 per month, according to research firm SNL Kagan. (News Corp. currently owns 22 regional sports networks across the country, which will help promote the new national channel.)

ESPN offered a muted response to Fox's challenge. "We like our position," ESPN spokesman Josh Krulewitz told the *AP*. "We have always had vigorous competition so there is really nothing substantially new here. Others are, however, beginning to recognize what we have long known: The power of live sports, especially in light of technological advances, is substantial and brings tremendous value in today's entertainment landscape."

In preparation for the launch, Murdoch has been systematically gathering broadcast rights for major sports teams. Last fall, the company re-signed a deal to televise Major League Baseball games, and announced a blockbuster pact to buy 49 percent of the Yankees Entertainment and Sports (YES) Network, the country's most valuable regional sports network. That deal, which values YES at a whopping $3 billion, allies Murdoch with the Bronx Bombers, arguably the most valuable professional sports franchise in the world.

"They've lined up an impressive amount of sports rights and they appear to be off to a good start," SNL Kagan analyst Derek Baine told Bloomberg. "But nobody expects them to be ESPN overnight."

So why did it take so long for Fox to challenge ESPN? For the last few years, Murdoch and News Corp. have been somewhat preoccupied with the U.K. phone-hacking scandal, which led to the closure of *News of the World*. Several former News Corp. employees have been charged with criminal conduct for illegally breaking into the cell phones of British celebrities and crime victims.

The debut of Fox Sports 1 comes as News Corp. is in the process of breaking itself into two independent companies. Fox Group will include the new sports channel, as well as the company's most lucrative entertainment businesses, including Hollywood movie studio 20th Century Fox, the FOX broadcast network, and cable news leader Fox News Channel. These businesses accounted for 90 percent of News Corp.'s operating income in 2012. A much smaller publishing entity, which will keep the name News Corp., will include the company's newspapers, its education business, and the HarperCollins publishing house.

4

The Concussion Culture

Associated Press

Adam Bartsch demonstrates a test for football helmet–to–helmet collisions.

Responsible Solutions to Concussion-Related Injuries

Concussion is the most common type of neurological injury, medically classified as traumatic brain injury (TBI) and defined generally as a head injury resulting in a temporary loss of brain function. While concussions have long been a concern in youth, college, and professional sports, especially contact sports such as football and boxing, modern research has helped to bring about greater public awareness regarding the dangers and frequency of concussions in all athletic competitions. As a result of medical research into brain science and concussion, participation in boxing, football, and other concussion-prone sports is down among both youth and professional leagues. In response, sports leagues are attempting to develop more effective strategies for preventing, detecting, and treating concussions.

Causes of Concussions

Concussions can be caused either by a blow to the cranial region or by violent shaking movement that causes the brain to shift within the skull. Concussions are not always accompanied by loss of consciousness. Symptoms associated with concussion differ between individuals and according to the severity of the injury.

The brain is surrounded by a layer of cerebrospinal fluid that serves to cushion the brain during movement and, ideally, prevents the brain from impact with the skull. If the body is shaken violently or an individual receives a blow to the skull, the brain and the skull may come into contact, causing injury to the soft tissues of the brain. The symptoms resulting from an impact of this type differ depending on the part of the brain affected and a variety of other variables including brain, body size, and cranial thickness.

Difficulty in Diagnosis

Because there are no symptoms that definitively indicate concussion, physicians tend to diagnose concussions by looking for patterns of symptoms. Data from American sports organizations and the Center for Disease Control indicate that concussions are exceedingly common in competitive sports. Between 1.4 and 3.8 million TBIs are diagnosed each year among athletes. At least 300,000 of these concussions affect athletes that are in nonprofessional leagues. Estimates indicate that 10 to 20 percent of athletes suffer a TBI an average of once per season.

Unconsciousness occurs in only 10 percent of concussions and mild concussions may manifest in generalized symptoms that do not clearly indicate injury, such as dizziness or headache. Some sports-medicine experts estimate that more than 85 percent of mild concussions are undiagnosed. Symptoms resulting from a TBI can last for hours, days, weeks, or months after the initial injury depending on the severity of the concussion. Cognitive symptoms include having difficulty thinking clearly or impaired short-term memory function. Concussion victims may experience emotional symptoms including mood fluctuations, depression, and anger. In children, this may manifest as difficulty controlling temper or excessive crying.

Concussions are also accompanied by physical symptoms that include headache, dizziness, nausea, vomiting, blurred or reduced vision, difficulty maintaining one's balance, and lethargy or fatigue. Concussions tend to affect sleep patterns; they may result in either an increased need for sleep or a reduced ability to sleep, depending on the specifics of the injury.

The traditional method of concussion diagnosis involves asking a series of questions to gauge the patient's physical and mental state. Physicians generally begin by performing tests to make sure that the individual has not suffered any potentially threatening circulatory or respiratory complications. If the symptoms seem to worsen during the period of observation, physicians may conduct additional tests, such as examining dilation in the eyes or the relative size of the patient's pupils, which can provide an indication of more extreme damage or hemorrhaging in the brain.

Other diagnostic tools include x-ray computed tomography, known as a CT scan, and magnetic resonance imaging, also known as MRI. Each of these scanning techniques is used to detect lesions in the brain. Brain lesions tend to form within twenty-four hours after the initial impact and brain scans are generally only conducted when the symptoms worsen or indicate the potential for more extreme damage. Medical imaging techniques may be unable to detect mild concussions and are most useful in cases where complications have occurred, indicating a more severe injury.

One of the most reliable ways to check for TBI is to obtain CT scans or MRI scans of an individual before and after an injury and to compare the results. Increasingly, professional sports organizations are performing scans on players before a concussion is suspected to enable this type of testing. Pre-participation exams (PPE) are common in professional and collegiate football, for instance, though some medical experts believe that existing PPEs do not sufficiently address concussion risk.

CT scans are costly and the equipment needed is cumbersome. For these reasons, many sporting organizations only use medical imaging when severe injury is suspected. A new technique revealed in 2013 by scientists at Notre Dame University may indicate the way that diagnostic techniques will evolve in the future. Computer scientists have developed a program that can be loaded onto a tablet and can be used to measure speech patterns before and after a potential brain injury. By measuring differences in speech, including nasality, imprecise consonants, and other indicators, the program can help to indicate whether a minor concussion has occurred.

Complications from Concussions

The treatment for a minor concussion generally involves giving the patient pain relievers and recommending rest to allow the brain to heal on its own. Allowing sufficient time for recovery can be a problem, especially since so many minor concussions are not diagnosed. An individual who suffers a TBI may feel relief from physical or mental symptoms long before the brain has completely healed. Some studies indicate that individuals who have suffered a concussion in the past may be more likely to suffer additional concussions. Though scientists do not fully understand this trend, it appears that past injury makes the brain more susceptible to future injury.

Research indicates that more than 20 percent of concussions are recurrent, including more than 13 percent of concussions suffered by high school athletes. Post-concussion brain scans in patients experiencing recurrent concussions indicate that individuals both do not recover as quickly as those who have isolated concussions and run an increased risk of suffering additional complications after their first concussion. These findings indicate the importance of determining an athlete's complete concussion history during an effective PPE. Sports medicine professionals are working to adjust interviews and other evaluation methods used to determine whether an individual has suffered previous concussions.

Chronic traumatic encephalopathy (CTE) is one of the most well-known complications of repeated concussion. CTE has been tentatively linked to repeated head trauma and known to occur in athletes involved in football, boxing, hockey, and other contact sports. CTE is a progressive, degenerative disease marked by the development of the abnormal protein "tau," which is often used as the primary diagnostic for the disease. CTE has been known to occur in boxers since the 1920s and has been studied in that population. Increasingly, occurrence of CTE has been discovered among former football players. The highly publicized suicides of former San Diego Chargers linebacker Junior Seau and former Chicago Bears safety Dave Duerson were both linked to emotional-psychological issues resulting from the onset of CTE. These suicides helped to bring the CTE issue to the forefront of the professional sports health debate.

Symptoms associated with CTE include memory loss, confusion, impaired judgment, motor-control issues, aggression, depression, and severe dementia. It is difficult to determine when an individual will experience the onset of CTE, and it is also difficult to determine why some individuals appear prone to the condition while others do not. The first symptoms of the disease may occur weeks, months, years, or even decades after traumatic brain injury, which provides an impediment to early diagnosis. In 2013, researchers at the North Shore Neurological Institute in Illinois found that they were able to detect signs of CTE development using low-radioactivity brain scans. Though this technique is not in general use, the team hopes that techniques like these will allow for earlier diagnosis and treatment in the future.

Implications for Professional Sports

Research indicating that concussions occur more frequently in sports than previously thought has important implications for the future of professional sports. Additionally, increased public knowledge about concussion-related diseases like CTE has brought the health risks of professional sports to the forefront of the public consciousness. Interest in amateur and professional boxing has been in decline for decades, largely linked to a growing public sentiment that boxing is an unhealthy and overly dangerous sport that often leads to debilitating injury. By contrast, the association between professional football and concussions had not been as clearly demonstrated, and only recently has the public begun to debate whether football might also be too dangerous to be considered a healthy sporting activity.

In 2013, more than four thousand players and their family members undertook a legal suit against the National Football League (NFL) stemming from concussion-related brain injuries suffered by players. The players and their families allege that the NFL acted irresponsibly, allowing players to continue participating on the field after suffering a concussion, thus increasing their risk of sustaining lasting neurological damage. In addition, the lawsuits allege that the NFL may have downplayed research indicating that football players suffered frequent concussions and that concussions were related to CTE. Though the legal liability of the NFL has not been decisively determined in the courts, ultimately the NFL may need to institute a variety of policy changes to protect the industry from future legal action. In March 2013, the NFL announced that it was partnering with General Electric Co. and undertaking a $60 million effort to improve the diagnosis of brain injury and to develop new ways to prevent head trauma.

Estimates derived from the National Sporting Goods Association indicate that overall participation in football, at all ages, decreased from 10.1 million in 2006 to less than 9 million in 2011. In addition, the National Federation of State High School Associations estimates that participation in high school football has also decreased, dropping by as many as ten thousand players per year. Studies indicate that the NFL and amateur football organizations have failed to mandate anticoncussion equipment, and the league's procedures continue to weaken the public perception of American football. Many health analysts and former players continue to argue that professional and student football programs need to make drastic changes to increase safety standards.

In recent years, an increasing number of athletes, former athletes, and public figures have spoken out about the dangers of football and have expressed trepidation about children and young athletes becoming involved in the game. Former NFL player Kurt Warner has said in interviews that, he would not allow his children to play football because he considers the sport too dangerous. In January 2013, President Barack Obama stated in an interview that although he described himself as a football fan, he was uncertain whether he would be able to allow a son, if he had one, to play the game because of the health risks. President Obama added that he believed football was going to need to evolve to address persistent health issues, perhaps reducing the focus on violent contact that has come to characterize the game. While Obama sympathized with those who believe changes of this nature might make football less exciting in some respects, most people agree that the league must take drastic steps to enhance safety if it hopes to stem the tide of eroding public opinion.

While the NFL and other organizations may be culpable for some of the injuries suffered by professional athletes, the inherent difficulty of diagnosing and recognizing concussions also contributes to the complexity of the head-injury phenomenon. The debate over concussions is partially the result of modern research indicating a new understanding of how concussions and repeated injuries affect the brain over long periods. Questions remain regarding whether or not new equipment and safety regulations can address health concerns in such a way that contact sports can still be practiced safely.

Former Packer Tauscher Backs Concussion Bill

By Scott Bauer
Associated Press, February 22, 2012

Longtime Green Bay Packer offensive lineman Mark Tauscher joined high school athletes, doctors and state lawmakers on Wednesday to push the Wisconsin Legislature to pass legislation designed to reduce concussions in youth sports.

The National Football League has been lobbying Wisconsin and 18 other states that have yet to adopt laws requiring that young athletes be immediately removed from their activity if they appear to be suffering from a head injury. In January, NFL Commissioner Roger Goodell and NCAA President Mark Emmert sent letters to the states' governors calling for passage of the laws.

To help make the case, former NFL players have been speaking out in support of similar laws across the country. Tauscher joined in Wednesday, saying awareness of the dangers posed by concussions has increased over the years, but more needs to be done.

Tauscher, 34, grew up in Wisconsin, played football for the University of Wisconsin and was drafted by the Packers in 2000 and played for 11 years before being released in 2011. He said there used to be a stigma attached to players who were viewed as not being tough if they didn't shake off a big hit.

"We, as players, have never understood the consequences of what's going on," Tauscher said at the Capitol news conference.

After suffering at least 10 concussions over three years, Richland Center High School senior Brock Rosenkranz said he was forced to stop playing football and basketball. He talked about his headaches, memory loss, depression and insomnia, and the medication he now takes to deal with his symptoms.

"People just don't really get this problem," he said, adding that he wants to help others understand the importance of the issue.

The Wisconsin bill is modeled after Washington state's 2009 "Zackery Lystedt Law," named for a middle school football player who sustained brain damage after he suffered a concussion and returned to play.

The bipartisan proposal easily passed the Wisconsin Assembly but has stalled in the Senate, where some Republicans expressed concern about placing new mandates on school districts.

The bill would require young athletes who suffer what appears to be a concussion or head injury to be immediately removed from practice or games and not be allowed to return until examined by a health care provider and given written clearance.

The bill would require young athletes who suffer what appears to be a concussion or head injury to be immediately removed from practice or games and not be allowed to return until examined by a health care provider and given written clearance.

The proposal would also require the state Department of Public Instruction, in conjunction with the Wisconsin Interscholastic Athletic Association, to develop guidelines and other information to educate coaches, athletes and parents about the risk of concussions and head injuries.

One alternative proposal circulated among Republican senators would give schools the option to develop policies, but they would not be required to do so. Student athletes also wouldn't be forced to leave the playing field after suffering an injury.

The original bill's sponsor, River Hills Republican Sen. Alberta Darling, said the mandate was necessary to protect children and teens. She said Wisconsin residents should contact their local lawmakers and urge them to pass the bill before the session ends in mid-March.

Concussions are caused by a hard blow to the head. The injury can affect memory, judgment, reflexes, speech, balance and muscle coordination, and the symptoms become worse if not properly treated. Young people, particularly girls, are more susceptible to long-term repercussions than adults.

The number of athletic children going to hospitals with concussions increased 60 percent in the past decade, according to a study released in October by the Centers for Disease Control and Prevention.

The CDC has reported that athletic activities lead to nearly 4 million concussions a year.

USA Football last week announced it was commissioning a full-season research study to examine player health and safety in organized youth tackle football. USA Football is the official youth football development partner of the NFL, the NFL Players Association and each of the league's 32 teams, as well as the Atlantic Coast Conference.

Reducing concussions both in the NFL and in youth sports is a priority of the league, NFL lobbyist Kenneth Edmonds said Wednesday.

A federal judge in Philadelphia last month consolidated four lawsuits blaming the NFL for concussion-related dementia and brain disease. The lawsuits represent more than 300 retired players or spouses, including two-time Super Bowl champion Jim McMahon.

The NFL has disputed claims of wrongdoing made in the lawsuits.

In November, Green Bay Packers great Forrest Gregg disclosed that he was fighting Parkinson's disease and he and his neurologist believe it may be related to numerous concussions he suffered during his nearly two-decade-long playing career.

In addition to the NFL and the Packers, other supporters of the Wisconsin bill include the Wisconsin Medical Society, the Medical College of Wisconsin, the University of Wisconsin, Children's Hospital of Wisconsin and other health care groups.

Genetic Research on Sports Injuries Takes an NFL Veteran to a California College

By David Glenn
Chronicle of Higher Education, April 1, 2011

From 1979 to 1985, James Kovach was a linebacker for the New Orleans Saints. But you wouldn't find him much at Mardi Gras or on Bourbon Street. During his off-seasons, he was back at his alma mater, the University of Kentucky, earning a medical degree. After he retired from football, he topped that off with a law degree from Stanford University.

Today Dr. Kovach spends many of his hours talking with friends and former teammates who are experiencing the long-term effects of concussions. He suffered four of them when he was a Saint. He says he hasn't detected any lasting damage in himself, but he has become an advocate for former players who have been demanding that the NFL take head injuries more seriously. (If you're an NFL veteran terrified of developing tremors and dementia, there is probably some comfort in having a doctor/lawyer/linebacker in your Rolodex.) He is also president and chief executive of Athleticode, a biotech start-up that sells athletes personalized genetic analyses that are intended to guide their gaining and warn them about their propensities to injury.

In January, Dr. Kovach began to play yet another role: adjunct professor of biology. At Dominican University of California, he has developed an undergraduate course on sports injuries. Such courses are reasonably common in kinesiology programs, but this one is different. Dr. Kovach is trying to reach a broad range of biology and health-science majors. The point isn't to teach about sports injuries per se, but to use the topic as a hook for lessons in epidemiology, physiology, genetics, and ethics.

At the age of 54, Dr. Kovach looks like an athlete, but it's hard to picture him as a football player. His hair is receding, his build is slim, and his general demeanor is more Northern California tech entrepreneur than Kentucky gridiron.

One thing that excites him about the course, he says, is the opportunity to teach students to read scientific research intelligently. "I've asked them to write literature reviews on some of the key questions here," he says. "Do football helmets prevent concussions? Does synthetic turf increase the rate of injury? The idea is not to write a persuasive paper, but just to write something accurate and analytical."

Dr. Kovach became familiar with Dominican when he was president of the nearby Buck Institute for Research on Aging, an independent center that often hires undergraduate researchers from the college. When Sibdas Ghosh, chair of

Dominican's natural-sciences department, invited him to create a course last year, he found the idea hard to resist.

The course is also proving to be a fruitful forum for discussing the ethics of genetic screening of athletes. Last year the NCAA began requiring all Division I programs to screen athletes for the sickle-cell trait, which has been linked to the deaths of several football players.

That is just the early frontier of genetic screening for athletes, Dr. Kovach says. Researchers have found associations between certain gene variants and tendencies toward concussions and anterior-cruciate-ligament injuries, commonly known as ACL injuries. (Such an injury forced him out of football in 1985.) In collaboration with Huntington E. Willard, director of Duke University's Institute for Genome Sciences and Policy, Dr. Kovach is searching for genetic markers that might indicate high vulnerability to long-term damage from concussions, including chronic traumatic encephalopathy.

Dr. Kovach's commercial venture, Athleticode, analyzes athletes' COL5A1 genes, certain variants of which are associated with an elevated risk of Achilles tendinitis. Many more such tests are likely to emerge.

But in the case of concussions, the genetic correlations are not likely to be fully understood for a long time. "On some of these questions, we won't be able to really say anything for 20 years," he says. Some post-concussion symptoms take decades to emerge, and the process of identifying genetic markers for those vulnerabilities might take just as long. Similarly, Dr. Kovach says, it will take years for scientists to assess the dangers faced by players at the high school and college levels.

"To know whether it's only the pro athletes or millions of amateur football players—it's going to be years before we know that," he continues. "But I think it's going to be a relentless series of bad news."

On the Side of Caution

Timothy E. Hewett, director of the Sports Medicine Dynamics Center at the Cincinnati Children's Hospital Medical Center, has studied genetic associations with ACL injuries. He says this area of research is "extremely promising, but I think we have to approach this with great caution."

What the research has shown more than anything else, Mr. Hewett says, is that environmental and genetic factors interact in highly complex ways. You can't create an exercise regimen simply by reading a genotype.

People with a certain gene variant tend to have unusually low levels of collagen in their ligaments, which, all else being equal, makes them vulnerable to ACL injuries. But Mr. Hewett notes that such vulnerability is contingent on other factors as well. For example, if the person has high levels of neuromuscular control and avoids hyperextending her joints, her vulnerability to injury might be no greater than the average person's.

"As scientists, we don't even come close to understanding these questions." he says. For that reason, he is skeptical of ventures like Dr. Kovach's Athleticode, which offers genetic counseling on a retail basis.

"We're going to hand all of this over to an individual and a family and expect them to understand what all this means?" Mr. Hewett asks.

Other scholars in the field agree that there are serious ethical hurdles in this work. Vicki L. Kristman, an assistant professor of public health at the University of Toronto, did a study a few years ago on the relationship between a certain gene variant and vulnerability to concussion. Participants in the study did not know initially whether they carried the gene, and Ms. Kristman and her colleagues decided not to tell them after the fact.

> *Some post-concussion symptoms take decades to emerge, and the process of identifying genetic markers for those vulnerabilities might take just as long.*

That was because the gene variant is also associated with Alzheimer's disease, which cannot be cured or prevented. "There seemed to be an ethical issue in giving people this information and saying, 'There you go. You may get Alzheimer's, but there's nothing you can do.'"

Dr. Kovach does not dispute the ethical challenges, but he says he will usually err on the side of patients' right to know. "I played with many of the people who have had problems, the most recent of whom is Dave Duerson, who committed suicide," he says. "And to be a parent—my son played football at Duke. I feel the world changing under my feet in terms of the kinds of things I would recommend for concussion safety. I'll always be on the side of caution."

Mr. Ghosh, the department chair who recruited Dr. Kovach to Dominican, says he hopes to expand the course from a one-credit to a three-credit offering.

Tasha Kahn, a senior biology major in the course, supports that idea. "The textbook is excellent, and there's a huge amount of material here, but it's not possible to cover it all when we meet just once a week," she says.

For her semester project, Ms. Kahn is reading scholarly research on whether certain types of stretching can prevent injuries in various sports. Her one complaint about the course: She would like to see attention given to sports beyond football. (But she cheerfully concedes that football is what the professor knows.)

Dr. Kovach says he relishes his conversations with students. "If you can get two or three things in the course that people will remember for a substantial period of time—just to help remember a few nuggets about the incredibly exciting time that humanity has now reached, and the implications of genetic science—that's what makes this worthwhile."

The NFL's Concussion Culture

By Nate Jackson
Nation, August 15, 2011

Many former players are degenerating at an early age, but the league doesn't seem to care.

A few months after former Chicago Bears star Dave Duerson committed suicide in February at age 50, researchers at Boston University confirmed that he had suffered from a form of dementia that has been linked to repeated brain trauma.

Until recently, the skeletons in the NFL's closet were easier to hide. Sure, something stunk, but no one quite knew what it was. But now players from the 1980s and '90s are turning up dead. And it's pretty hard to ignore the questions that spring from the shocking fact that the same brain disease that afflicted Duerson has been confirmed in at least twenty recently deceased players.

Why is it that men who were the strongest and fittest people alive when they were young degenerate so quickly? That's the million-dollar question. Ask NFL commissioner Roger Goodell, and you won't even get an answer. I guess I don't really blame him. What can he do, agree with the critics? Yup, football kills.

One of the NFL's latest plays, finalized in labor talks this past March, was to change the kickoff rules. Now the ball will be kicked off from the thirty-five-yard line, and the kickoff team will get only a five-yard running start instead of the unlimited start it had before (which rarely amounted to more than ten yards). This was all created by the "competition committee," a group of NFL coaches and executives who tweak the rules every year based on perceived trends and public relations needs.

For example, in 2009 the competition committee eliminated the "wedge" from kickoff returns. I recall one member citing Kevin Everett's 2007 spinal injury as an example of the perils of wedge returns. I was playing in that game in Buffalo when Kevin broke his neck, and I watched the play happen. The Bronco returner chose to carry the ball outside the wall of interlocked players, away from the "wedge" blocking formation that is now banned. He and Kevin Everett collided in a very routine football hit. The result was far from routine. By all accounts, Kevin nearly died on the field that day.

In a move that would symbolize the league's strategy in dealing with player health, the NFL made an arbitrary change to the rules, hoping that eliminating wedges would come across as a genuine attempt to protect players. This new kickoff rule smells exactly the same. Knowing the wide reach of sports media, committee members find forums on lapdog platforms like ESPN, the NFL Network and Pro Football Talk, and speak in earnest about their concern for player safety. They say they understand that players don't like it, but, geez guys, we're looking out for *you!*

If that were true, players would be better cared for when their bodies begin to fall apart in early middle age. They are forgotten on purpose because acknowledging the health issues of former players draws attention to a dirty little secret: when you sacrifice your body for the game, your brain goes with it. According to the Alzheimer's Association International Conference in Paris, retired NFL players are more likely than similarly aged men to develop mild cognitive impairment, a form of dementia that can lead to Alzheimer's disease. But don't look to us for help. You're on your own now, buddy. Unless you can still play, that is. Think you've got some juice left in the tank?

Every day, players are risking long-term injury by rushing themselves back on the field after being hurt. The average NFL career lasts only 3.5 years, and the window of opportunity to carve out a roster spot is dangerously thin. Minimum salary goes up with experience, so the trend is to push out the veterans and bring in younger, cheaper labor.

Under the recently expired collective bargaining agreement, vested players received five years of postfootball health coverage. So right about the time the player dug himself out of the hole he'd been living in after he realized his life peaked in his 20s, his healthcare ran out. And the real problems don't show up for twenty years anyway—plenty of time for him to be forgotten. (Players now have the option of buying into the NFL's health policy for life.)

For current players, the hypocrisy is equally disturbing. Players have little control over their bodies; they are the property of the team. When a player is injured, he is rushed back onto the field by an athletic trainer who is being pressured by the coach to get his guys playing again. The rehabilitation and surgical approaches for injuries are often decided by team doctors and trainers who are paid by the organization and have no vested interest in the long-term health of the man who is hurt.

Every day, players are risking long-term injury by rushing themselves back on the field after being hurt. The average NFL career lasts only 3.5 years, and the window of opportunity to carve out a roster spot is dangerously thin. Minimum salary goes up with experience, so the trend is to push out the veterans and bring in younger, cheaper labor.

Injured players are strapping it up every day because they are told by medical staff, voices they should be able to trust, that their injuries should be healed by now. And "split" clauses in many contracts severely cut pay if the player goes on injured reserve. In other words, players are punished for getting hurt and rewarded for acting like they're not even when they are.

Compounding the problematic medical approach to injury treatment is an in-stitutional pressure not to be a "pussy." How tough are you? Can you play on that broken ankle? That separated shoulder? With that concussion? Your headaches are gone, right? Because this is glory, son. This is what people will remember you for. And besides, if you can't suck it up and get it done, then we'll find someone else who can. Test an athlete like that, and of course he's going to make every effort to play.

But at what price comes the glory? And what glory is this, anyway, when no one can even remember who won the Super Bowl two years ago? The train keeps mov-ing along, pausing only to refuel with new talent and lose the dead weight of bro-ken bodies. But our football-adoring society sees only the refueling, because the NFL carefully crafts that image. For every rookie who makes a team this season, a veteran loses his job forever and packs his bag for a lifetime of physical pain. You'd think the NFL would try to lighten that load. But you'd be wrong.

Concussions in Youth Sports

By Matt Terl
Parks and Recreation, December 1, 2011

When Shane Caswell was a high school hockey player in upstate New York, a dirty hit put him headfirst into the boards, knocking him out. He quickly regained consciousness and skated off to the bench. "When I went back to the bench, I got very emotional," Caswell says now. "I was crying, I was swearing, which aren't normal behaviors for me. And in retrospect, I couldn't see and was having visual disturbances."

Today, these symptoms would immediately indicate concussion. In 1991, Caswell's coach put him back into the game almost immediately, only taking him out when it was clear that his disorientation was severe enough that he couldn't contribute.

"There was no medical care," Caswell says, "and really no understanding at the time of what a concussion was."

Caswell was fortunate and escaped with no ill effects, but the incident haunted him. Which is part of how he wound up as Dr. Caswell, in charge of the Sports Medicine Assessment Research and Testing (SMART) Laboratory at George Mason University, a multi-disciplinary sports medicine lab focused on injury prevention and human performance. One of Caswell's specialties is, of course, concussions.

It's a lively field to be involved in at the moment, at all levels of sport. Professional sports leagues have made strides to improve concussion awareness and regulate return to play. High schools have followed suit—and, increasingly, parks and recreation agencies are also getting involved in testing and concussion safety. Recently, for example, the Franklin Lakes (New Jersey) Recreation and Parks Department mandated cognitive baseline testing for athletes participating in their programs and facilities,

Cognitive baseline tests are used to detect subtle changes in the way information is processed by someone who has suffered a concussion. The test is first taken while healthy, establishing a baseline, and administered again as one of the final steps in determining when someone is no longer suffering a concussion's effects.

As public concern over concussions grows, other parks and recreation administrators and staffers might naturally be inclined to follow Franklin Lakes' lead.

Which might not be the best idea.

"These exams are a tool," Caswell explains. "They are designed to be used by a qualified and well-trained healthcare professional who understands concussions.

They're really not intended to be used by untrained and unqualified non-medical professionals, such as coaches, parents, and administrators."

James Kozlowski, an attorney specializing in the legal aspects of parks and recreation administration (and a regular *Parks & Recreation* contributor), agrees. "Right now I don't think it is the community's responsibility for doing it," Kozlowski says. "Just because some people are doing it doesn't mean you're negligent for not doing it."

In fact, Kozlowski explains, adding this requirement might open parks and rec agencies to more liability rather than less.

"In this whole area oftentimes less is more," he says. "At this point in time, there's no requirement that that be done. But if you assume that you're going to do it, you'd better do it right."

The popularity of cognitive baseline tests (ImPACT being the best-known brand) stems partly from their use on the professional level. But even NFL athletic trainers express skepticism that these tests are the best way to help younger athletes.

According to Larry Hess, head athletic trainer for the Washington Redskins, "The biggest thing now is heightened awareness. There's more awareness of the signs and symptoms and more education, and I think that's what we have to get across to the youth athletes and the people that are around them every day."

Again, Caswell agrees. SMART Lab has partnered with Central Loudoun (Virginia) Youth Football, a nonprofit league for ages 6–14 that uses municipal fields, and implemented a more holistic approach to concussions and sports injuries. The league maintains a safety commissioner, handling general league safety procedures, and has entered into an affiliate agreement with George Mason University, paying a portion of the tuition for one of Caswell's graduate assistants—a Certified Athletic Trainer—to serve as the medical authority at nearly all of their league games.

"There are multiple benefits," league president Roly Rigual explains. "Not only do we get the benefit and security of having a medically trained person at these contact games in case something really bad happens, but we're collecting data," which will be used in the future to identify trends and minimize risks.

Caswell has helped the league set up an online injury monitoring system, even tracking injuries incurred in practice. He has also provided mandatory coaching safety training, which he believes is the most important element parks and rec staffs can offer to their leagues and athletes. Specifically, Caswell believes that annual safety education sessions should be mandatory for coaches.

"Annual because the science is continually changing, particularly with regard to concussions," Caswell says.

One place where the education approach has worked well is the Newtown Township (Pennsylvania) Parks and Recreation Department, which in September partnered with Princeton Brain and Spine Care (PBSC) for a Concussion and Brain Injury Symposium.

Dr. Nirav Shah, a neurosurgeon and head of the Concussion Clinic at PBSC, helped to spearhead the event.

"One key resource that was very important was the parks and recreation department," Shah explains. "What they were able to do was get the word out to the parents, to the children, to get us in front of the local youth leagues, and really galvanize interest in the community—which is the most important thing you need for something like this."

The event was targeted at coaches, medical professionals, and parents of young athletes, and featured a roundtable discussion, a Q&A session, and a concussion care expo.

According to Larry Hess, head athletic trainer for the Washington Redskins, "The biggest thing now is heightened awareness. There's more awareness of the signs and symptoms and more education, and I think that's what we have to get across to the youth athletes and the people that are around them every day."

Newtown parks director Kathy Pawlenko judged the event a tremendous success. "I was so proud to be a part of this," Pawlenko says. "It's really raised the awareness in our community."

In the end, though, the education begins with one simple phrase: "Err on the side of caution," Caswell says.

Everyone around the league should be made aware of the classic symptoms of concussion; CDC offers free kits, training, posters, and more through its Heads Up program, which is an excellent place for parks and rec administrators to start, even if connecting with local medical professionals and organizing symposia is impractical.

Being let back out on the ice with a concussion wound up okay for Dr. Shane Caswell, but there is no reason that any modern athlete should face that kind of risk today.

Truth and Consequences of Concussions

Why Mild Traumatic Brain Injuries Should Be Taken Seriously

By Brianna Kerr
Horse-Canada.com, July/August 2012

There are as many different ways to fall off a horse as there are horses and riders, and the results can vary from amusing tales that stick with you for life, to injuries that threaten, change or end your life.

According to statistics, head injuries are the most common reason riders end up in the hospital or dead. While wearing a helmet can protect you from catastrophic brain injury, like a skull fracture, they can't protect you from mild traumatic brain injury, like a concussion.

You don't even have to actually hit your head to sustain a concussion—a severe jolt to the body is all it takes. The consequences can be long-lasting or permanent, and affect you physically, cognitively and emotionally.

So, it turns out concussions aren't actually as "mild" as you would think. In fact, repeated concussions can have devastating results. Brianna Kerr, who suffers from post-concussion syndrome, can attest to that. Here, she shares her story and explains why getting right back on the horse is not always the best medicine for a fall.

Living with Post-Concussion Syndrome

I have been riding horses for almost as long as I can remember. As a member of High County Pony Club for more than 15 years, I am no stranger to safety precautions, especially the importance of wearing a helmet while riding. Nonetheless, two years ago, I started a very difficult journey through post-concussion syndrome following a series of traumatic head injuries due to riding accidents.

In June 2001, I had my first major concussion at 11 years old, while riding at a Pony Club event. One of the games ponies got loose and ran up behind my mount, spooking her. She immediately started bucking and ran towards the trailers. I still can't remember what happened after she spooked, but my mother later told me she stopped suddenly and I went over her neck, head-first into a trailer and onto the ground. I didn't regain consciousness for more than five minutes. After a visit to the hospital, everything checked out, and the usual precautions of rest and monitoring were taken. I continued riding once the back injury I also sustained healed. I never thought anything of it again until many years later.

In July 2010, on a trail ride with my pony Cowboy and my friend Nevin on his mount Phoenix, we decided to let our ponies go for a run. We were soon laughing and galloping down a narrow path. My unruly, troublesome pony had a sudden and unexpected burst of energy and we found ourselves in the lead, excited by the fact that we were always the slower pair. I turned in my saddle to grin back at Nevin, not paying much attention to Cowboy. In that moment, we crossed over a shadowy area on the path and Cowboy stopped and turned on his haunches, throwing me headlong into a tree. Nevin dismounted, checked to make sure I was okay, and kept me still on the ground.

Immediately, I felt a thundering headache come on. I was dizzy, nauseated and very disoriented. I tried to gather myself as much as I could because I had no choice but to get back on and ride home. We were a two-hour ride from our farm, with no cell phone service and, worst of all, the sun was going down and a thunderstorm was rolling in. I remounted and we slowly picked our way home in the dark, cold rain.

I have always known the importance of wearing a helmet and have never gotten on a horse without one. My family doctor, as well as my neurologists and several other specialists I have seen, have stressed the gravity of the situation. They explained that if I had not been wearing a helmet, with such a severe hit, at such a speed, the chances of me surviving were very low, particularly because I had suffered from a severe head injury previously. Even though it was almost 10 years before, the neurologists explained that my brain had probably not fully healed from the trauma.

After my encounter with the tree, I did the worst possible thing anyone suffering from a concussion can do, I didn't rest. All my life, chiefly when I was young, every time I fell off, I was told to promptly get back on the horse—a phrase I am sure all riders are familiar with. It is a way of thinking that is instilled in us from our first fall—a way of thinking I have instilled in my students. Growing up, every time I took a tumble, my coaches told me, "Ninety-nine more and you will be a great rider." Not knowing I needed time to heal and rest, I didn't explain to my family how bad the fall had been. I never dreamt it would affect me so much in the future.

I continued to go to school, extremely focused on graduating in two more months. Worst of all, I kept riding. I continued to feel dizzy and nauseated, and I suffered from constant migraines, fatigue and blurred eyesight, as well as extreme confusion, memory loss, insomnia and lack of concentration. Sometimes, when the symptoms got really bad I could not even remember my own thoughts halfway through a sentence. All of this continued to worsen as I pushed myself.

From August to October, I received three more blows to the head. Two were from riding, as I was having difficulty with my performance due to my lost sense of balance. With every new injury, my symptoms got worse. At first, I blamed it on school, stress and lack of sleep from my final exams. I decided once I was done school I would start to feel better. I knew I had gotten several concussions by then, but I had never been told about how one concussion on top of another could be extremely damaging. After the brain is injured once, it is extremely sensitive to any and all jarring or trauma. At the time, I hadn't known this.

But my symptoms didn't get better and those around me began to notice a big difference in my behavior.

Trying to decide what the problem was, I explained my injuries to my family and they immediately took me to the doctor. I was told even if I rode and didn't fall, the jarring motion of riding could be dangerous. I have been through a series of scans and tests, and have seen several different doctors and specialists. They all say rest is the best thing. There is no way of telling how long it will take me to fully recover. There is also no guarantee that I will ever fully recover.

Almost two years later, the way I live my life is still dictated by the injuries I have sustained. I haven't ridden since September 2010, and because riding was a very large part of my life, it is an extremely difficult challenge. The head neurologist from the Acquired Brain Injury Physical Medicine and Rehabilitation Program, in Hamilton, ON, recently stated in her last letter: "Unfortunately, given the length of time from her last injuries and the persistence of her symptoms as well as repeated concussions, her prognoses is not particularly good at this time. Of course, she is told that there should be no more horse riding and this is a permanent restriction. She is also encouraged not to be involved in high risk activities at all."

Not only has the riding portion of my life been altered, but so has my ability to function day to day. I graduated from college as a cabinetmaking technician, but not knowing how long this will continue, I have no choice but to re-train in a different field. The large saws and power tools that I operate in cabinetmaking are not safe for me to use for long periods of time or when I am getting dizzy spells without warning. I currently cannot drive, or be active in any sports, or do anything mentally stressing for too long, like read, for example, A lot of the activities I used to do I can't do or have difficulty doing now. There are countless things I took for granted that are only slowly coming back to me.

> *It is a way of thinking that is instilled in us from our first fall—a way of thinking I have instilled in my students. Growing up, every time I took a tumble, my coaches told me, "Ninety-nine more and you will be a great rider." Not knowing I needed time to heal and rest, I didn't explain to my family how bad the fall had been. I never dreamt it would affect me so much in the future.*

Every day, I deal with migraines, dizzy spells, nausea, mental confusion, fatigue, insomnia, memory loss and lack of concentration. The symptoms of post-concussion syndrome are heightened when I am mentally or physically over-stimulated. Sometimes, it takes as little as a 10-minute walk to send my head spinning. I have large amounts of bruising, which takes a long time to heal in brain tissue. There is also excess fluid and pressure in my brain, which causes the dizziness and pain. From the trauma, the muscles and the bones in my head, neck and back are locked in a tight pulling position. Not allowing for natural movement, this causes pressure build-up and, in turn, pain and discomfort all over. With time, the symptoms have lessened very slowly, with the help of multiple supplements, medications and ongoing physiotherapy. No one can tell me for sure what the end result will be. It continues to be a long and trying journey.

If I had taken the time to rest and heal after I hit my head on the tree, I might not have been as bad as I am today There is a great possibility I would have been back to normal in no time. The most important thing to do after sustaining any kind of head injury is to rest. Do not get back on a horse until all symptoms have gone away, and you have seen a doctor. You will end up waiting a lot less time to return to your regular routine that way. Your brain runs your entire body, and if it's hurting and injured, nothing can function properly. Learn from my experience and always wear a helmet and always rest after a fall. You will never regret it. You might even be grateful to it for truly saving your life, and your way of life, one day.

5

The Doping Era

Lance Armstrong riding past the Arc de Triomphe waving the Texas flag after he won the Tour de France cycling race in Paris in 2001.

Race to the Top: Performance-Enhancing Drugs in Professional Sports

The use of illegal performance-enhancing drugs (PEDs) in sports, commonly known as "doping," is one of the most prominent issues in professional athletics. All organized sporting organizations have regulations prohibiting the use of PEDs. During the early twenty-first century, many sports developed new regulations to counter the use of new PEDs. Critics of doping argue that PEDs pose a health risk to athletes, provide an unethical and unfair advantage over athletes who compete without using them, and threaten the integrity of athletics as a test of natural human ability.

Major Doping Scandals in the Twenty-First Century

In 2007, Major League Baseball (MLB) published the Mitchell Report, the results of a two-year investigation into the use of PEDs by American professional baseball players. The investigation was led by former Maine senator George J. Mitchell. The Mitchell Report also evaluated the successes and failures of the MLB's Drug Prevention and Treatment Program. The report lists eighty-nine major league baseball players known to have used performance-enhancing drugs and indicates prominent personal trainers and clubhouse employees were among the most important sources of drugs within the teams in the late 1990s and early 2000s.

Doping scandals in professional baseball continued into the second decade of the 2000s. The sport's steroid controversy culminated in the 2011 conviction of seven-time National League Most Valuable Player Barry Bonds on charges of obstructing justice. According to a court ruling, Bonds lied to officials during an investigation of the Bay Area Laboratory Co-operative, a company believed to have provided the steroid tetrahydrogestrinone (also known as THG, or "clear") to a number of MLB players. During the baseball doping scandals of the era, the use of THG was uncovered in a number of other sports. Olympic sprinter Marion Jones admitted in 2007 to having used THG before her winning race in the 2000 Summer Olympics in Sydney, Australia.

A number of high-profile doping accusations have occurred within the world of international professional cycling. In 2007, Danish Tour de France competitor Michael Rasmussen was suspended from the national team over his alleged use of performance-enhancing drugs. In 2013, Rasmussen admitted to having used a number of different drugs from 1998 to 2010 and agreed to cooperate with the Danish government's investigation of drug use in professional sports.

One of the most widely publicized doping scandals in modern history involved allegations of drug use by professional cyclist Lance Armstrong. Suspicions of drug use followed Armstrong throughout his cycling career. Following an investigation

by the US Anti-Doping Agency (USADA), Armstrong admitted to using PEDs during each of seven of his Tour de France victories between 1999 and 2005. As a
result, the Union Cycliste Internationale stripped Armstrong of his titles and tro-
phies. During a 2013 interview with Oprah Winfrey, Armstrong admitted he had
used erythropoietin (EPO), human growth protein (HGP), blood transfusions, and
a variety of other drugs over his career.

Types of PEDs

Not all performance-enhancing substances are prohibited. State, federal, and international agencies evaluate new drugs and stimulants to determine which should be
prohibited. Some PEDs are illegal even when used outside athletic competitions,
while other substances are legal for general use but are prohibited for athletes in
competition.

Stimulants increase circulatory and nervous-system functioning, increase alert-
ness, and reduce fatigue. Some stimulants, like caffeine, are legal and therefore not
prohibited by anti-doping regulations. Narcotic stimulants like cocaine are considered illicit drugs. Some stimulants, like ephedrine and methylephedrine are legal
and prescribed for medicinal purposes, but they are banned in some sports for use
in competition.

Narcotic analgesics are another category of controlled substances used to control or suppress pain. They are often taken by athletes hoping to continue performing despite injury. There are a number of analgesics that can be used legally by
professional athletes. These include common analgesics in pain relievers such as
aspirin, ibuprofen, codeine, and dihydrocodeine. While many analgesics are legal
and are permitted, athletes may abuse analgesics, resulting in addiction or physical
injury.

Anabolic agents, or steroids, are taken to increase muscle mass, enhance weight
loss, and increase endurance, permitting longer periods of training or performance.
The use of anabolic steroids is generally prohibited both in and out of competition,
as they are believed both to provide an unfair advantage and to pose health risks to
athletes. Common examples of anabolic enhancers include THG, the PED used in
the widely reported Bonds and Jones scandals. Other examples include metenolone
and oxandrolone. In certain cases, individuals may need to take various types of anabolic steroids to cope with physiological conditions, and athletes may be permitted
to use certain types of anabolic agents if they can demonstrate that the drugs are
being used to address a legitimate medical need.

Peptide hormones can also help to increase muscle mass but are more often
taken to increase oxygenation of the blood and blood flow. Some peptide hormones,
like human growth hormone (HGH), increase the growth of muscle tissue, while
circulatory hormones like EPO increase the production of red blood cells—the
component of the blood that carries oxygen. Ingestion of EPO speeds oxygenation
of the blood and enhances endurance. Another hormone used by athletes is insu-
lin, which regulates production of carbohydrates and fat in the body. Peptide hormones stimulate the production of naturally occurring hormones and are sometimes

necessary medical treatments. Regulation and prohibition is therefore restricted to the nonmedical use of these substances.

Glucocorticosteroids are substances typically used as anti-inflammatory agents, helping to reduce pain and discomfort due to tissue inflammation. Common gluco-corticosteroids are used to treat hay fever, asthma, and arthritis. When taken by athletes, glucocorticosteroids can mask the results of pain and illness, allowing athletes to perform in situations where their physical condition would otherwise prevent peak performance. While many glucocorticosteroids are legal and prescribed medically, the use of glucocorticosteroids is generally prohibited in athletic competition, as they are believed to provide an unfair advantage.

There are a variety of drugs known collectively as "masking agents" that can be taken to disguise the use of prohibited substances. This class of drugs includes diuretics like probenecid, which help to rid the body of substance traces by increasing urinary output. Another masking agent is epitestosterone, an inactive product of the testosterone production process in the human body. Drug tests searching for excess testosterone use the ratio of testosterone and epitestosterone to assess whether an athlete has been taking exogenous testosterone. Therefore, athletes sometimes attempt to take epitestosterone in an effort to equalize the balance of these chemicals and thereby avoid detection for substance use. The use of masking agents is prohibited both in an out of competition and detection of masking agents has repeatedly been used to initiate investigations into the use of prohibited substances.

One of the most controversial performance-enhancing procedures involves the use of blood transfusions to obtain oxygenated blood or to enhance the oxygen capacity of the blood immediately before competition. Known as "blood doping," this process was outlawed in the United States in 1986. Athletes have found ways to subvert testing procedures that have been used to detect blood doping by examining certain key blood characteristics. Armstrong was one of the most prominent athletes to have admitted using prohibited blood transfusion procedures to enhance his performance.

The Health Risks of PEDs

Each of the major categories of performance enhancing substances can cause dangerous side effects in athletes. The use of stimulants, for instance, can lead to increased blood pressure and cause cardiovascular damage if use continues over an extended period. Narcotics can be highly addictive, and continued use can lead to a loss of balance and coordination. Narcotic overdose has also been linked to loss of consciousness, coma, and death.

The side effects of anabolic steroid use include mood swings and increased aggression, commonly known as "roid rage." Use of anabolic steroids can also lead to unusual sexual characteristics, such as the development of enlarged breasts in men (gynocomastia) or the development of facial hair and deeper voices in women. In both sexes, steroid use has been associated with infertility, sexual dysfunction, and loss of hair. If used continually for an extended period, peptide steroids can cause abnormal growth patterns in the hands, head, and feet. There have also been links between the use of peptide steroids and an increased risk of stroke.

Blood doping, which has been used since the 1970s, has unique side effects that relate to the transfusion process. In some cases, clotting and overload of the circulatory system can occur. Those who use transfusions may also experience kidney or other circulatory-system damage as a result.

Ethics of Performance-Enhancing Drugs

Regulations against the use of performance-enhancing drugs are generally based on the principle that it is unfair for athletes utilizing drugs to compete with other athletes who rely on their natural physical fitness and conditioning. Anti-doping organizations like the USADA argue that, in addition to posing health risks, PEDs diminish a primary goal of sporting competition, which is to gauge and develop the natural potential of the human body.

In response to those who argue that doping changes the natural balance of sporting competitions, some suggest that the practice of banning PEDs is based on subjective decisions about what is ethical and moral. For instance, there are no prohibitions against elective surgery aimed at enhancing an athlete's performance. For example, athletes may undergo surgery to enhance their vision, even in cases where their existing visual acuity falls within the normal range of athletes in their particular sport.

In addition, the use of inhaled substances used to control the symptoms of asthma have been shown to enhance performance in endurance sports. Athletes who have a medical condition and use an inhaler to control this condition may use the drug, but it is not permitted for another athlete to use the same substance, despite the substance having the same physiological effect. From the perspective of the anti-doping majority, this distinction is irrelevant, because one person requires the drug and is permitted to use it while another is not.

The argument that PEDs are unhealthy has also been countered by individuals who argue that athletes are allowed, and even encouraged, to engage in behaviors that are equally likely to result in physical injury. Training regimens and dietary practices in some professional sports fields can pose a risk to circulatory, digestive, muscular, and skeletal health. Some have argued that the use of PEDs is not substantially different from an athlete having access to any other advanced and inherently dangerous technique or training aid.

Anti-doping advocates often argue that the use of performance-enhancing drugs eliminates a level playing field in sports, creating a situation where athletes will be forced to use potentially dangerous chemicals to stay at the top of their game. The large number of leading athletes who have been discovered using PEDs lends credence to this argument. On the other hand, some have argued that it is an illusion to believe that it is possible to create a naturally level playing field. In some ways, unequal access to coaching and training aids constitutes an imbalance in the playing field of professional sports, creating a gap between individuals based on the availability of resources. Some critics and journalists have argued that these socioeconomic and resource-related differentials are not substantially different from the gap between individuals who choose to use PEDs and those who do not.

Wherever one stands on the ethical issues related to fair competition and PEDs, doping has become increasingly common in modern sports and combating their use has become increasingly difficult. Manufacturers are currently in the process of marketing new designer drugs and dietary supplements that must be reviewed and evaluated to ensure that none of the ingredients should be prohibited. Future developments in the field, including gene therapies, enhancement surgeries, and new varieties of natural enhancement drugs, will likely continue to blur the line between unfair advantage and acceptable enhancement.

Armstrong's Ahab

By Bill Saporito
Time, October 29, 2012

Travis Tygart's first office at the United States Anti-Doping Agency (USADA) had a poster of Lance Armstrong in it featuring a version of this quotation: "Everybody wants to know what I am on. What am I on? I am on my bike, busting my ass six hours a day."

But over the past four months, Tygart, a lawyer who is now the CEO of USADA, has been the one doing the busting, driven by the same relentlessness and competitiveness that are Armstrong's hallmarks. Tygart has redrawn the heroic cyclist—cancer survivor, philanthropist and seven-time Tour de France winner—as a poster boy for cheating. Citing Tygart's "seemingly insurmountable evidence," longtime Armstrong sponsor Nike dropped him. The cyclist resigned as chairman of Livestrong, the cancer-treatment advocacy organization he co-founded. (Disclosure: I am a Livestrong donor.)

In June, Tygart concluded what seemed to be a never-ending investigation of Armstrong (it began in spring 2010) by charging him with doping, orchestrating a drug ring for his US Postal Service team from 1998 to 2005 and even strong-arming a potential witness during a Tour stage. "It was a culture of drug use, and the moral creed was, You do it if you want to be on this team, and if you don't, the community is going to attempt to destroy you," Tygart tells *Time* from his Colorado Springs office.

Armstrong, who has denied doping charges for more than a decade and who never flunked a drug test, responded in July with a lawsuit accusing Tygart of leading an unconstitutional witch hunt. When that suit was tossed from federal court, he announced that he would not contest the allegations. "At every turn, USADA has played the role of a bully, threatening everyone in its way and challenging the good faith of anyone who questions its motives or its methods, all at US taxpayers' expense," he said.

In essence, the two men have accused each other of team tyranny, doing whatever serves their cause regardless of consequences. Tygart's riposte has been to unleash an avalanche of evidence, from e-mails and bank records to eyewitness accounts, drawing inferences of guilt that lacked any nuance or ambiguity. It was, in USADA's term, a "reasoned decision" that did not rely on drug tests. He lined up 11 former cycling teammates to testify against their team leader. There are 200 pages of detailed allegations of secret blood-doping sessions, EPO use, manipulation of drug tests and evasion of authorities. "So ends one of the most sordid chapters in sports history," Tygart concluded.

Not quite, since the International Cycling Union, which governs the sport globally, can appeal the charges. And what certainly hasn't concluded is the debate over whether Tygart's pursuit of Armstrong was a gratuitously expensive obsession—do Americans really care about bike races, in France, more than a decade ago?—or the pervasive culture of cheating in cycling and other elite sports needed to be crushed at any cost. "It's not personal," says Tygart. "That totally misses the point. It's about a mission and the belief that the rules should be upheld and that athletes want to compete clean and should have that right."

Tygart comes to that view as a lawyer rather than an elite athlete. Although he played sports in high school and coached for several years when he was a high school teacher in his native Jacksonville, Florida, it was while working as a public defender that he first understood why people break rules. "You obviously saw that people put in bad situations make bad decisions sometimes." He says USADA has empathy for athletes who feel compelled by teammates to dope. That's one reason, he says, that Armstrong's former teammates got off with six-month suspensions—a slap on the wrist, claim critics, for ratting out Armstrong. Says Tygart: "We called him and talked to his four lawyers and asked him to come in and sit down with us and be truthful, and he refused. He made it about himself. He refused to be part of the solution."

The Level Playing Field

USADA is an independent agency created in 2000 to take over anti-doping operations for the US Olympic Committee, allowing it to avoid any potential conflicts of interest. It was created during a particularly ugly period when US track athletes were being busted regularly. One of its first celebrity cases involved sprinter Marion Jones. Terry Madden, USADA's first boss, faced the same kind of "witch hunt" accusations, says Norm Bellingham, a former USOC operating officer. "Nobody put Terry up on a pedestal for doing that," says Bellingham. For the same reason, he says, Tygart "swallowed pretty hard before going down that path with the cyclists."

But once on that path, he never veered. When the federal case against Armstrong folded without charges being filed, Tygart leaped in. And even if he didn't think it was personal, the Armstrong legal team did, mentioning him by name, calling him out. "We expect it. It's part of the job. We never like it," Tygart says. "We don't let it deter us."

He broke the case by getting cyclist and Armstrong foil Floyd Landis to tell all by convincing him that USADA would not protect anyone. "That was a big break in the code of silence," says Tygart. And then he did what every prosecutor worth his badge does: he used Landis as the wedge to turn other witnesses, including Armstrong's long-serving lieutenant, George Hincapie.

Tygart's high-profile, high-cost investigation again raises the issue of how much tax money—USADA gets some government funding—should be spent policing jocks. It's not against the law to cheat at sports. That's not a justification to ignore it,

> *[Tygart] broke the case . . . He broke the case by getting cyclist and Armstrong foil Floyd Landis to tell all by convincing him that USADA would not protect anyone. "That was a big break in the code of silence," says Tygart. And then he did what every prosecutor worth his badge does: he used Landis as the wedge to turn other witnesses, including Armstrong's long-serving lieutenant, George Hincapie.*

Tygart says, pointing to rationalizations that led to ethical breakdowns at athletic programs at Penn State and his alma mater, the University of North Carolina.

Tygart is not alone in seeing sport as something bigger than playing games—it teaches values, ethics, dedication to a larger goal—but if sports want to allow doping, fine by him. "If people want to change the rule, change the rule," he says. "If you want to go that route, that's the sport's decisions. Just stop the charade. At USADA, it's not a charade."

Olympic gold medalist Edwin Moses, a USADA board member and longtime anti-doping crusader, says athletes have always craved a level playing field—with a few notable exceptions. "There's really nothing unusual or special about this case. I've seen the baddest and biggest all come and go. Travis has done a fantastic job."

Armstrong has another term for that job: hatchet. "The toughest event in the world, where the strongest man wins. Nobody can ever change that. Especially not Travis Tygart," he stated in one response. But Armstrong currently stands banned for life from cycling and triathlons, his titles voided, his legacy shattered. And that is especially because of Travis Tygart.

Steroids Loom Large over Programs

Associated Press, December 20, 2012

With steroids easy to buy, testing weak and punishments inconsistent, college football players are packing on significant weight—30 pounds or more in a single year, sometimes—without drawing much attention from their schools or the NCAA in a sport that earns tens of billions of dollars for teams.

Rules vary so widely that, on any given game day, a team with a strict no-steroid policy can face a team whose players have repeatedly tested positive.

An investigation by The Associated Press—based on dozens of interviews with players, testers, dealers and experts and an analysis of weight records for more than 61,000 players—revealed that while those running the multibillion-dollar sport believe the problem is under control, that is hardly the case.

The sport's near-zero rate of positive steroids tests isn't an accurate gauge among college athletes. Random tests provide weak deterrence and, by design, fail to catch every player using steroids. Colleges also are reluctant to spend money on expensive steroid testing when cheaper ones for drugs like marijuana allow them to say they're doing everything they can to keep drugs out of football.

"It's nothing like what's going on in reality," said Don Catlin, an anti-doping pioneer who spent years conducting the NCAA's laboratory tests at UCLA. He became so frustrated with the college system that it drove him in part to leave the testing industry to focus on anti-doping research.

Catlin said the collegiate system, in which players often are notified days before a test and many schools don't even test for steroids, is designed to not catch dopers. That artificially reduces the numbers of positive tests and keeps schools safe from embarrassing drug scandals.

While other major sports have been beset by revelations of steroid use, college football has operated with barely a whiff of scandal. Between 1996 and 2010—the era of Barry Bonds, Mark McGwire, Marion Jones and Lance Armstrong—the failure rate for NCAA steroid tests fell even closer to zero from an already low rate of less than 1 percent.

The AP's investigation, drawing upon more than a decade of official rosters from all 120 Football Bowl Subdivision teams, found thousands of players quickly putting on significant weight, even more than their fellow players. The information compiled by the AP included players who appeared for multiple years on the same teams, making it the most comprehensive data available.

For decades, scientific studies have shown that anabolic steroid use leads to an increase in body weight. Weight gain alone doesn't prove steroid use, but very rapid weight gain is one factor that would be deemed suspicious, said Kathy Turpin, senior director of sport drug testing for the National Center for Drug Free Sport, which conducts tests for the NCAA and more than 300 schools.

Yet the NCAA has never studied weight gain or considered it in regard to its steroid testing policies, said Mary Wilfert, the NCAA's associate director of health and safety. She would not speculate on the cause of such rapid weight gain.

The NCAA attributes the decline in positive tests to its year-round drug testing program, combined with anti-drug education and testing conducted by schools.

"The effort has been increasing, and we believe it has driven down use," Wilfert said.

Big Gains, Data Show

The AP's analysis found that, regardless of school, conference and won-loss record, many players gained weight at exceptional rates compared with their fellow athletes and while accounting for their heights. The documented weight gains could not be explained by the amount of money schools spent on weight rooms, trainers and other football expenses.

Adding more than 20 or 25 pounds of lean muscle in a year is nearly impossible through diet and exercise alone, said Dan Benardot, director of the Laboratory for Elite Athlete Performance at Georgia State University.

The AP's analysis corrected for the fact that players in different positions have different body types, so speedy wide receivers weren't compared to bulkier offensive tackles. It could not assess each player's physical makeup, such as how much weight gain was muscle versus fat, one indicator of steroid use. In the most extreme case in the AP analysis, the probability that a player put on so much weight compared with other players was so rare that the odds statistically were roughly the same as an NFL quarterback throwing 12 passing touchdowns or an NFL running back rushing for 600 yards in one game.

In nearly all the rarest cases of weight gain in the AP study, players were offensive or defensive linemen, hulking giants who tower above 6-foot-3 and weigh 300 pounds or more. Four of those players interviewed by the AP said that they never used steroids and gained weight through dramatic increases in eating, up to six meals a day. Two said they were aware of other players using steroids.

"I just ate. I ate 5–6 times a day," said Clint Oldenburg, who played for Colorado State starting in 2002 and for five years in the NFL. Oldenburg's weight increased over four years from 212 to 290, including a one-year gain of 53 pounds, which he attributed to diet and two hours of weight lifting daily. "It wasn't as difficult as you think. I just ate anything."

Oldenburg told the AP he was surprised at the scope of steroid use in college football, even in Colorado State's locker room. "College performance enhancers were more prevalent than I thought," he said. "There were a lot of guys even on my team that were using." He declined to identify any of them.

The AP found more than 4,700 players—or about 7 percent of all players—who gained more than 20 pounds overall in a single year. It was common for the athletes to gain 10, 15 and up to 20 pounds in their first year under a rigorous regimen of weightlifting and diet. Others gained 25, 35 and 40 pounds in a season. In roughly 100 cases, players packed on as much 80 pounds in a single year.

In at least 11 instances, players that AP identified as packing on significant weight in college went on to fail NFL drug tests. But pro football's confidentiality rules make it impossible to know for certain which drugs were used and how many others failed tests that never became public.

What is bubbling under the surface in college football, which helps elite athletes gain unusual amounts of weight? Without access to detailed information about each player's body composition, drug testing and workout regimen, which schools do not release, it's impossible to say with certainty what's behind the trend. But Catlin has little doubt: It is steroids.

"It's not brain surgery to figure out what's going on," he said. "To me, it's very clear."

Football's most infamous steroid user was Lyle Alzado, who became a star NFL defensive end in the 1970s and '80s before he admitted to juicing his entire career. He started in college, where the 190-pound freshman gained 40 pounds in one year. It was a 21 percent jump in body mass, a tremendous gain that far exceeded what researchers have seen in controlled, short-term studies of steroid use by athletes. Alzado died of brain cancer in 1992.

The AP found more than 130 big-time college football players who showed comparable one-year gains in the past decade. Students posted such extraordinary weight gains across the country, in every conference, in nearly every school. Many of them eclipsed Alzado and gained 25, 35, even 40 percent of their body mass.

Even though testers consider rapid weight gain suspicious, in practice it doesn't result in testing. Ben Lamaak, who arrived at Iowa State in 2006, said he weighed 225 pounds in high school and 262 pounds in the summer of his freshman year on the Cyclones football team. A year later, official rosters showed the former basketball player from Cedar Rapids weighed 306, a gain of 81 pounds since high school. He graduated as a 320-pound offensive lineman and said he did it all naturally.

"I was just a young kid at that time, and I was still growing into my body," he said. "It really wasn't that hard for me to gain the weight. I had fun doing it. I love to eat. It wasn't a problem."

In addition to random drug testing, Iowa State is one of many schools that have "reasonable suspicion" testing. That means players can be tested when their behavior or physical symptoms suggest drug use.

Despite gaining 81 pounds in a year, Lamaak said he was never singled out for testing.

The associate athletics director for athletic training at Iowa State, Mark Coberley, said coaches and trainers use body composition, strength data and other factors to spot suspected cheaters. Lamaak, he said, was not suspicious because he gained a lot of "non-lean" weight.

"There are a lot of things that go into trying to identify whether guys are using performance-enhancing drugs," Coberley said. "If anybody had the answer, they'd be spotting people that do it. We keep our radar up and watch for things that are suspicious and try to protect the kids from making stupid decisions."

There's no evidence that Lamaak's weight gain was anything but natural. Gaining fat is much easier than gaining muscle. But colleges don't routinely release information on how much of the weight their players gain is muscle, as opposed to fat. Without knowing more, said Benardot, the expert at Georgia State, it's impossible to say whether large athletes were putting on suspicious amounts of muscle or simply obese, which is defined as a body mass index greater than 30.

Looking solely at the most significant weight gainers also ignores players like Bryan Maneafaiga.

In the summer of 2004, Maneafaiga was an undersized 180-pound running back trying to make the University of Hawaii football team. Twice—once in preseason and once in the fall—he failed school drug tests, showing up positive for marijuana use. What surprised him was that the same tests turned up negative for steroids.

He'd started injecting stanozolol, a steroid, in the summer to help bulk up to a roster weight of 200 pounds. Once on the team, where he saw only limited playing time, he'd occasionally inject the milky liquid into his buttocks the day before games.

"Food and good training will only get you so far," he told the AP recently.

Maneafaiga's coach, June Jones, meanwhile, said none of his players had tested positive for doping since he took over the team in 1999. He also said publicly that steroids had been eliminated in college football: "I would say 100 percent," he told *The Honolulu Advertiser* in 2006.

Jones said it was news to him that one of his players had used steroids. Jones, who now coaches at Southern Methodist University, said many of his former players put on bulk working hard in the weight room. For instance, adding 70 pounds over a three- to four-year period isn't unusual, he said.

Jones said a big jump in muscle year-over-year—say, 40 pounds—would be a "red light that something is not right."

Jones, a former NFL head coach, said he is unaware of any steroid use at SMU and believes the NCAA is doing a good job testing players. "I just think because the way the NCAA regulates it now that it's very hard to get around those tests," he said.

The Cost of Testing

While the use of drugs in professional sports is a question of fairness, use among college athletes is also important as a public policy issue. That's because most top-tier football teams are from public schools that benefit from millions of dollars each year in taxpayer subsidies. Their athletes are essentially wards of the state. Coaches and trainers—the ones who tell players how to behave, how to exercise and what to eat—are government employees.

Then there are the health risks, which include heart and liver problems and cancer.

On paper, college football has a strong drug policy. The NCAA conducts random, unannounced drug testing and the penalties for failure are severe. Players lose an entire year of eligibility after a first positive test. A second offense means permanent ineligibility from sports.

In practice, though, the NCAA's roughly 11,000 annual tests amount to just a fraction of all athletes in Division I and II schools. Exactly how many tests are conducted each year on football players is unclear because the NCAA hasn't published its data for two years. And when it did, it periodically changed the formats, making it impossible to compare one year of football to the next.

Even when players are tested by the NCAA, people involved in the process say it's easy enough to anticipate the test and develop a doping routine that results in a clean test by the time it occurs. NCAA rules say players can be notified up to two days in advance of a test, which Catlin says is plenty of time to beat a test if players have designed the right doping regimen. By comparison, Olympic athletes are given no notice.

"Everybody knows when testing is coming. They all know. And they know how to beat the test," Catlin said, adding, "Only the really dumb ones are getting caught."

Players are far more likely to be tested for drugs by their schools than by the NCAA. But while many schools have policies that give them the right to test for steroids, they often opt not to. Schools are much more focused on street drugs like cocaine and marijuana. Depending on how many tests a school orders, each steroid test can cost $100 to $200, while a simple test for street drugs might cost as little as $25.

When schools call and ask about drug testing, the first question is usually, "How much will it cost," Turpin said.

Most schools that use Drug Free Sport do not test for anabolic steroids, Turpin said. Some are worried about the cost. Others don't think they have a problem. And others believe that since the NCAA tests for steroids their money is best spent testing for street drugs, she said.

Wilfert, the NCAA official, said the possibility of steroid testing is still a deterrent, even at schools where it isn't conducted.

"Even though perhaps those institutional programs are not including steroids in all their tests, they could, and they do from time to time," she said. "So, it is a kind of deterrence."

For Catlin, one of the most frustrating things about running the UCLA testing lab was getting urine samples from schools around the country and only being asked to test for cocaine, marijuana and the like.

"Schools are very good at saying, 'Man, we're really strong on drug testing,'" he said. "And that's all they really want to be able to say and to do and to promote."

That helps explain how two school drug tests could miss Maneafaiga's steroid use. It's also possible that the random test came at an ideal time in Maneafaiga's steroid cycle.

Enforcement Varies

The top steroid investigator at the US Drug Enforcement Administration, Joe Rannazzisi, said he doesn't understand why schools don't invest in the same kind of testing, with the same penalties, as the NFL. The NFL has a thorough testing program for most drugs, though the league has yet to resolve a long-simmering feud with its players union about how to test for human growth hormone.

"Is it expensive? Of course, but college football makes a lot of money," he said. "Invest in the integrity of your program."

For a school to test all 85 scholarship football players for steroids twice a season would cost up to $34,000, Catlin said, plus the cost of collecting and handling the urine samples. That's about 0.2 percent of the average big-time school football budget of about $14 million. Testing all athletes in all sports would make the school's costs higher.

When schools ask Drug Free Sport for advice on their drug policies, Turpin said she recommends an immediate suspension after the first positive drug test. Otherwise, she said, "student athletes will roll the dice."

But drug use is a bigger deal at some schools than others.

At Notre Dame and Alabama, the teams that will soon compete for the national championship, players don't automatically miss games for testing positive for steroids. At Alabama, coaches have wide discretion. Notre Dame's student-athlete handbook says a player who fails a test can return to the field once the steroids are out of his system.

"If you're a strength-and-conditioning coach, if you see your kids making gains that seem a little out of line, are you going to say, 'I'm going to investigate further? I want to catch someone?'" said Anthony Roberts, an author of a book on steroids who says he has helped college football players design steroid regimens to beat drug tests.

There are schools with tough policies. The University of North Carolina kicks players off the team after a single positive test for steroids. Auburn's student-athlete handbook calls for a half-season suspension for any athlete caught using performance-enhancing drugs.

Wilfert said it's not up to the NCAA to determine whether that's fair.

"Obviously if it was our testing program, we believe that everybody should be under the same protocol and the same sanction," she said.

Fans typically have no idea that such discrepancies exist and players are left to suspect who might be cheating.

"You see a lot of guys and you know they're possibly on something because they just don't gain weight but get stronger real fast," said Orrin Thompson, a former defensive lineman at Duke. "You know they could be doing something but you really don't know for sure."

Thompson gained 85 pounds between 2001 and 2004, according to Duke rosters and Thompson himself. He said he did not use

The top steroid investigator at the US Drug Enforcement Administration, Joe Rannazzisi, said he doesn't understand why schools don't invest in the same kind of testing, with the same penalties, as the NFL. The NFL has a thorough testing program for most drugs, though the league has yet to resolve a long-simmering feud with its players union about how to test for human growth hormone.

steroids and was subjected to several tests while at Duke, a school where a single positive steroid test results in a yearlong suspension.

Meanwhile at UCLA, home of the laboratory that for years set the standard for cutting-edge steroid testing, athletes can fail three drug tests before being suspended. At Bowling Green, testing is voluntary.

At the University of Maryland, students must get counseling after testing positive, but school officials are prohibited from disciplining first-time steroid users. Athletic department spokesman Matt Taylor denied that was the case and sent the AP a copy of the policy. But the policy Taylor sent included this provision: "The athletic department/coaching staff may not discipline a student-athlete for a first drug offense."

By comparison, in Kentucky and Maryland, racehorses face tougher testing and sanctions than football players at Louisville or the University of Maryland.

"If you're trying to keep a level playing field, that seems nonsensical," said Rannazzisi at the DEA. He said he was surprised to learn that what gets a free pass at one school gets players immediately suspended at another. "What message does that send? It's OK to cheat once or twice?"

Only about half the student athletes in a 2009 NCAA survey said they believed school testing deterred drug use.

As an association of colleges and universities, the NCAA could not unilaterally force schools to institute uniform testing policies and sanctions, Wilfert said.

"We can't tell them what to do, but if [we] went through a membership process where they determined that this is what should be done, then it could happen," she said.

"Everybody Around Me Was Doing It"

Steroids are a controlled substance under federal law, but players who use them need not worry too much about prosecution. The DEA focuses on criminal operations, not individual users. When players are caught with steroids, it's often as part of a traffic stop or a local police investigation.

Jared Foster, 24, a quarterback recruited to play at the University of Mississippi, was kicked off the team in 2008 after local authorities arrested him for giving a man nandrolone, an anabolic steroid, according to court documents. Foster pleaded guilty and served jail time.

He told the AP that he doped in high school to impress college recruiters. He said he put on enough lean muscle to go from 185 pounds to 210 in about two months.

"Everybody around me was doing it," he said.

Steroids are not hard to find. A simple Internet search turns up countless online sources for performance-enhancing drugs, mostly from overseas companies.

College athletes freely post messages on steroid websites, seeking advice to beat tests and design the right schedule of administering steroids.

And steroids are still a mainstay in private, local gyms. Before the DEA shut down Alabama-based Applied Pharmacy Services as a major nationwide steroid supplier, sales records obtained by the AP show steroid shipments to bodybuilders, trainers and gym owners around the country.

Because users are rarely prosecuted, the demand is left in place after the distributor is gone.

When Joshua Hodnik was making and wholesaling illegal steroids, he had found a good retail salesman in a college quarterback named Vinnie Miroth. Miroth was playing at Saginaw Valley State, a Division II school in central Michigan, and was buying enough steroids for 25 people each month, Hodnik said.

"That's why I hired him," Hodnik said. "He bought large amounts and knew how to move it."

Miroth, who pleaded no contest in 2007 and admitted selling steroids, helped authorities build their case against Hodnik, according to court records. Now playing football in France, Miroth declined repeated AP requests for an interview.

Hodnik was released from prison this year and says he is out of the steroid business for good. He said there's no doubt that steroid use is widespread in college football.

"These guys don't start using performance-enhancing drugs when they hit the professional level," the Oklahoma City man said. "Obviously it starts well before that. And you can go back to some of the professional players who tested positive and compare their numbers to college and there is virtually no change."

Maneafaiga, the former Hawaii running back, said his steroids came from Mexico. A friend in California, who was a coach at a junior college, sent them through the mail. But Maneafaiga believes the consequences were nagging injuries. He found religion, quit the drugs and became the team's chaplain.

"God gave you everything you need," he said. "It gets in your mind. It will make you grow unnaturally. Eventually, you'll break down. It happened to me every time."

At the DEA, Rannazzisi said he has met with and conducted training for investigators and top officials in every professional sport. He's talked to Major League Baseball about the patterns his agents are seeing. He's discussed warning signs with the NFL.

He said he's offered similar training to the NCAA but never heard back. Wilfert said the NCAA staff has discussed it and hasn't decided what to do.

"We have very little communication with the NCAA or individual schools," Rannazzisi said. "They've got my card. What they've done with it? I don't know."

The Doping Dilemma

Game Theory Helps to Explain the Pervasive Abuse of Drugs in Cycling, Baseball and Other Sports

By Michael Shermer
Scientific American, April 1, 2008

For a competitive cyclist, there is nothing more physically crushing and psychologically demoralizing than getting dropped by your competitors on a climb. With searing lungs and burning legs, your body hunches over the handlebars as you struggle to stay with the leader. You know all too well that once you come off the back of the pack the drive to push harder is gone—and with it any hope for victory.

I know the feeling because it happened to me in 1985 on the long climb out of Albuquerque during the 3,000-mile, nonstop transcontinental Race Across America. On the outskirts of town I had caught up with the second-place rider (and eventual winner), Jonathan Boyer, a svelte road racer who was the first American to compete in the Tour de France. About halfway up the leg-breaking climb, that familiar wave of crushing fatigue swept through my legs as I gulped for oxygen in my struggle to hang on.

To no avail. By the top of the climb Boyer was a tiny dot on the shimmering blacktop, and I didn't see him again until the finish line in Atlantic City. Later that night Jim Lampley, the commentator for ABC's Wide World of Sports, asked what else I might have done to go faster. "I should have picked better parents," I deadpanned. We all have certain genetic limitations, I went on, that normal training cannot overcome. What else could I have done?

Plenty, and I knew it. Cyclists on the 1984 US Olympic cycling team had told me how they had injected themselves with extra blood before races, either their own—drawn earlier in the season—or that of someone else with the same blood type. "Blood doping," as the practice is called, was not banned at the time, and on a sliding moral scale it seemed only marginally distinguishable from training at high altitude. Either way, you increase the number of oxygen-carrying red blood cells in your body. Still, I was already 30 years old and had an academic career to fall back on. I was racing bikes mostly to see how far I could push my body before it gave out. Enhancing my performance artificially didn't mesh well with my reasons for racing.

But suppose I had been 20 and earning my living through cycling, my one true passion, with no prospects for some other career. Imagine that my team had made performance-enhancing drugs part of its "medical program" and that I knew I could be cut if I was not competitive. Finally, assume I believed that most of my competitors were doping and that the ones who were tested almost never got caught.

That scenario, in substance, is what many competitive cyclists say they have been facing since the early 1990s. And although the details differ for other sports such as baseball, the overall doping circumstances are not dissimilar. Many players are convinced that "everyone else" takes drugs and so have come to believe that they cannot remain competitive if they do not participate. On the governance side, the failure of Major League Baseball to make the rules clear, much less to enforce them with extensive drug testing throughout the season, coupled with its historical tendency to look the other way, has created an environment conducive to doping.

Naturally, most of us do not want to believe that any of these stellar athletes are guilty of doping. But the convergence of evidence leads me to conclude that in cycling, as well as in baseball, football, and track and field, most of the top competitors of the past two decades have been using performance-enhancing drugs. The time has come to ask not if but why. The reasons are threefold: first, better drugs, drug cocktails and drug-training regimens; second, an arms race consistently won by drug takers over drug testers; and third, a shift in many professional sports that has tipped the balance of incentives in favor of cheating and away from playing by the rules.

Gaming Sports

Game theory is the study of how players in a game choose strategies that will maximize their return in anticipation of the strategies chosen by the other players. The "games" for which the theory was invented are not just gambling games such as poker or sporting contests in which tactical decisions play a major role; they also include deadly serious affairs in which people make economic choices, military decisions and even national diplomatic strategies. What all those "games" have in common is that each player's "moves" are analyzed according to the range of options open to the other players.

The game of prisoner's dilemma is the classic example: You and your partner are arrested for a crime, and you are held incommunicado in separate prison cells. Of course, neither of you want to confess or rat on the other, but the D. A. gives each of you the following options:

1. If you confess but the other prisoner does not, you go free and he gets three years in jail.

2. If the other prisoner confesses and you do not, you get three years and he goes free.

3. If you both confess, you each get two years.

4. If you both remain silent, you each get a year.

The table below, called the game matrix, summarizes the four outcomes:

PRISONER'S DILEMMA

		MY OPPONENT'S STRATEGY	
		COOPERATE (remain silent)	DEFECT (confess)
MY STRATEGY	COOPERATE (remain silent)	One year in jail (High Payoff)	Three years in jail (Sucker Payoff)
	DEFECT (confess)	No jail time (Temptation Payoff)	Two years in jail (Low Payoff)

With those outcomes, the logical choice is to defect from the advance agreement and betray your partner. Why? Consider the choices from the first prisoner's point of view. The only thing the first prisoner cannot control about the outcome is the second prisoner's choice. Suppose the second prisoner remains silent. Then the first prisoner earns the "temptation" payoff (zero years in jail) by confessing but gets a year in jail (the "high" payoff) by remaining silent. The better outcome in this case for the first prisoner is to confess. But suppose, instead, that the second prisoner confesses. Then, once again, the first prisoner is better off confessing (the "low" payoff, or two years in jail) than remaining silent (the "sucker" payoff, or three years in jail). Because the circumstances from the second prisoner's point of view are entirely symmetrical to the ones described for the first, each prisoner is better off confessing no matter what the other prisoner decides to do.

Those preferences are not only theoretical. When test subjects play the game just once or for a fixed number of rounds without being allowed to communicate, defection by confessing is the common strategy. But when testers play the game for an unknown number of rounds, the most common strategy is tit-for-tat: each begins cooperating by remaining silent, then mimics whatever the other player does. Even more mutual cooperation can emerge in many-person prisoner's dilemma, provided the players are allowed to play long enough to establish mutual trust. But the research shows that once defection by confessing builds momentum, it cascades throughout the game.

In cycling, as in baseball and other sports, the contestants compete according to a set of rules. The rules of cycling clearly prohibit the use of performance-enhancing drugs. But because the drugs are so effective and many of them are so difficult (if not impossible) to detect, and because the payoffs for success are so great, the incentive to use banned substances is powerful. Once a few elite riders "defect" from the rules (cheat) by doping to gain an advantage, their rule-abiding competitors must defect as well, leading to a cascade of defection through the ranks. Because of the penalties for breaking the rules, however, a code of silence prevents any open communication about how to reverse the trend and return to abiding by the rules.

It was not ever thus. Many riders took stimulants and painkillers from the 1940s through the 1980s. But doping regulations were virtually nonexistent until Tom Simpson, a British rider, died while using amphetamines on the climb up Mont Ventoux in the 1967 Tour de France. Even after Simpson's death, doping controls in the 1970s and 1980s were spotty at best. With no clear sense of what counted as following the rules, few perceived doping as cheating. In the 1990s, though, something happened to alter the game matrix.

The EPO Elixir

That "something" was genetically engineered recombinant erythropoietin: r-EPO. Ordinary EPO is a hormone that occurs naturally in the body. The kidneys release it into the bloodstream, which carries it to receptors in the bone marrow. When EPO molecules bind to those receptors, the marrow pumps out more red blood cells. Chronic kidney disease and chemotherapy can cause anemia, and so the development of the EPO substitute r-EPO in the late 1980s proved to be a boon to chronically anemic patients—and to chronically competitive athletes.

Taking r-EPO is just as effective as getting a blood transfusion, but instead of hassling with bags of blood and long needles that must be poked into a vein, the athlete can store tiny ampoules of r-EPO on ice in a thermos bottle or hotel minifridge, then simply inject the hormone under the skin. The effect of r-EPO that matters most to the competitor is directly measurable: the hematocrit (HCT) level, or the percentage by volume of red blood cells in the blood. More red blood cells translate to more oxygen carried to the muscles. For men, the normal HCT percentage range is in the mid-40s. Trained endurance athletes can naturally sustain their HCT in the high 40s or low 50s. EPO can push those levels into the high 50s and even the 60s. The winner of the 1996 Tour de France, Bjarne Riis, was nicknamed Mr. 60 Percent; last year he confessed that he owed his extraordinary HCT level to r-EPO.

The drug appears to have made its way into professional cycling in the early 1990s. Greg LeMond thinks it was 1991. Having won the Tour de France in 1986, 1989 and 1990, LeMond set his sights on breaking what would then have been a record of five Tour de France victories, and in the spring of 1991 he was poised to take his fourth. "I was the fittest I had ever been, my split times in spring training rides were the fastest of my career, and I had assembled a great team around me," LeMond told me. "But something was different in the 1991 Tour. There were riders from previous years who couldn't stay on my wheel who were now dropping me on even modest climbs."

LeMond finished seventh in that Tour, vowing to himself that he could win clean the next year. It was not to be. In 1992, he continued, "our [team's] performance was abysmal, and I couldn't even finish the race." Nondoping cyclists were burning out trying to keep up with their doping competitors. LeMond recounted a story told to him by one of his teammates at the time, Philippe Casado. Casado learned from a rider named Laurent Jalabert, who was racing for the Spanish cycling team ONCE, that Jalabert's personal doping program was entirely organized by the ONCE team. That program, LeMond said, included r-EPO, which LeMond refused to take, thereby consigning himself to another DNF ("did not finish") in 1994, his final race.

Some who did go along with the pressure to dope paid an even higher price. Casado, for instance, left LeMond's team to join one that had a doping program—and died suddenly in 1995 at age 30. Whether his death resulted directly from doping is not known, but when HCT reaches around 60 percent and higher, the blood becomes so thick that clots readily form. The danger is particularly high when the heart rate slows during sleep—and the resting heart rates of endurance athletes are renowned for measuring in the low 30s (in beats per minute). Two champion Dutch riders died of heart attacks after experimenting with r-EPO. Some riders reportedly began sleeping with a heart-rate monitor hooked to an alarm that would sound when their pulse dropped too low.

Trapped in an Arms Race

Just as in evolution there is an arms race between predators and prey, in sports there is an arms race between drug takers and drug testers. In my opinion, the testers are five years away from catching the takers—and always will be. Those who stand to benefit most from cheating will always be more creative than those enforcing the rules, unless the latter have equivalent incentives. In 1997, because there was no test for r-EPO (that would not come until 2001), the Union Cycliste International (UCI), the sport's governing body, set an HCT limit for men of 50 percent. Shortly afterward, riders figured out that they could go higher than 50, then thin their blood at test time with a technique already allowed and routinely practiced: injections of saline water for rehydration. Presto change-o.

Willy Voet, the soigneur, or all-around caretaker, for the Festina cycling team in the 1990s, explained how he beat the testers in his tell-all book, *Breaking the Chain*:

> Just in case the UCI doctors arrived in the morning to check the riders' hematocrit levels, I got everything ready to get them through the tests. I went up to the cyclists' rooms with sodium drips—the whole transfusion would take twenty minutes, the saline diluting the blood and so reducing the hematocrit level by three units—just enough. This contraption took no more than two minutes to set up, which meant we could put it into action while the UCI doctors waited for the riders to come down from their rooms.

How did the new rules of the doping game change the players' strategies? I put the question directly to Joe Papp, a 32-year-old professional cyclist currently banned after testing positive for synthetic testosterone. Recalling the day he was handed the "secret black bag," Papp explained how a moral choice becomes an economic decision: "When you join a team with an organized doping program in place, you are

> *Just as in evolution there is an arms race between predators and prey, in sports there is an arms race between drug takers and drug testers. In my opinion, the testers are five years away from catching the takers—and always will be. Those who stand to benefit most from cheating will always be more creative than those enforcing the rules, unless the latter have equivalent incentives.*

simply given the drugs and a choice: take them to keep up or don't take them and there is a good chance you will not have a career in cycling."

When Papp came clean, professional cycling slapped him with a two-year ban. But the social consequences were far worse than that. "The sport spit me out," he lamented to me. "A team becomes a band of brothers,... but with a team of dopers there's an additional bond—a shared secret—and with that there is a code of silence. If you get busted, you keep your mouth shut. The moment I confessed I was renounced by my friends because in their mind I put them at risk. One guy called and threatened to kill me if I revealed that he doped."

Papp was never a Tour-caliber cyclist, however, so perhaps the game matrix—with its implications for the rider's own cycling career—is different at the elite level. Not so, as I learned from another insider. "For years I had no trouble doing my job to help the team leader," said Frankie Andreu, who was the superdomestique, or lead pacer, supporting Lance Armstrong throughout much of the 1990s. "Then, around 1996, the speeds of the races shifted dramatically upward. Something happened, and it wasn't just training." Andreu resisted the temptation as long as he could, but by 1999 he could no longer do his job: "It became apparent to me that enough of the peloton [the main group of riders in a cycling race] was on the juice that I had to do something." He began injecting himself with r-EPO two to three times a week. "It's not like Red Bull, which gives you instant energy," he explained. "But it does allow you to dig a little deeper, to hang on to the group a little longer, to go maybe 31.5 miles per hour instead of 30 mph."

The Doping Difference

One of the subtle benefits of r-EPO in a brutal three-week race like the Tour de France is not just boosting HCT levels but keeping them high. Jonathan Vaughters, a former teammate of Armstrong's, crunched the numbers for me this way: "The big advantage of blood doping is the ability to keep a 44 percent HCT over three weeks." A "clean" racer who started with a 44 percent HCT, Vaughters noted, would expect to end up at 40 percent after three weeks of racing because of natural blood dilution and the breakdown of red blood cells. "Just stabilizing [your HCT level] at 44 percent is a 10 percent advantage."

Scientific studies on the effects of performance-enhancing drugs are few in number and are usually conducted on nonathletes or recreational ones, but they are consistent with Vaughters's assessment. (For obvious reasons, elite athletes who dope are disinclined to disclose their data.) The consensus among the sports physiologists I interviewed is that r-EPO improves performance by at least 5 to 10 percent. When it is mixed in with a brew of other drugs, another 5 to 10 percent boost can be squeezed out of the human engine. In events decided by differences of less than 1 percent, this advantage is colossal.

Italian sports physiologist Michele Ferrari, as knowledgeable on doping as he is controversial (because of his close affiliation with elite athletes who have tested positive for doping or been accused of same), explains it this way: "If the volume of [red blood cells] increases by 10 percent, performance [the rider's net gain in output of useful kinetic energy] improves by approximately 5 percent. This means a gain of about 1.5 seconds per kilometer for a cyclist pedaling at 50 kilometers per hour in a time trial, or about eight seconds per kilometer for a cyclist climbing at 10 kph on a 10 percent ascent."

In the Tour de France, those numbers imply that a cyclist who boosts his HCT by 10 percent will cut his own time by 75 seconds in a 50-kilometer (31-mile) time trial, a race typically decided by a few seconds. On any of the numerous 10-kilometer (six-mile) climbs in the Alps and the Pyrenees, on grades as steep as 10 percent, that same blood difference would gain the rider a whopping 80 seconds per climb. If any of the top cyclists are on the juice, their erstwhile competitors cannot afford to give away such margins. That is where the game matrix kicks into defection mode.

Nash Equilibrium

In game theory, if no player has anything to gain by unilaterally changing strategies, the game is said to be in a Nash equilibrium. The concept was identified by mathematician John Forbes Nash, Jr., who was portrayed in the film *A Beautiful Mind*. To end doping in sports, the doping game must be restructured so that competing clean is in a Nash equilibrium. That is, the governing bodies of each sport must change the payoff values of the expected outcomes identified in the game matrix [see matrix on page 153]. First, when other players are playing by the rules, the payoff for doing likewise must be greater than the payoff for cheating. Second, and perhaps more important, even when other players are cheating, the payoff for playing fair must be greater than the payoff for cheating. Players must not feel like suckers for following the rules.

In the game of prisoner's dilemma, lowering the temptation to confess and raising the payoff for keeping silent if the other prisoner confesses increases cooperation. Giving players the chance to communicate before they play the game is the most effective way to increase their cooperation. In sports, that means breaking the code of silence. Everyone must acknowledge there is a problem to be solved. Then drug testing must be done and the results communicated regularly and transparently to all until the test results are clean. That will show each player that the payoff for playing fair is greater than the payoff for cheating, no matter what the other players do.

Here are my recommendations for how cycling (and other sports) can reach a Nash equilibrium in which no one has any incentive to cheat by doping:

- Grant immunity to all athletes for past (pre-2008) cheating. Because the entire system is corrupt and most competitors have been doping, it accomplishes nothing to strip the winner of a title after the fact when it is almost certain that the runners-up were also doping. With immunity, retired athletes may help to improve the antidoping system.

- Increase the number of competitors tested—in competition, out of competition, and especially immediately before or after a race—to thwart countermeasures. Testing should be done by independent drug agencies not affiliated with any sanctioning bodies, riders, sponsors or teams. Teams should also employ independent drug-testing companies to test their own riders, starting with a preseason performance test on each athlete to create a baseline profile. Corporate sponsors should provide additional financial support to make sure the testing is rigorous.

- Establish a reward, modeled on the X prizes (cash awards offered for a variety of technical achievements), for scientists to develop tests that can detect currently undetectable doping agents. The incentive for drug testers must be equal to or greater than that for drug takers.

- Increase substantially the penalty for getting caught: one strike and you're out—forever. To protect the athlete from false positive results or inept drug testers (both exist), the system of arbitration and appeals must be fair and trusted. Once a decision is made, however, it must be substantive and final.

- Disqualify all team members from an event if any member of the team tests positive for doping. Compel the convicted athlete to return all salary paid and prize monies earned to the team sponsors. The threat of this penalty will bring the substantial social pressures of "band of brothers" psychology to bear on all the team members, giving them a strong incentive to enforce their own antidoping rules.

That may sound Utopian. But it can work. Vaughters, who is now director of the US cycling team Slipstream/Chipotle, has already started a program of extensive and regular in-house drug testing. "Remember, most of these guys are athletes, not criminals," he says. "If they believe the rest are stopping [the doping] and feel it in the speed of the peloton, they will stop, too, with a great sigh of relief."

Hope springs eternal. But with these changes I believe the psychology of the game can be shifted from defection to cooperation. If so, sports can return to the tradition of rewarding and celebrating excellence in performance, enhanced only by an athlete's will to win.

Key Concepts

- An alarming number of sports—baseball, football, track and field, and especially cycling—have been shaken by doping scandals in recent years.

- Among the many banned drugs in the cycling pharmacopoeia, the most effective is recombinant erythropoietin (r-EPO), an artificial hormone that stimulates the production of red blood cells, thereby delivering more oxygen to the muscles.

- Game theory highlights why it is rational for professional cyclists to dope: the drugs are extremely effective as well as difficult or impossible to detect; the payoffs for success are high; and as more riders use them, a "clean" rider may become so noncompetitive that he or she risks being cut from the team.

- The game theory analysis of cycling can readily be extended to other sports. The results show quantitatively how governing bodies and antidoping agencies can most effectively target efforts to clean up their sports.

Steroid Era's Lineup

Who's Who on Hall Ballot's Cast of Doping Characters

By Gabe Lacques
USA Today, November 29, 2012

It will be known—immediately and for the foreseeable future—as the Baseball Hall of Fame's Doping Class.

The Hall on Wednesday released its 2013 ballot that will be sent to 10-year members of the Baseball Writers' Association of America, who must decide how best to handle a long list of players tied directly, indirectly or circumstantially to performance-enhancing drugs.

Indeed, the debate will not die after balloting results are released Jan. 9.

And the support each player receives likely won't remain static, either. A player must be named on 75 percent of ballots to earn induction to the Hall or 5 percent to remain on the ballot, for up to 15 years. Over that course of time, the voting pool will change, as could the attitude of the electorate.

Here's a guide to the users, suspected and otherwise, that voters will be basing their ballots upon.

Keep it close at hand. Some debates might not go away for the next 15 years.

No-Doubters

Rafael Palmeiro: Tested positive for Stanozolol in 2005, the first whale nailed by baseball's drug testing program. His 3,020 career hits and 569 home runs would make him a Hall lock; instead, his positive test—and sanctimonious denials of PED use in a 2005 congressional hearing—reduced him to vote totals of 11 percent and 12.6 percent in his first two years on the ballot.

Mark McGwire: His nebulous testimony about steroid use in the same hearing that set Palmeiro up for his fall from grace all but discounted his 583 career home runs. McGwire peaked at 23.7 percent of the vote in 2010. Coming clean did not help his cause, either. After he admitted in January 2010 that he took steroids and growth hormone in his career, his total dipped to 19.8 percent and 19.5 percent the last two years.

Legally Ensnared

Barry Bonds: Bonds dodged a perjury conviction in a federal trial related to his testimony in the Bay Area Laboratory Co-Operative doping scandal, but he was

---

found guilty of obstruction of justice, a conviction that is under appeal. However, the crux of that trial
was based on whether he know-
ingly took steroids. The book *Game
of Shadows* breaks down in excru-
ciating detail the arc of Bonds' alleged used, which it claims began
after the 1998 season. For what it's
worth, Bonds had a near–Hall of
Fame career (411 home runs, 445
steals, .966 on-base-plus-slugging
percentage) from 1986 to 1998,
years in which he was ostensibly
clean. By the time his 22-year career wrapped up in 2007, he had a
record 762 home runs and a 1.051
OPS.

*[McGwire's] nebulous testimony
about steroid use in the same
hearing that set Palmeiro up for
his fall from grace all but discounted his 583 career home runs.
McGwire peaked at 23.7 percent
of the vote in 2010. Coming clean
did not help his cause, either.
After he admitted in January 2010
that he took steroids and growth
hormone in his career, his total
dipped to 19.8 percent and 19.5
percent the last two years.*

Roger Clemens: The biggest
name ensnared in baseball's 2007 Mitchell Report on PED use, Clemens will learn
this winter if his successful fight to avoid federal perjury convictions—and his seven
Cy Young awards—resonate with voters more than allegations from his former trainer that he took steroids and growth hormone between the years of 1998 and 2001.
Clemens won 354 games over his career, including 213 wins and four Cy Young
awards before he was accused of using PEDs. But voters must weigh whether Brian
McNamee's allegations—at least partially corroborated by former teammate Andy
Pettitte—resonate more than Clemens' June 2012 acquittal on six charges of lying
to Congress and obstruction.

Circumstantially Linked

Sammy Sosa: McGwire was admittedly doped up when he slugged a then-record
70 home runs in 1998. The only player who could keep pace with him? Sosa, who
finished with 66. Seven years later, both testified before Congress about PED use.
While Sosa emerged a bit better than McGwire, his suddenly faulty English and
statement that he had not "broken the laws of the United States or the laws of the
Dominican Republic," where steroids can be legally purchased, did not help his
cause.

Nothing but Whispers

Jeff Bagwell: There has been no evidence that Bagwell used PEDs during a career
in which he hit 449 home runs, had a .297 batting average, won an MVP award
and finished in the top three two other times, all easily Hall credentials. But his
bulky physique and the large disconnect between his minor league and major league

production (he hit six home runs in 731 minor league at-bats) have tailed him. Bagwell received 41.7 percent and 56 percent of the vote his first two years on the ballot, and barring PED evidence emerging, figures to eventually win election. But in a 2010 interview with ESPN.com, Bagwell seemed to sense that he might be a victim of his era when it came to Hall of Fame voting. "I know a lot of people are saying, 'His body got bigger,'" Bagwell said then. "Well, if you're eating 30 pounds of meat every single day and you're working out and bench-pressing, you're going to get bigger. You can go to every single trainer, and they'll say, 'He was the first here and last to leave, and that dude worked his ass off.'"

Mike Piazza: Like Bagwell, Piazza had famously modest amateur credentials— he was drafted in the 62nd round by the Los Angeles Dodgers in 1988. He developed into arguably the greatest-hitting catcher of all time as baseball's steroid era blossomed. That has put him in the crosshairs of suspicion, though he has denied using PEDs. One on-the-record assertion that Piazza doped came in a 2009 book on Clemens, *The Rocket Who Fell to Earth*. Reggie Jefferson, a major league first baseman–outfielder from 1991 to 1999, said Piazza's use was widely assumed by his peers. "He's a guy who did it, and everybody knows it," Jefferson said.

Is Doping-Free Sport a Utopia?

By Stephen Seiler, Ralph Beneke, Shona L. Halson, Franco M. Impellizzeri, Inigo Mujika, David B. Pyne, and Carl Foster

International Journal of Sports Physiology and Performance, January 1, 2013

In October, what was a doping myth fueled by suspicion, but lacking hard evidence, became a doping-related fact beyond reasonable doubt. The impressive legend of 7-time Tour de France winner Lance Armstrong died, replaced by an equally impressive legacy of shameless lying and cheating on a grand scale, team doping orchestration and discipline on and off the road, and conspiracy to fool the world while earning tens of millions of dollars. As sport scientists watching cycling during Armstrong's decade of domination, we tried to maintain neutrality and probably wanted to believe that his negative doping tests were strong evidence of "innocence." It made for a nice story, even if the numbers never added up: *such large powers in the big climbs... so consistently, and beating others who we knew were doping*. Like fans of science-fiction films, we suspended our disbelief.

But the harsh reality is that the doping-control system did not catch arguably the biggest, boldest, and most brazen drug cheat in the history of sport. Hundreds of analytical doping tests performed over nearly a decade in state-of-the-art laboratories failed to reveal his charade. And the same system failed to catch any of his teammates as long as they were on his team. Riders have confessed under oath how easily the tests could be manipulated. Doping testing failed miserably. A federal investigation compiling 1000 pages of evidence and testimony from 26 different cycling teammates and support staff finally caught Armstrong. All of this evidence is now public.[1] If one of the world's most visible athletes evaded detection despite "500 doping tests" (probably the real number was about half that) over all those years while the whole world watched and the doping-control officials took blood and urine samples, why should we have any confidence that the situation is better today? Was the professional peloton doping free(er) in 2011 and 2012? Were the London Olympics "a cleaner games"? The editorial staff at *IJSPP* wants to believe so. But many of us wanted to believe Lance Armstrong's claim, "What am I on? I'm on the bike 6 hours a day." Alas, he proved once and for all that if the prize is big enough, the entire system can be corrupted. Still, we think there is some reason for cautious optimism moving forward. Just as there was inconclusive evidence throughout the 1990s and early 2000s that strongly suggested that doping was rampant even when positive tests were nearly absent, in

Have we eliminated doping, or just forced the doses to become smaller? Even more concerning, we have to ask ourselves whether USADA inadvertently wrote a 1000-page textbook for would-be dopers? When the performance effect of doping is so large, the difference between first and sixth so small, and the economic rewards so large, the temptation to cheat will remain powerful.

the last few years, we see glimpses of encouraging anecdotes pointing in the right direction.

SRM power data from tour riders[2] and analyses of often-repeated stages such as the famous Alpe d'Huez and Tourmalet are one cause for careful optimism. Ross Tucker has analyzed the power-output-to-weight ratio fingerprint for the Tour de France from 1989 and forward.[3] We do not subscribe to the idea that performance above some fixed power-output threshold clearly indicates doping. However, large shifts in performance capacity that happen in the peloton over a short time are not easily explained by any of the strategies that are legal that we study as scientists. The contours seen in the Tucker analysis are well explained by a rise in doping over the timeline that doping confessions now support and a decline in performances in most recent years that can most reasonably be seen as a return to "reasonable" levels[4] of doping, whatever that is. In numbers, the power-to-weight ratio for the best cycling climbers in the world on their hardest, most decisive climbs rose from about 5.8 W/kg in the late 1980s and early 1990s quite rapidly to >6.3 W/kg by the mid-1990s and remained there to the mid-2000s, before beginning to fall again to 5.8 to 6.0 W/kg in the most recent tours. This anecdote suggests that EPO plus consumption/injection of anabolic agents facilitating accelerated recovery may have been "worth" as much as a 10 percent increase in sustainable power over climbs of 30 to 40 minutes. The Festina doping scandal of 1998 seemed to scare the peloton straight in 1999, because climbing power (otherwise) inexplicably dropped about the same 10 percent, before rising again in 2000 and thereafter. That is a measurable, chronologically precise blip that adds some contrast to the doping fingerprint. With the exception of doping-positive Alberto Contador, the fastest climbs in Tour history were performed during the 1996–2006 time window, with slower climbing times since by the best climbers and the Tour de France winners in the last 2 years. So we interpret these anecdotal data as reason for very cautious optimism.

The now infamous argument we heard so often was that "I have been tested 500 times and never had a positive test." Even if the number was exaggerated, no official positives "stuck" to Armstrong despite frequent testing. That seems to suggest total failure of the doping-detection system. But was Armstrong's often-repeated line even true? Sadly, no. There can be little doubt that detecting EPO use and other forms of blood doping (as well as microdosing of anabolic steroids) is extremely challenging.[5] And yet, Armstrong's doping violations *were* detected by antidoping laboratories on several occasions. But these results appear to have been systematically swept under the rug at a higher level. A broom-shaped checkbook may have been used, as evidenced by large "financial contributions" by Armstrong to the International Cycling Union (UCI). This would mean not that doping testing systematically failed but that the *system* was corrupt. The UCI has agreed to commission an independent investigation of its own role in the failure of drug testing. We think this is a second small piece of evidence that the drug labs can go a long way toward keeping cycling and all sports cleaner, provided that the sport-governing bodies they serve are 100 percent clean.

A third source of encouragement amid all the gloom is that the culture of collective "tight lips" among athletes has collapsed. In addition to a substantial increase in positive tests since 2006, a large share of a generation of top cyclists has confessed their doping practices. And more are confessing every day. One third of the top 10 finishers in the tour since 1998 have either been officially linked to doping or admitted using performance-enhancing drugs in their careers.[6] It is telling that the UCI will not award the 7 Tour de France victories stripped from Armstrong to *anyone*. At least when compared with that dismal backdrop, the peloton's rules of professional ethics seem to have changed. A long-standing code of silence has now been broken. We can read from the extensive witness testimony that Lance Armstrong both threatened teammates with and depended on this code more than any other method of deception. The collapse of the code of silence may have an even more powerful effect than better analytical chemistry.

Effective doping on the immense scale uncovered with Team US Postal (and subsequent versions of Team Armstrong) exemplifies how critical the cooperation of athletes, sport scientists, doctors, and coaches is to achieving the combined goals of extensive and effective doping on one hand and detection avoidance on the other.[5] Clearly, doctors and sport scientists reading this journal have à crucial role to play in preventing the development of new doping collusions. We are either part of the solution or part of the problem.

The editors of *IJSPP* are big fans of great athletic performances. A number of us are directly involved with national sports federations, professional teams, and Olympic federations in research or consulting capacities. A few of us are directly involved with the training process of individual performers. Whether the prize is the yellow jersey or a gold medal, winning at the highest levels of sport is an increasingly expensive enterprise, measured in energy and in dollars. It can also be very lucrative for the winners. Good sport science and the open dissemination of research and best-practice methodology in all aspects of athlete preparation have probably contributed to making the race to the top of the international podium more expensive. The top-20 medal-winning countries are winning a smaller share of the total medals in the Olympics, from 90 percent in 1992 down to 75 percent in 2012. This is great for sport and in part a result of better sport-science support in a larger number of countries, all along the path from talent identification to physiological and technical development, to performance peaking, to race management. The difference between a gold medal and finishing out of the medals is smaller than ever before. Good sport science can make the tiny difference between gold and fourth place on a given day. The problem is that doping is just about a sure thing; its effects are so relatively huge that athletes and their support teams can often be persuaded to take the "calculated risk" that drives so much of the athletic doping culture. At the world-class level, the performance-enhancing effects of doping clearly exceed what cutting-edge sport science can achieve with further optimization of training programs, recovery methods, etc. Any training program a cyclist or cross-country skier chooses will look more effective if she or he is using low-dose anabolic steroids to enhance recovery and EPO to push their hemoglobin concentrations up to just under the legal limit. We also know that designer drugs are still out there. The only reason that THG, or "the Clear," as it was called by BALCO labs, was identified back in 2003 was because a sample of it was leaked to the UCLA drug-testing lab. The resulting drug test then helped roll up dozens of track-and-field athletes and may have kept the record for single-season home runs in American professional baseball from exceeding 100 today.

So we are cautiously optimistic that sport is cleaner and freer of doping today than 10 years ago, but we are not naive. Seiler et al.[7] showed convincingly that women's sprint performances in Olympic and World Championship finals had actually deteriorated after the "steroid peak" of the late 1980s. The most reasonable explanation was improved doping control. We think it is definitely harder to get away with cheating today than 10 years ago . . . if you are a woman. Interestingly, though, that same study showed that men's sprint performances had continued to improve linearly. Have we eliminated doping, or just forced the doses to become smaller? Even more concerning, we have to ask ourselves whether USADA inadvertently wrote a 1000-page textbook for would-be dopers. When the performance effect of doping is so large, the difference between first and sixth so small, and the economic rewards so large, the temptation to cheat will remain powerful.

IJSPP publishes performance-oriented research investigating training methodology, the physiology and methodology of recovery optimization, talent identification and development, technology innovation, and other avenues that contribute to helping athletes achieve the *Citius, Altius, Fortius* that makes sport the attraction that it is. Cycling is not alone in facing challenges to its integrity due to doping. But the doping crisis now facing cycling and threatening numerous professional and amateur sports can help bring sport science even more to the forefront. Can great sport science boost athlete performances 5 percent to 10 percent in an 8-week cycle? No, it cannot. The last time "sport science" appeared to achieve something like that was perhaps around the time when Ron Hill first employed "glycogen loading" to win the Boston Marathon in 1970.[8] But if doping is effectively reined in, the real differences that optimization of training organization, recovery methods, nutrition, pacing, and all the research areas in which *IJSPP* endeavors to provide cutting-edge science will become even more important in determining who rises to the top of the podium. For the sake of sports, we hope that good sport science, and not just good chemistry, matters more in the future.

References

1. http://cyclinginvestigation.usada.org.
2. http://www.srm.de/index.php/us/srm-in-action/competition-with-srm/road.
3. www.sportsscientists.com.
4. http://www.sportsscientists.com/2009/07/tour-de-france-2009-power-estimates. html.
5. Lundby C, Robach P, Saltin B. "The Evolving Science of Detection of "Blood Doping." *Br J Pharmacol.* 2012; 165. 1306–1315.
6. http://www.nytimes.com/interactive/2012/08/24/sports/top-finishers-of-the-tour-de-france-tainted-by-doping. html.
7. Seiler S, de Koning JJ, Foster C. "The Fall and Rise of the Gender Difference in Elite Anaerobic Performance." 1952–2006. *Med Sei Sports Exerc.* 2007. 39 (2): 534–540.
8. Karlsson J, Saltin B. "Diet, Muscle Glycogen, and Endurance Performance." *J Appl Physiol.* 197. 31 (2): 203–206.

The Man Who Fell to Earth

By Michael Hall
Texas Monthly, March 1, 2013

"Hey, babe," Lance Armstrong called to his girlfriend, Anna Hansen. "I'll take the girls. Do they have all their gear? Shoes and whatnot?" He stood in the door of the den of his West Austin home at 3:45 on a Thursday afternoon. It was almost time for his eleven-year-old twin daughters, Grace and Isabelle, to be at basketball practice, and I could hear the girls in the kitchen, talking with a friend. "Okay," he said, "five minutes."

Lance closed the door, walked back to the couch, and sat down. It was January 31, just two weeks since his two-part interview with Oprah Winfrey, in which, after more than a decade of fierce denials, he had finally admitted to an audience of 28 million people that he had used performance-enhancing drugs for most of his cycling career. Six months earlier, Lance had been widely regarded as one of the greatest champions the world had ever known. But then he'd been stripped of his seven Tour de France titles and his Olympic medal and dropped by his corporate sponsors. The Oprah interview, the ultimate revelation in Lance's drawn-out, painfully awkward downfall, had been the most talked-about mea culpa since Bill Clinton admitted to having sex with Monica Lewinsky.

Except Clinton had fared better. In print and on the Internet, across the country and around the globe, reviews of Lance's cold, careful performance had been universally scathing: he was a narcissist, a sociopath, a douche bag. He had selectively told the truth; he hadn't seemed contrite. The most common refrain was that he hadn't shown enough emotion. In the days after the interview, Lance had fled Austin to his home in Hawaii. His Twitter feed was uncharacteristically silent.

Sitting on the couch now, however, in black shorts, a black hoodie, and slippers, Lance was the picture of ease. He had about five days of beard on his chin, and his short hair was awash in gray. He had just come from a round of golf with a friend. As we talked, he seemed unfazed by the reaction to his confession. "It's been a bloodbath," he said. "But we expected that. You gotta put that stake in the ground and say, 'Okay, we're turning it around.' That had to happen first."

He paused. "There are days I think, 'I shouldn't have done the interview.' But then I see my kids, see the way they're acting, the way they're interacting. I see the way my son plays basketball, the way he hustles, the way he's focused. I see a different kid."

He was talking about Luke, his thirteen-year-old. Lance had told Oprah that the reason he was confessing was his children. In the one moment during the interview that he had shown any real feeling, Lance's eyes had welled with tears as he related how he had told his oldest son to stop defending him at his middle school.

I told Lance that a close friend of his had informed me that, in 23 years, he'd never seen that happen. "I'm not that emotional of a person," Lance replied. "It wasn't ever gonna be one or two or three hours of grabbing tissues."

His life since the interview, he said, had remained pretty much the same as before. He swam, ran, and biked. He hung out with his kids. He occasionally went out with Anna and friends to a handful of local establishments—Whole Foods for lunch, Uchi for dinner, Deep Eddy for beers. So far, he'd experienced minimal fall-out from the confession. "No one's come up to me and said, 'Hey, f—er,'" he said. "Though I'm sure that'll happen."

He was proud of his cancer charity work with the Lance Armstrong Foundation and peeved that all of a sudden people didn't seem to want to give him any credit for it. Still, he was realistic about his situation. "The stain's not going away—my girls will grow into it. My two little ones will grow into it. This stain will live forever. I'll never get rid of it. I'll just try and do the best for my family, my community, my constituency—whatever that may be."

Twelve years ago, when we'd first met, there wasn't a doubt who Lance's constituency was. He was on top of the world back then, and as part of a story I was doing on him, I attended the Ride for the Roses gala, a high-dollar, star-studded fund-raising party for the foundation. Lance came out at the start of the evening to almost giddy applause. "This night is going to be unbelievable," he said. The crowd clapped wildly at everything—the inspirational videos, the audience members who had raised large sums for the foundation. Lance was treated as a savior. "Lance does something to those of us who know him," said emcee Harry Smith, "and those of us who admire him." Shawn Colvin played a song partly inspired by Lance. Survivors came out and told their stories; when Cara Dunne-Yates spoke (she was a blind Paralympic medal winner fighting her third round with cancer), nearly everyone in the room had tears in his eyes. Lance followed her to close the night. "Stories like this are what get me on the bike every day and get us out there." At the very end, a man yelled out, "Tear it up, Lance!"

Lance always had his doubters, but it's not an exaggeration to say that back then he was almost universally beloved in Austin. That spring he took me along on a training ride across town (at one point when I couldn't keep up he'd had to literally push me up a long incline with his hand on my back). Twice we were hailed by locals. The first time was two burly white guys in a moving truck. "Hey, Lance!" the passenger called. Lance smiled. "How's it going?" he shouted. A few minutes later a black guy in a Delta 88 drove past, slowed, pulled over ahead of us, and got out. He asked if he could take Lance's picture. Sure, Lance said, and stopped. "Appreciate it!" the man called as we rode away. "Thank you!"

As the years went on, Lance became more than just a local hero—he became a personification of the city itself. Fit, driven, cool, fast, young, weird: Lance and

Austin were made for each other. On any given day now it seems as if everyone in town is running or biking on the ten-mile hike-and-bike trail around Lady Bird Lake. Packs of colorful cyclists cruise the streets at all hours. Austin is home to healthy businesses like Whole Foods and RunTex and healthy weirdos like Willie Nelson. It's a hip, high-tech, liberal city in a conservative state, a city without a big-time professional sports team—but with a famous athlete whose sport is revered in Europe and mostly ignored in the US. Lance gave Austin swagger and Austin gave Lance a home. It was, he announced after his 2005 Tour win, "the greatest city on the planet."

But now the incredible feats of athleticism and courage that built his reputation have been wiped out, his foundation is fighting for its existence, and those who loved and admired him are trying to figure out what happened to their idol. For many in Austin, it is an impossible and agonizing puzzle: What does it mean that the things that ultimately led to his downfall—his will, his arrogance, his fighting streak—were the very things that had once made him great? That his single-mindedness harmed so many of his teammates and peers yet benefited so many cancer survivors? That the same defiance that inspired his rise now seems to prevent him from showing remorse like a normal, decent human being? Who is the real Lance, anyway?

I told Lance how I think people in Austin want to like him again. "You were a hero here," I said.

He shook his head. "That was too perfect," he replied. "Now the media, certain people out there, my enemies, my foes want me to be a monster." He paused.

"Mike, I wasn't a hero, and I'm not a monster."

Lance was an eighteen-year-old cycling prodigy when he moved to Austin not long after graduating from high school, in 1989. He had grown up in Oak Cliff, Richardson, and Plano and wanted out of the flatlands of North Texas but also didn't want to go too far from his mother. Austin was ideal—hilly, sleepy, cool. "In Austin nobody seemed to care what I wore," he wrote in his 2000 autobiography, *It's Not About the Bike*, "or whether I 'belonged' or not." The terrain was excellent for training, and he loved the city's bike trails. He got a small place near Pease Park, in downtown Austin.

Even back then the brash, hotheaded showboater had a knack for getting under people's skin. He would do anything to win—ride down other cyclists and force them into the ditch, throw f-bombs, and even punches, with abandon. No one was going to get in his way. "I never backed down," he later wrote. After finishing fourteenth in the 1992 Olympics, he turned pro, winning various European races and a couple of stages at the Tour de France. He spent most of his time training and racing in Europe. At that point in his career, Lance was exceptionally good at short, fast races but couldn't compete in the longer ones; he didn't have the endurance and couldn't climb the mountains.

Few people in Austin knew his name back then, but he became a more ubiquitous presence after he won the US Cycling Triple Crown, in 1993, racing for

Motorola. The winnings made him a millionaire, and the next year he brought his team with him to train in the Hill Country. He would lead them on rides on Texas Highway 71 northwest to Marble Falls. He was building a 4,300-square-foot house on Lake Austin with 29 palm trees and a pool. "I'll never work again," he told a reporter. When he finally moved into his new home, in 1996, he was earning more than $2 million a year in salary and endorsements and driving a Porsche 911.

Still, he remained relatively obscure. Texans, after all, loved football, not cycling. That changed in October 1996, when Lance was diagnosed with testicular cancer, which had spread to his lungs. Almost overnight he became a symbol of tenacity and heroism in the face of a deadly disease. A few days after surgery, he held a press conference. "I want you all to know that I intend to beat this disease," he said, "and further, I intend to ride again as a professional cyclist." While recuperating, he read up on testicular cancer, which prompted him to seek a second opinion; this led to the discovery that the disease had spread to his brain. His chance of survival dropped to 50 percent. Surgeons removed two lesions on his brain, then arranged for chemo to kill the dozen tumors in his lungs and chest. Lance was characteristically cocky about the chemo: "Whatever you give to other people, give me double," he told the nurses. Nike, one of Lance's sponsors, announced that he was "one of the most courageous athletes ever." The *Austin American-Statesman* opined, "Armstrong is one of life's true heroes." Exactly one year after his diagnosis, doctors declared him cancer-free. His girlfriend, Kristin Richard, threw him a party to celebrate. She and Lance danced while Lyle Lovett played.

The experience changed the trajectory of his career. Shortly after his recovery, Lance assembled a board of directors for a new foundation that would fight cancer. The board included Austin mayor Kirk Watson, also a survivor of testicular cancer. In May 1998 the Lance Armstrong Foundation kicked off its first Ride for the Roses, holding it on a weekend that featured a silent auction, a Rock for the Roses concert, and a 56K criterium in downtown Austin, for which Sprint, the sponsor, donated $100,000. School kids sold lemonade and gave money to the cause. Cancer survivors got their old bikes out of the garage and rode with their hero. They spoke of Lance with awe. He had made it part of his routine to call or write people with cancer. "If somebody comes up to me and says, 'I have a friend and he needs your help—they just need some encouragement,' I'll call. I do that on a daily basis," he said. That summer, the foundation gave two $50,000 grants to fund research on testicular and prostate cancer.

The powerful symbiotic relationship between Lance and Austin had begun, and it was about to get a whole lot stronger. In 1999 Lance, now married to Kristin and a member of the US Postal Service Pro Cycling team, began his comeback in earnest with the Tour de France. All over town, people watched the race on tape delay. Six hundred fans crowded into the Copper Tank Brewing Company, which was decorated with yellow balloons and crepe paper. After the tenth stage, when Lance had opened up a massive lead, the *Statesman* rhapsodized, "His achievement is a triumph of the human spirit." He was welcomed home with a huge parade down Congress Avenue—five thousand cyclists, including children, amateurs, and cancer survivors, followed by Lance in a white Mercedes convertible. Watson declared August 9 Lance Armstrong Day. The first words out of Lance's mouth to the adoring crowd were "*Vive le* Austin, Texas!"

Within a month Lance had signed $6 million worth of endorsement deals and a new $2 million contract with US Postal. He appeared on boxes of Wheaties. He gave $250,000 to the foundation, which went into hyperdrive. Lance's cancer mission gained even more momentum the following year, when *It's Not About the Bike* was released. It became a bible for how to fight the daily battles and humiliations of cancer. There were two options, Lance wrote: "Give up or fight like hell." His foundation began to change its focus—less on research and more on "survivorship," or how to help those diagnosed with cancer navigate the frustrating and byzantine world of hospitals, treatments, and insurance companies. How to fight like hell.

Lance won Tour after Tour, and as he morphed into a megabrand, his success helped reinforce the city's sense of its own growing importance. Austin had always been a hip place to live, but Lance helped take it to a new level. His agent, Bill Stapleton, began branching into concert promotion, teaming up in 2002 with promoter Charlie Jones to put on the first Austin City Limits Music Festival. The following year the event drew 150,000 people. REM was the headliner, and guess who introduced them?

If you lived in Austin during this time, you had a ringside seat to a global phenomenon. In 2004 Nike came out with the Livestrong wristbands. The "Livestrong" idea, which was the brainchild of a local firm, Milkshake Media, was a perfect fit for Lance's attitude about how to survive and compete. The yellow bracelets were a huge hit, not just locally (Bicycle Sport Shop sold two thousand in one day) but nationally as well (Matt Damon and Serena Williams wore them). By the end of the year Nike had sold 30 million at $1 each. All proceeds went to the foundation, which continued to grow in strength and influence, scoring a notable victory in 2005, when it threw its weight behind a successful bid to ban smoking in Austin clubs and restaurants.

Lance retired in 2005, after winning his seventh Tour, and returned to Austin. He seemed to be everywhere. His image covered almost every inch of wall space at the four local 24 Hour Fitness gyms, which were branded with his name. He walked the sidelines at Darrell K Royal–Texas Memorial Stadium with Matthew McConaughey. He helped launch the Street Smarts Task Force with Mayor Will Wynn, which aimed to make Austin a more bike-friendly town, and within a year, the city had created more than twenty miles of new lanes. Lance opened his own bike shop, Mellow Johnny's, a kind of downtown cycling hub with showers and a locker room for commuters. And he campaigned for the state to pass a massive cancer initiative that would dole out $300 million a year for ten years to research institutions working to find a cure. Those were austere times, but Lance went to the Capitol, shook hands, met legislators one-on-one, called Speaker Tom Craddick when the bill was in danger, and spoke emotionally before the Senate Finance Committee. He did, in short, whatever it took to get the bill passed, and when it went before the voters that fall, he barnstormed the state in a bus called Survivor One. As the 2008 presidential campaign heated up, he held candidate forums for both parties in Iowa. He went on the *Charlie Rose* show and talked about health care. Many thought Lance was preparing for his own run in politics, for governor or US senator. Given his dramatic life so far, Mr. Armstrong Goes to Washington had an air of inevitability to it.

Of course, the story wasn't really as rosy as all that. Lance had a win-at-all-costs mentality, and for years he was able to keep the costs mostly out of view. When I reported my 2001 story about him, though, I learned enough to become skeptical about his success. I went to Paris and talked to a couple of French journalists. I spoke with other European cycling fanatics and journalists. Of course he dopes, they said; everybody does. These people didn't have any evidence, but they knew the culture, and they knew what was possible. "He's not a machine," said one journalist. "He's not a mutant."

After our ride through Austin, Lance and I went to Hula Hut, a bar and restaurant on the lake where he liked to hang out. I remember how nervous I was when we talked about doping, which he denied, looking me straight in the eye. "Even if they found a foolproof test for everything, which I would love," he said, "these guys are always going to come up with something. If it's not EPO then it's ABC or XYZ or MNO." He called the widely abused performance-enhancing drug EPO a substance "absolutely undetectable and unbelievably beneficial." So why, I asked, wouldn't you use it? "It's pretty scary," he replied. "People have died. I'm not lining up for that job." That was essentially the alibi he gave every time he was asked.

Of course, as we know now, the skeptics were correct. Lance wasn't just doing EPO, he was also doing testosterone, steroids, and blood transfusions, and he was pushing other riders to do them too. And he was lying about it constantly—dozens of times he was asked if he used performance-enhancing drugs, and dozens of times he looked the questioner in the eye, just as he had with me, and said he didn't. He routinely intimidated people in the cycling world who hindered his progress or threatened to reveal his secret—non-dopers, journalists, those who worked for him. It could be physical or mental intimidation, name-calling, lawsuits, you name it.

The most charitable explanation for this behavior is that Lance was simply determined to do whatever it took to win. He believed it was impossible to win the Tour de France without doping, so he doped, which meant he had to lie about doping to keep winning. There's a cold logic to this. Lance had bullied his way through the cancer and the peloton; now he bullied his way past the haters who were trying to bring him down.

And not just the haters. Even as he was emerging as Austin's biggest star and most prolific philanthropist, Lance was developing a reputation around town as, well, a jerk. The capital is a small town, and stories of his boorish behavior spread fast. There was the time at La Zona Rosa nightclub in 2008, when a doorman tried to stop him from leaving with a drink. According to witnesses, Lance grew incensed and waved his finger in the doorman's face, shouting, "You'll never work at this bar again!" After word of the incident began to circulate, Lance called the *Statesman* and apologized. But this was far from the only story of its kind. In one widely gossiped-about incident, he demanded the forcible reassignment of a woman who refused to allow him access to the VIP area at the music venue the Backyard ("She needs to go," Lance told club management, according to one witness). Lance denies this story, as he denies most of these stories (such as the one about trying to get a TV cameraman fired after he asked for an autograph), but they persist, passed around Austin with relish—and a little fear.

He was unquestionably a hero, but he was increasingly seen in Austin as a self-absorbed one. After a divorce from Kristin, in 2003, followed by a two-year relationship with rock star Sheryl Crow, Lance went on a very public dating binge with the likes of Tory Burch, Ashley Olsen, and Kate Hudson, earning himself a new reputation as a playboy. More and more, Lance seemed to believe he was special, entitled, invincible. Many saw an example of this in the watering controversy of 2008. Like much of Texas, Austin was going through a terrible drought and had instituted water restrictions, and that summer the *Statesman* ran a story on the city's biggest water users. Lance, who now owned an eight-thousand-square-foot, three-story Spanish colonial mansion with a pool and rows of cypress trees framing the path to a cabana, was the number one water pig, using 222,900 gallons a month—the equivalent of 26 average local households.

Still, despite it all, he remained one of the most admired figures in town. As Howard Chalmers, a former president for the foundation, said in 2008, "The boy has been cut a lot of slack and will continue to be cut a lot of slack because of the good he does."

If Lance felt restless under the scrutiny of his love life and his utilities, he didn't let on. Before his divorce from Kristin, they had had three children, and he devoted his time to building a life with them in the tony world of West Austin. He had started dating Anna, and soon he had two more children, Max and Olivia. "He's a genuinely good dad," says the father of one of Luke's friends. Lance would show up at his kids' athletic events, sit in the stands, and cheer them on. He'd host sleepovers at his massive home, which other kids loved to attend. He was a regular guy—though one whose upstairs game room had on the wall seven jerseys from the Tour de France.

Lance believes he never would have gotten caught if he hadn't tried to make another comeback. Had he stayed in retirement, he told Oprah, "We wouldn't be sitting here." In September 2008 he decided to try to win another Tour de France, though it was not to be. Racing for Astana, he finished third in 2009; the next year, racing for RadioShack, he finished twenty-third and retired again.

Unfortunately for Lance, Floyd Landis, who had raced with him on the US Postal team, also wanted a comeback. Landis had won the Tour in 2006 but then failed a drug test and was suspended from cycling. In 2009, hoping to return, he asked Lance to put him on the Astana squad. When Landis didn't make the team, he fired off a series of emails to cycling officials in April 2010, in which he formally confessed to doping and implicated Lance. The US Anti-Doping Agency opened an investigation, as did Jeff Novitzky, a special agent with the US Food and Drug Administration who had brought about the indictments of Barry Bonds and Marion Jones.

The federal investigation, for fraud and drug trafficking, picked up steam that summer as various former teammates of Lance's were called to testify before a grand jury. Since lying carried jail time, they started talking—and for the first time, investigators got a peek into cycling's secret world.

In May 2011 Tyler Hamilton, one of Lance's lieutenants in the glory years, went on *60 Minutes* and also confessed to doping, implicating Lance. The show revealed that George Hincapie, one of Lance's closest and most loyal riders, had testified before the grand jury as well. Though the federal investigation was called off in February 2012, USADA kept on, and in June the agency filed anti-doping charges against Lance. He could have taken the charges to an arbitration panel, but in August—perhaps aware he was in a fight he couldn't win—he chose not to, saying he was "finished with this nonsense." He was, in fact, just plain finished. The next day USADA stripped Lance of his titles and banned him from competition for life.

Though the legal battles were over (at least for the time being), Lance's undoing would play out dramatically over the next several months. In September Hamilton's long-awaited book about doping, *The Secret Race,* came out, full of damning details about Lance. One of the people who read the book was Mark McKinnon, a board member for the foundation and one of Lance's most loyal defenders. McKinnon had served on the board since 2004, after his wife, Annie, had been diagnosed with cancer and given a 15 percent chance of survival. She was still alive, in no small part because of the attitude Lance had brought to survivorship. "Lance's example was 'You can do it,'" McKinnon told me. "That's what he was all about, the idea of hope. Hope is life."

Now, though, he was shocked at what he read in Hamilton's book. "I'd resisted the truth for years," he said. "A lot of us in that universe were guilty of confirmation bias—pick out the information you want, ignore the rest." McKinnon called up other board members—had they read the book?

One who had was Jeff Garvey, one of Lance's oldest friends and a board member since the foundation's first days, in 1997. Garvey had also watched the *60 Minutes* report. "That was the first time I said to myself, 'There may be more to this'—mostly because of Hincapie, who had utter credibility," he told me.

A month later, on October 10, USADA released its one-thousand-page report, with affidavits from eleven former teammates who said that they and Lance had used performance-enhancing drugs. "The evidence shows beyond any doubt that the US Postal Service Pro Cycling team ran the most sophisticated, professionalized, and successful doping program that sport has ever seen," said the group's CEO, Travis Tygart.

Garvey, McKinnon, and their fellow board members held an emergency conference call. "We were struggling

Of course [Lance] dopes, they said; everybody does. These people didn't have any evidence, but they knew the culture, and they knew what was possible. "He's not a machine," said one journalist. "He's not a mutant."

not just with what was right for the foundation," said McKinnon, "but what was right morally." They concluded that Lance had become a liability and should step down as head of the board. Reluctantly, Lance agreed. On October 17, he resigned as chairman. That same day, he was dropped by Nike and his other corporate sponsors.

Two nights later, in perhaps the worst case of bad timing in Austin history, the foundation held its most important fund-raising event, the Livestrong Gala, a glitzy affair that had always been one of the big moments in the social season for Austin's elite. It was an awkward night, as 1,800 sleek, athletic-looking, impeccably dressed men and women gathered at the Austin Convention Center to eat food created by celebrity chefs; gawk at guests like Bo Jackson, Sean Penn, and Matthew McConaughey; and see what Lance would do. They were supposed to be celebrating Livestrong; instead they focused on Armstrong, who briefly acknowledged his troubles ("I've been better, but I've also been worse") and gamely ad-libbed his way through some embarrassing AV problems with McConaughey. "The whole night was a train wreck," one longtime Livestrong supporter told me.

The board knew it had to go further. "A handful of us talked about it, and it was obvious," remembered McKinnon. Lance couldn't be on the board at all. He had to leave the foundation. Garvey agreed. "There was not a doubt in my mind—we had to establish separation. He had to voluntarily resign."

Lance reacted predictably: he fought like hell. This was his foundation, the one he'd created after climbing out of his deathbed and built into one of the best cancer charities in the world. On November 4, calling the board members "cowards," he gave in and resigned, apologizing the next day for his language. By then the split was complete, and his brainchild had begun taking steps to officially change its name to the Livestrong Foundation, trying desperately to save itself.

Lance's once-adoring city was also distancing itself. By the end of the month, most people in Austin had changed their minds about their hero, officially a doper, a cheat, and a bully. "Is it okay now to say you don't like him?" asked a friend of mine. One West Austin dad, whose son plays with Luke, said it wasn't the doping that bothered him and the other parents. "We didn't care that he doped," he told me. "Lance did it because everyone else did. But when it came out that he had been the ringleader and pressured other guys to dope, we reconsidered how we felt about him."

On November 10, Lance tweeted to his almost four million followers a photo of himself relaxing on a couch under his seven Tour jerseys. The caption read "Back in Austin and just layin' around." It was a sign of how tone-deaf he'd become. "He looks like the loneliest man in the world," my wife said when she saw the picture, which brought to mind the image of Nixon at the end of his presidency, alone in the White House with the world closing in, muttering to portraits of his predecessors. The next morning, readers of the *Statesman,* which had supported Lance for so long, opened the paper to the headline "Time to Rename the Lance Armstrong Bikeway." At that same moment, inside the 24 Hour Fitness gyms across Austin, workers were literally scraping Lance's image off the walls. Exercisers going to their workouts passed pieces of Lance's face lying on the floor, waiting to be swept up and tossed in the garbage.

Finally, two months later, Lance decided to grant an interview to Oprah. I went to Nelo's Cycles, in North Austin, to watch the interview with sixty or seventy cyclists (some in their racing uniforms) and cycling fans. These were people who had ridden with Lance, who had admired him, who had become fans because of him. They had loved Lance.

Not anymore. For the first few minutes, the crowd—sitting before the TV, standing behind the counter and along the walls and next to the expensive bikes—watched in stunned silence as Lance admitted to doping. It was one thing to suspect it, as everyone there did. It was another to hear it from his lips, the lips that had denied it so forcefully for so many years. It didn't take long for the mockery to begin. When Lance insisted that the US Postal doping system wasn't the most sophisticated but that it was smart, a woman called out, "He's totally proud of it." She leaned back in her chair, a look of disgust on her face. When Lance claimed to have been clean in 2009 and 2010, everyone laughed. "But this time I'm telling the truth!" a man called out. When Lance acknowledged that he had been a bully, again everyone laughed—this time derisively.

I was surprised at the depth of the anger. "I'm angry because I got fooled," said cyclist Ira Kaplan, during a commercial. "I wanted to believe, like everyone else, that he could do it clean. Now he's just saving his ass." For most watchers it wasn't about the drugs; it was about how he'd compelled others to do the same and gone after those who objected. "We can understand the doping," said Gary Obernolte, another cyclist. "But the bullying—an athlete shouldn't do that. A human being shouldn't do that."

Ultimately, no one seemed ready to forgive. All over the country, people watched the show and had similar reactions. He hadn't shown enough remorse. He hadn't said enough of the right things. He showed the same face he had in all those other interviews when he'd denied doing anything wrong. It was the face of a man who was still trying to game the system, the face of a man who was still trying to win.

Not everyone in Austin is angry. There are people around town who have known Lance for ten or fifteen or twenty years, who saw him through the worst days of his life and then saw him do the most amazing things a human being could do, who are heartbroken and dumbfounded. "I can't sort him out," said a man who was close with Lance but hasn't talked with him since October. "I don't want to call him because I'm worried about being untruthful. I don't want to find myself saying to him, 'It's okay.' Because I don't think it's okay. I'm disgusted and upset. But for some reason I still love him."

Lance sundered relationships with many who were connected to the foundation or inspired by the work he did. "So many of us wanted to believe in the myth because it provided inspiration to so many," said McKinnon. "Absent the myth, we want to believe there is a human redemption story. We feel conflicted, even a bit guilty—we don't want to abandon him. But he abandoned us."

Who is Lance Armstrong? He's an arrogant bastard who would do anything to win, including lie, cheat, and make others miserable. He's also an inspirational survivor who has saved people, literally. Laurey Masterton just fought her third bout with cancer; this one was particularly hard, and she wound up depending on Livestrong's counseling services. One counselor in particular helped her. "I got back on my feet, started believing I could get through this. Lance inspired this incredible organization. He saved my life because he started Livestrong, and he has helped a lot of other people all over the world. I don't know what he could do to lose my support."

Asher Price, who writes about energy and the environment for the *Statesman*, was diagnosed with testicular cancer in 2006. After surgery, he got an email: "Hi, it's Lance Armstrong here." Lance recommended a trip to Indiana to see his doctor, Larry Einhorn, but when Price—who had learned that the cancer had spread to his lymphatic system—tried to get an appointment, the nurse said he'd have to wait six weeks. Price asked Lance for advice; Lance emailed Einhorn. One week later, Price was being examined by the doctor. Now Price is cancer-free. Like everyone in Austin, he has wrestled with his relationship with Lance. "My feeling is, the good things he did, whether it was helping me or inspiring someone else in their struggle, or nudging people to get a checkup or donate money—all of that was real. It really happened, and it helped people," he told me. "Yes, there's a stained quality to his victories. But people think that makes everything false. It doesn't."

Many in Austin are less concerned about Lance than about Livestrong, hoping that the tragedy of the man will not be the tragedy of the foundation. Indeed, the charity seems to be in a no-win situation: Lance was unparalleled as a passionate, charismatic leader and fund-raiser, yet he is also damaged goods. Livestrong needs Lance—yet Livestrong needs Lance like a hole in the head. What may save the organization is the fact that it actually began the process of separating from Lance in 2004, back when the Livestrong wristbands came out. "It established an independent identity early on," said Leslie Lenkowsky, a professor of philanthropic studies at Indiana University. "It also established a broad funding base and set up strong alliances with other groups, like the American Cancer Society and the YMCA." Ken Berger, the president and CEO of Charity Navigator, agreed: "It has been able to do what other charities haven't—change the brand. Also, it has a tremendously large reserve, more than $90 million." Neither man thinks it will be easy, but Livestrong will survive—even if, as Berger adds, "It won't be as large or able to do as much."

Meanwhile, over in West Austin, Lance thinks about redemption. Kind of. "I think about it because I get asked about it all the time," he told me. "It's 'the road to redemption,' 'the path to redemption.' It's 'Act 3.' It's all these things that people think about in Shakespearean terms."

For most people, redemption involves atonement and remorse for doing wrong. But Lance is not like most people. And the truth is, Lance doesn't feel like he did much wrong: in his mind, the doping leveled the playing field. He also says now that the way he treated people wasn't so bad. "I prefer the word 'defiance' to 'bullying,'" he told me, "but I'm sure there was some. I used that word a lot in the interview.

That might be something I'd say less now. I don't think those situations have been accurately portrayed. The facts are out there. People can decide."

Most have already decided. "I want to see contrition," said McKinnon, "the sense that he has gone to a place where he knows he has to sacrifice, knows he has to serve a cause greater than himself. I don't think that's happened yet. But I think Lance can get there. I've seen flashes of deep humanity and humility when he visits with cancer patients. It's powerful. It's within him." Another former friend told me, "He needs to change his point of view. He's not showing remorse, and I think it's horseshit. Life is a son of a bitch, and he has been given so many gifts."

Lance bides his time, chauffeuring his kids and training for races he can't run because he's still banned for life. "Now is the time to do nothing," he said. "Stop the bleeding. Let things settle down, plot a course, write a book." What would this one be about, I asked. "That's what I gotta figure out. I know I'm gonna do it, but I don't know what I'm gonna say."

He's also waiting for various shoes to drop. Although one federal investigation ended with no charges, two more potential ones wait in the wings: the Department of Justice may still join a whistle-blower suit brought by Landis, and on February 5 ABC News reported that federal agents were "actively investigating Armstrong for obstruction, witness tampering, and intimidation." SCA Promotions, a Dallas-based company that paid Lance bonuses for winning the Tour, is suing for $12 million. The *Sunday Times* is suing for $1.5 million over a libel settlement.

Elizabeth Christian, of the Austin firm Elizabeth Christian and Associates Public Relations, thinks Lance's best option at the moment is to pull out his wallet (he has a reported $125 million in the bank). "Honestly," she said, "the only thing he could do at this point to save himself is call a press conference and sit there with a PowerPoint presentation. On the first slide, show all his money, and on the second slide, show all the people he hurt. Then start writing checks."

Lance believes his road back will come with good works and the passage of time. "Ultimately," he told me, "people forgive and forget and remember the good stuff you did." He looks to Bill Clinton as his model. "Is it hard to do?" he asked. "Yeah. But Clinton did it—he loves to work, he loves people, he loves to hustle. He's a hero of mine. He's a tough guy, he's smart, surrounded himself with good people. And ten years later, he's president of the world. It can be done."

Our interview was over, and he opened the door. "All right, girls, you ready?" We headed for the kitchen, where his daughters and their friend picked up their backpacks and moved toward the front door. As they walked, Lance's three-year-old son, Max, wearing a diaper and T-shirt, followed. He looked up at Lance. "Wait, Daddy. Can I go too?" he asked.

"Sure, come on," Lance replied. The five headed out the door and got into a black Denali SUV. Lance eased down the driveway, out the gate, and onto the streets of Austin. I watched him drive away. Father and chauffeur. Survivor and doper. Hero and bully. Champion and cheat.

6

The Rise of Fantasy Sports

AP Images for NFL

Fantasy Sports, the Internet, and Casino Gambling

Fantasy sports is a competitive recreational activity in which individuals create virtual sports teams and compete against other virtual team owners using statistics derived from the outcome of real-world professional games. Fantasy baseball and fantasy football, the two most popular types of fantasy sports, first emerged in the 1960s. Each evolved from games that were played as far back as World War II. In addition to football and baseball, fantasy hockey, basketball, soccer (known outside the United States as football), and other sports are used as the model for fantasy sports leagues.

The number of fantasy sports players worldwide grew substantially with the advent of the internet, resulting in countless websites and web services catering to the hobby and companies selling statistical and hosting services for fantasy leagues. Despite the widespread popularity of fantasy sports, some critics have objected to the hobby, believing that it encourages potentially dangerous gambling behavior. In addition, certain sports organizations have objected to unlicensed use of statistics taken from professional games.

The Pen and Paper Origins of Fantasy Sports

The basic idea of creating fantasy sports games based on statistics from real-time professional contests can be traced to the early 1940s, but these early hobbyists did not organize into formal leagues. According to Alan Schwarz, who investigated the history of statistical analysis in baseball, Harvard sociologist William Gamson was the first to create a competitive fantasy sports club, which measured wins by calculating year-end statistics for athletes.

Fantasy football began independently of fantasy baseball and had its origins in California. In 1959, *Oakland Tribune* writer Scotty Sterling, Oakland Raiders public relations manager Bill Tunnell, and Oakland Raiders shareholder Wilfred Winkenbach developed a game in which fantasy owners drafted players from real-life football teams. Statistics from each real football game were then compiled to calculate a winner of the fantasy league at the end of each season. In 1962, the three friends involved *Oakland Tribune* sports editor George Ross and formed the Greater Oakland Professional Pigskin Prognosticator's League, the first fantasy football league in the United States. Winkenbach served as the league's commissioner.

Journalist Daniel Okrent of Massachusetts is the person most responsible for the evolution of fantasy baseball. Okrent learned the basics of the game played at Harvard by Gamson through one of Gamson's former students. Between the 1979 and 1980 baseball seasons, Okrent wrote a series of articles about a fantasy baseball league that he and his friends had created, which met at a New York restaurant named La Rotisserie Francaise. Okrent restructured Gamson's system such that league owners followed the progress of their players throughout the season, rather than simply computing a winner based on statistics compiled at the end of the season.

Taking its name from La Rotisserie restaurant, Okrent's game became known as the "Rotisserie League." This term was later adopted by similar groups around the country and remains in use today. Okrent taught his version of the game to a number of journalists in New York and the surrounding region. During the 1981 baseball strike, Okrent wrote an article about his Rotisserie League in an issue of *Inside Sports*, which included the basic rules for playing the game. Having little else to write about during the strike, other baseball journalists followed suit and produced content about the growing hobby of fantasy baseball.

Finding that readers were unexpectedly interested and enthusiastic about the articles written by Okrent and others, Okrent's Rotisserie League decided to publish a guidebook for the sport in 1984. That same year, Tom Kane and Cliff Charpentier wrote *Fantasy Football Digest*, the first book on fantasy football and a major source of inspiration behind the creation of leagues across the country. As the popularity of fantasy sports increased, leagues began to make use of more comprehensive forms of statistical analysis. In 1988, *USA Today* reported that there were more than 500,000 fantasy sports players in the United States.

Corporate and Internet Expansion

By the 1990s, what started as a simple statistical hobby among dedicated sports fans had morphed into a burgeoning industry. *Fantasy Sports Magazine* published its debut issue in 1989, beginning a publication craze that would lead to hundreds of books and magazines on the subject. *USA Today* debuted a fantasy sports column in 1992, further representing the hobby's transition into the mainstream.

In the mid-1990s, the rapid spread of the internet brought about the next major milestone in fantasy sports, allowing players to use virtual rosters and web-based statistical analysis programs. Players increasingly began retrieving their statistics from specialized companies like STATS Inc., a leading provider and analyst of sports statistics.

Professional sports organizations were at first critical of fantasy sports, fearing that participation in the leagues would reduce interest in sports broadcasts and publications. In 1996, the National Basketball Association sued STATS Inc. over the company's distribution of NBA statistics through wireless devices. A court ruling established STATS Inc. could legally distribute statistics from professional games. This decision paved the way for a number of other companies to begin competing in the sports statistics industry. The controversy over corporate distribution of sports statistics continued to be a point of contention between major sports organizations and fantasy sports leagues into the twenty-first century.

In 1997, the Missouri-based company CDM Sports held a conference involving a number of fantasy sports companies and organizations, including Sports Buff

Fantasy Sports, Prime Sports Interactive, Sportsline, and the *Sporting News*, to discuss the issues facing the burgeoning fantasy sports industry. This meeting resulted in the formation of the Fantasy Sports Trade Association (FSTA) in 1999. Since that time, the FSTA helped to organize collective bargaining to protect the rights of hobbyists as well as provide demographic and economic data regarding the fantasy sports industry.

In the 2000s, the relationship between professional sports organizations and fantasy sports groups began to change, largely buoyed by studies indicating that participation in fantasy sports increased television viewership and the sale of sports-related periodicals. As a result, some sports organizations began to market to fantasy sports players through print and television advertisements. While sports organizations were beginning to embrace the fantasy sports industry, some of the sports organizations, including Major League Baseball (MLB), continued to oppose the distribution of statistics in hopes that they could establish legal ownership over player and game information and could then profit by selling this information directly to fantasy sports leagues. The issue reached the US Supreme Court in 2008. The Court ruled that citizens had a First Amendment right to utilize public information, including game statistics and player data, without the permission of professional sports organizations.

The State of Fantasy Sports in the Modern Era

The FSTA is still the industry leader in collecting and analyzing statistics regarding the growth and demographics of the industry. The FSTA has compiled statistics through 2012 indicating that more than 35 million people play fantasy sports each year in the United States and Canada, which is an increase from an estimated 9 million in 2005. Internationally, the sport attracts more than 10 million additional players, with fantasy football (soccer) and cricket being the most popular international sports. Baseball and football are the most popular sports among players in North America. While fantasy sports leagues attract players of all ages, the majority of players are between eighteen and thirty-four years of age.

Approximately 72 percent of fantasy sports players focus on football as their primary fantasy game, while 37 percent primarily play fantasy baseball. Fantasy auto racing, basketball, and golf are also popular games among fantasy sports players. Data also indicates that 92 percent of fantasy sports players are college graduates, a statistic that may reflect the mathematical and statistical skills needed to participate competitively in fantasy leagues. In the United States and Canada, more than 88 percent of fantasy sports players are upper- and middle-class Caucasians, and more than 87 percent of players are male, though female participation has grown.

Estimates vary regarding the overall economic impact of the fantasy sports industry. In general, fantasy sports generates more than $3 billion in annual monetary transactions. The average fantasy sports player will spend more than $400 per season in league and contest fees. Fantasy sports players are also among the most important sources of income for companies and individuals who specialize in compiling and analyzing sports statistics.

Fantasy Sports and Gambling

Since the beginning of fantasy sports, leagues have offered prizes for the most successful owners in each season. Monetary contests have remained one of the central facets of the hobby into the twenty-first century. In the mid-2000s, the US government was forced to address the emergence of online gambling websites in an effort to prevent the internet gambling industry from violating state-specific gambling laws.

According to the Unlawful Internet Gambling Enforcement Act of 2006, signed into law by President George W. Bush, individuals are allowed to bet on sports contests and fantasy sports contests because these types of competitions are based on differential knowledge and skill rather than random outcomes. However, wagering on the outcome of a single game or a single player is not allowed under the 2006 law. The prizes for fantasy sports contests must be determined beforehand and cannot be determined by the number of participants.

Since 2006, a number of states have asked the courts to revisit the issue of legality in fantasy sports as a proliferation of websites have emerged that offer alternative betting arrangements that allow players to bet on the outcome of fantasy sports contests without owning teams or participating in a traditional fantasy league. Major League Baseball Advanced Media, which is the internet and alternative media wing of MLB, has also objected to the non traditional fantasy sports sites that allow daily betting scenarios. An example is FanDuel, which received more than $11 million in investments in 2013 and was one of the fastest growing fantasy sports sites. FanDuel allows players to wager on the daily performance of players, rather than offering prizes for achievements during season-long contests.

According to the FSTA, daily fantasy sports betting accounts for more than 490 million of the industry's $1.6 billion in annual revenues. The popularity of daily betting sites has increased in recent years. In addition, the proliferation of daily betting sites for fantasy sports has begun to attract attention from professional gamblers, who have begun to take an increased interest in fantasy sports gambling because internet poker sites and other internet-betting venues have been forced to close.

In March 2013, a group of casinos in Atlantic City, New Jersey, announced that they would begin offering fantasy sports betting as a new casino attraction. The decision came after casino management began to realize the potential of daily fantasy sports contests reflected in the popularity of FanDuel, DraftDay, and other daily betting sites for fantasy sports. Under current gambling regulations, casinos are allowed to host their own games and are free to collaborate with existing gambling sites. While casino management hopes that fantasy sports offerings will attract additional visitors to casinos, further association between fantasy sports may increase some critics' objections that the hobby is evolving from a game of skill to a game of chance.

A Winning Strategy in a Quarterback Age

By Gene Menez
Sports Illustrated, June 6, 2012

The e-mails start flooding my in-box in early August. My friend Erika from Denver annually contacts me, and so does my father-in-law, John, from Chicago. The messages, whomever they are from, all share the same urgent request: "My fantasy football draft is coming up. Help!"

This is one of the by-products of being the editor of this 156-page fantasypedia, as well as—I humbly submit—the back-to-back champion of the fantasy league I play in. I'm more than happy to share my title-winning secrets. These friends and relatives, after all, don't play against me.

That got me thinking, If I'm going to help them, why wouldn't I help you, too? So here you have it: the proven title-winning strategies that you need to follow to have a successful 2012 season. Learn them, live them, love them. Please don't forget the tip jar.

Play It Safe in the First Round

Don't be cute and try to hit a home run by selecting, say, A.J. Green because you think he's this year's Rob Gronkowski. Take the most reliable point producer that you can, regardless of position.

Draft One of the Fab Five Quarterbacks

Place high value on the top quarterbacks this season: Aaron Rodgers, Tom Brady, Drew Brees, Matthew Stafford and Cam Newton. Because the NFL has become a passing league, elite QB production can be more predictable than, say, elite running back numbers. Just ask yourself this: Whom do you trust more to produce a big year, Brees or Ryan Mathews? The drop-off from Newton to my sixth-ranked quarterback (Michael Vick) is steep.

Don't Overreach for a Tier 2 Running Back at the End of Round 1

The combination of passing-friendly NFL rules, an unusually high number of runners returning from injury and the evolution of backfields-by-committee has left only three elite backs, in my opinion—Ray Rice, Arian Foster and LeSean McCoy—who should be taken at the top of the draft. After that you have a runner who's a workhorse for an offense that may not score many points (Jacksonville's

No matter how much you prepare or how well your draft goes, you just cannot control whether your stud performers get hurt or whether you'll catch an unfavorable matchup during the fantasy playoffs. Of all the strategies, having good luck may be the most important of all.

Maurice Jones-Drew) and another back (Chris Johnson) who could be extraordinary (as he was in 2009) or ordinary (2011).

Both Jones-Drew and Johnson are worthy of late-first-round picks, but it's hard to make a case for anyone else. Don't draft injury-prone Darren McFadden or unproven Trent Richardson at the end of round 1 just because, say, six of the first eight picks are backs. You're better off with a Tier 1 QB or receiver or Gronkowski.

Also, remember that running backs miss games due to injury more than any other fantasy position, so as the season wears on, you can add contributors to your team with pickups off the waiver wire. Last season my top four backs at the start of the season were Shonn Greene (third round in a 12-team league), Tim Hightower (fourth), Fred Jackson (seventh) and James Starks (eighth). Starks was bad, Greene was mediocre, and Hightower and Jackson were lost to season-ending injuries. So I patched together a backfield that received key late-season contributions from C.J. Spiller, Felix Jones, Ben Tate and—even in my title game—Evan Royster, all of whom I picked up off the wire.

Back up Your Stud Running Backs

If you're lucky enough to land Rice, Foster, McCoy or anyone who emerges as a featured back, you need to support that selection by also taking his backup. Otherwise you're at risk of losing significant production if that starter is lost to injury.

This season the key backups for this strategy will be Bernard Pierce (Rice), Tate (Foster), Dion Lewis (McCoy), Rashad Jennings (Jones-Drew), Javon Ringer (Johnson) and Robert Turbin (Marshawn Lynch). If at any point in the season one of these players is available on the waiver wire and you have the roster space to add him, do it. As we saw last year, nagging injuries pile up over the course of the season.

Grab One of the Top Three Tight Ends

The gap between the tier 1 tight ends—Gronkowski, Jimmy Graham and Vernon Davis in that order on my personal draft board—and the rest is significant. So pull the trigger on one of these three in the first three rounds. If you're unsuccessful at that, you can wait a few rounds to address the area because the position is very deep—so deep in fact that if you're in a league in which you can start a tight end in a flex spot, it's often smart to start two tight ends because a second tight end is often more productive than a third receiver. Two seasons ago I started both Gronkowski and Jason Witten because my receivers were pass-catching dogs. This year I personally like Brandon Pettigrew.

Avoid Running Back Time-Share Situations

You're better off drafting what looks like an unsexy running back who gets the lion's share of his team's carries—Donald Brown of Indy, for example—than trying to choose between guys in a time-share. Good luck trying to decipher the Patriots' backfield of Joseph Addai, Stevan Ridley, Shane Vereen and Danny Woodhead, for example.

Select a Quality QB2

Since most leagues allow teams to start only one quarterback, it's the easiest position at which to own a quality backup and therefore the easiest in which to have a tradeable asset that can help you fill a hole elsewhere in your lineup.

Work the Waiver Wire with Abandon

Replace underachieving players with those off the wire and don't be afraid to cut bait if an early-round pick is not performing. If you're doing well in your league and are one of the last to act in the waiver wire every week, you'll need to be extra smart and think two or even three weeks ahead.

Mix and Match DSTS, if Necessary

Owners who wait until the penultimate round to draft a defense are often stuck with a mediocre unit. If your DST is not producing consistently, dump it and, instead, pick up a defense that has a favorable matchup against a poor offense. Repeat weekly though the end of the season. Even poor DSTs can have huge stat lines against inept teams.

Get Lucky

No matter how much you prepare or how well your draft goes, you just cannot control whether your stud performers get hurt or whether you'll catch an unfavorable matchup during the fantasy playoffs. Of all the strategies, having good luck may be the most important of all.

The Like List

The editor's picks for players to target in 2012:

Quarterback

Matthew Stafford: Lions

I would be happy with any of the top five QBs but have a soft spot for Stafford, who led my team to the 2011 title. His numbers will be right in line with those of Aaron Rodgers, Tom Brady and Drew Brees, and if you reach the fantasy playoffs, Stafford faces the Cardinals and the Falcons in Weeks 15 and 16.

Running Back

Darren Sproles: Saints
If you're in a PPR league, this pass-catching mighty mite in the Saints' scoring circus is an absolute must-have.

DeMarco Murray: Cowboys
In a perfect world, you could grab Murray in the third or fourth round as an RB2. Be sure to pick up Felix Jones for insurance later in the draft.

Donald Brown: Colts
The 2009 first-round pick finally came around a bit last year, and fumble-prone Delone Carter is no threat to take the starting job, meaning you may be able to draft a feature back, a rarity these days, as late as the eighth round.

Receivers

Victor Cruz: Giants
His 2011 season was not a fluke, folks. Read the coach's comment on Cruz in the Giants' Enemy Lines section, and if he's available in the third round, run, don't walk.

Demaryius Thomas: Broncos
Mile High Megatron came on at the end of last year with Tim Tebow throwing to him, and now he gets the upgrade to Peyton Manning. Thomas will provide third-round production at a fifth-round price.

Malcom Floyd: Chargers
New San Diego receiver Robert Meachem is getting all the hype, which is great for the Floyd lovers, who will gladly steal Philip Rivers's top target this year in the eighth round.

Tight End

Brandon Pettigrew: Lions
If any tight end this year is going to make a Gronk- or Graham-like leap to the next level, it's Pettigrew, who has a high-quality quarterback throwing to him and already plays a major role in a pass-first offense.

The Spike List

The editor's picks for players to avoid in 2012:

Quarterback

Matt Ryan: Falcons
That breakout season that many have been expecting may never come. He has the receiving weapons to be intriguing, but the word out of Atlanta is that the team will focus on the run. I'd rather take a shot with Jay Cutler or Ben Roethlisberger.

Robert Griffin III: Redskins
Don't Draft RG3 thinking he's Cam Newton II. Griffin is not a power-running bull-dozer like the Panthers quarterback is, and he doesn't have the weapons or the offensive line that Newton had last year. Unless you're in a dynasty league, pass.

Running Back

Any Back Coming off a Major Injury
The list is long: Darren McFadden, Rashard Mendenhall and Adrian Peterson, to name three. The seriousness of the injuries and the proliferation of time-share backfields make it unwise to gamble before the third round on one of these backs.

Shonn Greene: Jets
Nothing about Greene screams "every-down back." This comes from someone who owned him last year and was disappointed week after week after week.

James Starks: Packers
Aaron Rodgers & Co. rarely run the ball, even at the goal line, and when they do, either Rodgers or John Kuhn punches it in. Green Bay isn't changing philosophies; forget Starks.

Receivers

Any Brown or Jaguar
Until the quarterback play on these teams improves from poor to mediocre, none of the receivers are usable in fantasy, unless you're in a 16-team league.

Brandon Lloyd: Patriots
Part of me thinks he's going to have a nice year with Tom Brady throwing to him. Another part of me thinks that there are too many mouths to feed for him to have a 70-catch season.

Tight End

Antonio Gates: Chargers
He's likely to be the third or fourth tight end drafted, and that's too steep a price to pay for a player who has battled foot problems the last two seasons.

Daily Fantasy Sports Become a Gambling Reality

By Oskar Garcia
Associated Press, September 24, 2010

Sports fans are betting online each night on athletes' performances—and it's all legal.

The bets are an exception to laws banning online gambling because they take the form of fantasy sports—where participants pick a team of real-life players in baseball, football or other sports and compete based on their real-life statistics. Such competitions typically last a season, but more websites are springing up that offer prize money for teams that last only one night.

Drawn by the possibility of quick cash payouts, instead of just end-of-season glory, fans ready for more-than-casual rivalries among friends or co-workers are building new nightly online betting into a hit for the $800 million fantasy sports industry.

More than a dozen websites have sprung up to manage daily fantasy sports wagers and grab a percentage, says Paul Charchian, president of the Fantasy Sports Trade Association, which represents 120 companies. Those commissions amount to $35 per player per month at one of the largest new sites, FanDuel.com, according to its CEO. And with nearly 7 million Americans and Canadians already playing fantasy sports for money by 2008, the total is expected to soar.

"It's always been a little murky, so I think a lot of companies didn't have the stomach for it," said Charchian. "People now are jumping on board."

Gambling on fantasy sports online has been explicitly legal in all but six states since 2006, thanks to an exception built into that year's federal ban on most online gambling.

But Charchian says most website operators remained worried about the legality of wagering of any kind until one popular fantasy sports site, Fanball.com, launched a daily game in late 2008 called Snapdraft, and attracted players instead of trouble. Charchian, who co-founded Fanball in 1993 and had left in 2007, said Fanball didn't jump into daily betting sooner because the legal issues hadn't been resolved.

A far less popular site run by Fantasy Day Sports Corp., FantasySportsLive.com, launched daily games with gambling in mid-2007.

Here's how fantasy sports gambling online works. As in the office pool, fans compile teams of their favorite professional athletes and advance or fall back based on how the athletes perform in reality. A few major portals, including Yahoo.com and ESPN.com, have long offered platforms for the hobby without betting. But the newest online games pay cash each day to the participants whose teams for that night include the highest-achieving individual players.

"This isn't replacing their leagues with family and friends," Charchian said. "You don't play these kinds of games for the fun of it; you play it for the profit."

This isn't considered sports gambling, like Las Vegas casinos offer, because gamblers can't wager on scores or team wins or losses, and they can't create fantasy teams that mirror real-world teams. Not that they'd want to if they expect to win. These are what-if teams, where individual performance is the most important factor.

Dave Nutini, a 31-year-old former

> *Players who gamble on fantasy sports were spending an average of $134 per year on their leagues, an Ipsos study found in 2008, when the daily gambling sites were just starting to take off. Ipsos found that of the 27 million Americans and nearly 3 million Canadians who play fantasy sports each year, about three-quarters do it just for bragging rights.*

bank contract manager who quit his job three weeks ago to play poker professionally, said he plans to wager $200 to $300 per week on fantasy football using FanDuel this season. He sees players who take the games seriously making a steady income off FanDuel soon.

"I think it's pretty similar to the online poker thing," Nutini said. "I've looked on there, and there are a few guys who are making a significant amount every month."

Right away, Nutini scored $500 in cash plus a trip to Las Vegas to compete for $25,000 on a $10 wager when he won the first week of the FanDuel Fantasy Football Championship. Even counting his losses on two other $25 bets, Nutini is well ahead—though his winnings are nowhere close to steady yet.

"I'm obviously not doing that for a living—my bankroll management on that stinks," he said. "I think eventually, once I get the hang of it, I wouldn't mind."

FanDuel launched in the spring with $1.8 million in venture capital funding and now averages 20,000 users per month who have placed more than 65,000 bets worth more than $1 million to their winners since play started, CEO Nigel Eccles told The Associated Press.

Eccles said the site's use increased 10-fold with the start of the NFL season this month.

"Whereas season-long drafts have already had their single bite ... our daily draft model enables us and our partners to continue to add players throughout the NFL season," Eccles said.

Football is by far the most popular fantasy sport.

Players who gamble on fantasy sports were spending an average of $134 per year on their leagues, an Ipsos study found in 2008, when the daily gambling sites were just starting to take off. Ipsos found that of the 27 million Americans and nearly 3 million Canadians who play fantasy sports each year, about three-quarters do it just for bragging rights.

FanDuel just launched in Canada and expanded in the US this fall. It now has deals with seven major US newspapers to attract players. The papers promote Fan-Duel on their pages, often quite prominently, while FanDuel customizes the look of the site for each outlet and oversees the wagering and customer service. The two businesses evenly split the commission FanDuel collects on each bet.

Yoni Greenbaum, vice president of product development for Philly.com, the website of the *Philadelphia Inquirer* and *Philadelphia Daily News*, said its revenue from FanDuel is small, but the partnership gives readers something new and different.

"It's a niche that fits into a larger strategy," he said. The hope is that links like this will get readers to make Philly.com part of their daily routine; already some players have complained that they can't bet enough each night, he said.

Eccles expects FanDuel to become profitable in the next year, though he says he often still must convince customers they won't get in trouble for gambling on the site.

"It's not straightforward, and I think most people, they don't understand where the legal situation is," he said.

Fantasy Football Gaining in Popularity with Kids

By Beth Teitell
Boston Globe, October 23, 2012

Young brothers Nick and Theo Kennedy love watching football on Sundays, but the afternoons are anything but relaxing. When the Patriots are on, the TV in their Westwood living room is tuned to that game, but they regularly flip to the NFL's RedZone, a live highlights channel, and each boy constantly checks his tablet, monitoring ESPN for updates on more than 50 players leaguewide.

"They look like bookies," said their mother, Kimberly Kennedy.

No money is at stake. But like a growing number of children, Nick, 13, and Theo, 11, are playing for something more important: fantasy football bragging rights. "We like to razz each other at school," Theo said.

About 25 million people, ages 12 and over, play in fantasy football leagues around the United States, according to Paul Charchian, president of the Fantasy Sports Trade Association. That's up from about 16 million in 2007. And kids make up the second-biggest age category, behind 18-to 35-year-olds. Charchian estimates that almost 3.5 million kids play fantasy football and says their numbers are growing as the sport charms a football-obsessed nation.

Back in 2003, the number of kids playing fantasy football was "nonsignificant," according to Kim Beason, a University of Mississippi professor who has conducted surveys on the sport. In his most recent survey, in 2010, one quarter of the almost 1,100 respondents reported that their sons were playing, as were 4 percent of their daughters. More kids are playing, he said, because fantasy football has shed its nerdy image. "It was geek originally," Beason explained, "because of the statistic-heavy way the game was played [pre-Internet]. That has disappeared using today's technology."

Fantasy football has gone so mainstream, Charchian said, that playing has become a way of keeping up with friends. "Dropping a league is like ending a dozen friendships."

For those who aren't on a fantasy football team, here's how it works: Players join or create a league, and then get to act like owners of actual teams, "drafting" real NFL players and making game-day decisions. Points are earned on the basis of how the players perform in their real-life games that day.

The demand from the youth market is so strong that in 2007 the NFL added a kid-focused fantasy game on its popular NFLRush site, and this year launched mobile apps, the better to check on how your players are doing from the sidelines of travel soccer, or, like Christian Abbate, a Hanover 15-year-old, while you're out to dinner with your grandfather.

"I said 'Put the phone down,'" recalled his mother, Lisa Zajonc, the manager of a Disney store in Braintree. "He's always checking something."

But with fantasy football a constant source of youth conversation, a kid needs to do what a kid needs to do. "It's a superstitious thing for me," Abbate explained. "I think by checking, I'll help my players."

Here's another sign that fantasy football has taken hold of the kiddie set: It has become a source of friction between kids and parents. On a recent morning in Newton, Bret Miller, at 11, already a four-year fantasy veteran, and his father, Andrew, were bickering over a player the elder Miller had insisted they acquire for the team the two comanage.

"You cost me the game," Bret said, blaming Pop for Detroit Lions running back Mikel Leshoure's poor performance. "He got no points."

But a moment later, Bret conceded that his father—president of the Newton-based Football Nation LLC, which owns www.fooballnation.com, www.ffslots.com, and www.coldhardfootballfacts.com—isn't totally useless.

"I look at my dad's sites and they help me," Bret said when asked where he gets his football information.

Yahoo! Sports fantasy expert Brad Evans calls fantasy football the "sports cards of the 21st century." Considering that cards were just cards, and that fantasy football has invaded so many aspects of modern life, from smartphones to sitcoms, it's like cards on steroids.

Although parents rightfully worry about all sorts of online distractions, many take solace in fantasy's potential to teach math and strategic skills.

In the mid-1990s, Dan Flockhart, a middle-school math teacher in Northern California, increased his students' motivation by combining math and fantasy football.

"They consistently tested in the 80th percentile and above against other private-school students," he said.

He went on to write a master's thesis on the subject, which led to a Fantasy Sports and Mathematics series (available on Amazon.com).

"When I wrote the first book, people thought I was nuts," he said, pointing to two University of Mississippi surveys, in 2007 and 2009, that found fantasy helped with math skills and made learning more enjoyable.

And there's another plus, he added.

"I have had fathers tell me that fantasy sports has given them quality time with their adolescent sons and daughters, who previously wanted nothing to do with them."

The National Football League also plays up the educational component of fantasy football. The league awards a $10,000 college scholarship to the overall winner of the fantasy competition on the NFLRush site, and gives $1,000 scholarships to weekly winners.

Last year, with Tom Brady as his quarterback, Joseph Chiarenza, then 11, of Medford, won one of those $1,000 scholarships. Asked what advice he'd give other youth players, Chiarenza sounded like an athlete in a post-game press conferences. "Have fun," he said.

Meanwhile, fantasy football has become so popular that Jeremy Rosenstock Doughty, a Brookline seventh-grader who plays in three leagues, says he's surprised when he talks to a kid who doesn't have a team.

"It's such a part of me," he said. "My dad plays in a couple of leagues, and I've always wanted to be just like him."

At the same time, he added, he'd like to try to watch football for the beauty of the sport, rather than to see how his players are scoring.

Here's another sign that fantasy football has taken hold of the kiddie set: It has become a source of friction between kids and parents. On a recent morning in Newton, Bret Miller, at 11, already a four-year fantasy veteran, and his father, Andrew, were bickering over a player the elder Miller had insisted they acquire for the team the two comanage.

"This might sound weird," he said, "but I seem kind of tense on Sundays."

Fantasy Sports Leagues Challenged as Illegal Gambling

By Anita M. Moorman
Sport Marketing Quarterly, December 2008

Introduction

The fantasy sports industry continues to present interesting legal issues for sport managers. Last year, this [article] featured a discussion of *C.B.C. Distribution and Marketing, Inc. v. Major League Baseball Advanced Media, LP.* (2006, 2007) which held that an operator of a fantasy sports league was not infringing on the players' state law publicity rights and that the 1st Amendment to the United States Constitution preempted the players' state law publicity rights (Grady, 2007). The case that is the subject of this [article] identifies yet another issue surrounding fantasy sports. In *Humphrey* v. *Viacom* (2007) the plaintiff, Humphrey, alleged that online fantasy sports leagues were engaged in an illegal gambling enterprise prohibited by state wagering and gambling laws.

History of the Case and Factual Background

Charles E. Humphrey filed his lawsuit in 2006 against numerous online fantasy sports league providers, including Viacom, CBS, Sportsline.com, ESPN, and Vulcan Sports Media (hereinafter referred to as "the league defendants"). Online fantasy sports providers allow individuals to pay an entry fee in exchange for participation in a fantasy sports league. Participants' fee purchases a fantasy sports team and the related services necessary to manage the fantasy team, including access to "real-time" statistical information, expert opinions, analysis, and message boards for communicating with other participants.

The online leagues mimic actual professional leagues. Participants select players for their virtual teams and pit them against opposing virtual teams. Winners accrue points after each game and the participant with the most points at the end of the season receives a set prize. The success of a fantasy sports team depends on the participants' skill in selecting players for his or her team, trading players over the course of the season, adding and dropping players during the course of the season, and deciding who among his or her players will start and which players will be placed on the bench. The virtual team with the best performance is declared the winner at the season's end and typically receives small prizes, such as T-shirts or bobble-head dolls. Managers of the best teams in each sport across all leagues are awarded larger prizes, such as flat-screen TVs or gift certificates. All prizes are predetermined and announced before the fantasy sports season begins and are guaranteed to be awarded.

Humphrey's Legal Arguments

Humphrey sought recover from these fantasy sports leagues, under *qui tarn* laws, which allow individuals to recoup losses sustained while gambling. The case challenged the fantasy leagues based upon *qui tarn* statutes from multiple states—Georgia, Illinois, Kentucky, Massachusetts, New Jersey, Ohio, South Carolina—and the District of Columbia, but was tried in the United States District Court for New Jersey. The league defendants filed a motion to dismiss Humphrey's case for failure to

> *According to the district court, gambling represents an activity where parties voluntarily make a bet or wager. The act of doing so inherently involves a monetary risk: participants can lose the wager and receive no corresponding reward. When multiple parties bet, they may pool their collective monies, creating a purse to be awarded to the winning party. All participants have the opportunity to win or lose the purse.*

state a claim. In resolving the motion to dismiss, the district court only discussed the *qui tam* statute for the State of New Jersey since it was determined that the essential elements of the New Jersey law was the same in the other states.

England originally established *qui tam* laws in 1710. The United States subsequently adopted comparable statutes, and New Jersey introduced its own in 1797. The statute's intended purpose was to protect gamblers and their families from debilitating gambling losses, which could lead to the families seeking financial assistance from their local governments. The laws permitted gamblers to pursue reimbursement from the winning parties. States introduced *qui tam* laws during a time when governments offered only limited protection to individuals experiencing gambling losses. The district court advised that for Humphrey to succeed under the *qui tam* laws, he needed to (1) demonstrate that paying an entry fee to a league equated to incurring a gambling loss, (2) provide details for every individual represented in the suit, and (3) file within six months of when each individual first suffered the loss. This [article] focuses solely on the court's resolution of the first element, which is whether entry fees paid to participate in an online fantasy sports league is properly defined as a wager or gambling activity under the New Jersey *qui tam* statute.

Fantasy Sports League Fees and Gambling

The league defendants argued that Humphrey failed to state a claim under New Jersey's *qui tam* statute because, as a matter of law, the payment of an entry fee to participate in a fantasy sports league is not wagering, betting, or staking money. New Jersey allows recovery only of "wagers, bets or stakes made to depend upon any race or game, or upon any gaming by lot or chance, or upon any lot, chance, casualty or unknown or contingent event" (N.J.Stat. § 2A: 40–l).

The district court acknowledged that the New Jersey state courts have not addressed the three-factor scenario of (1) an entry fee paid unconditionally, (2) prizes guaranteed to be awarded, and (3) prizes for which the game operator is not competing. Courts throughout the country, however, have long recognized that it would be "patently absurd" to hold that "the combination of an entry fee and a prize equals gambling" (*State v. Am Holiday Ass'n, Inc.*, 1986). The district court cautioned that to hold otherwise would result in countless contests engaged in every day being construed as unlawful gambling, including "golf tournaments, bridge tournaments, local and state rodeos or fair contests,... literary or essay competitions,... livestock, poultry and produce exhibitions, track meets, spelling bees, beauty contests and the like," and contest participants and sponsors could all be subject to criminal liability (*Humphrey*, pp. 19–20).

According to the district court, gambling represents an activity where parties voluntarily make a bet or wager. The act of doing so inherently involves a monetary risk: participants can lose the wager and receive no corresponding reward. When multiple parties bet, they may pool their collective monies, creating a purse to be awarded to the winning party. All participants have the opportunity to win or lose the purse. Conversely, with online fantasy sports leagues, the court interpreted the fee as part of a contractual agreement between the online provider and the participant—not a wager or bet. The participant pays the fee, and the provider in turn offers services, including conducting a virtual draft where participants select players for their respective teams, providing player and team statistical data, and determining weekly and total season winners. Neither side places a bet or assumes a monetary risk with online fantasy sports. Both parties know in advance the terms of the agreement, and both benefit mutually from the arrangement. Additionally, the parties do not form a purse from the collective wagers. The provider establishes the prizes to be awarded in advance.

Courts have distinguished between *bona fide* entry fees and bets or wagers, holding that entry fees do not constitute bets or wagers where they are paid unconditionally for the privilege of participating in a contest, and the prize is for an amount certain that is guaranteed to be won by one of the contestants (but not the entity offering the prize). When the entry fees and prizes are unconditional and guaranteed, the element of risk necessary to constitute betting or wagering is missing. Therefore, online fantasy sports leagues are not gambling, and league participants do not suffer gambling losses.

The district court also rejected Humphrey's attempt to compare the operations of a fantasy league to a lottery that involves prize, chance, and consideration. The district court quickly distinguished the cases relied upon by Humphrey as inapplicable since those cases had been decided based upon a lottery statute rather than a gambling statute. New Jersey has an entirely separate statute that identifies certain types of prohibited lottery activities and recovery of losses. The district court declined to address whether the fantasy league activities would be prohibited under the New Jersey lottery statutes and stated "although Defendants deny that fantasy sports leagues are games of chance, this Court need not reach this issue in deciding Defendants' motions" (*Humphrey,* p. 24). The district court also relied upon the Unlawful Internet Gambling Enforcement Act of 2006, which prohibits internet gambling. The federal law confirms that fantasy sports leagues do not constitute an illegal bet or wager as a matter of law. Therefore, the court concluded that "as a matter of law, the entry fees for Defendants' fantasy sports leagues are not 'bets' or 'wagers' because 1) the entry fees are paid unconditionally; 2) the prizes offered to fantasy sports contestants are for amounts certain and are guaranteed to be awarded; and 3) Defendants do not compete for the prizes" (*Id.,* pp. 24–25).

Implications for Sport Marketers

Issues involving fantasy sports leagues have even recently emerged on the college sports front with the announcement in July of CBSSports.com's plans to offer an online fantasy game utilizing the actual names and statistics of college football players (Carey, 2008). Ironically, CBS is the NCAA's national broadcast partner. CBS has based its decision squarely on the legal precedent set in the *C.B.C. Distribution v. MLBAM* decision. The NCAA has vigorously opposed CBSSports.com's use of college player names and statistics, citing violations of its regulations governing amateurism (Carey, 2008). While lack of legal standing has ultimately stymied the NCAA from pursing the issue in court, and while amateurism issues have been the NCAA's stated objections, the emergence of college-based fantasy games further extends the boundaries of real and perceived gambling activities connected to sport.

The burgeoning industry of insured sport promotions has also raised new challenges based on claims of illegal gambling. An increasing number of retail companies are tying the offer of full or partial refunds on products purchased during a certain time period to a particular outcome of a game or season. For example, Massachusetts-based Jordan's Furniture offered consumers a full refund on furniture purchased between March 7 and April 16 *if* the Boston Red Sox won the 2007 World Series (which the team did, hence generating millions of dollars in free publicity for Jordan's Furniture) (Tedesco, 2007). These types of insured promotional offers are coming under increased scrutiny by legal commentators and state attorney generals' offices who view such promotions as potentially being an illegal lottery and susceptible to legal challenge. A lottery consists of three key elements: a prize, an element of chance, and consideration, usually the payment of money (Mohl, 2007). In specifically analyzing Jordan Furniture's promotion, one legal scholar noted that it may potentially qualify as a lottery because customers who bought furniture (the consideration) during the designated time period would receive a full rebate (the prize) if the Red Sox won the World Series (the element of chance) (Bortman, 2008). The *Humphrey* court declined to address a similar lottery argument.

Conclusion

The *Humphrey* case again demonstrates the complex legal issues surrounding online fantasy games. The *Humphrey* case together with the previous *C.B.C.* case also highlights the dual challenge professional sports leagues and collegiate sports may face to distance themselves from perceived gambling activities while proactively protecting intellectual property interests connected to online sports and entertainment services.

References

Bortman, E. (2008, Spring). The Jordan's Furniture "Monster Deal": Illegal gaming? Taxable income? *Business Law Review, 41*, 31–43.

Carey, J. (2008, July 30). College football fantasy game will set a new precedent. *USA Today.* Retrieved October 26, 2008, from http://www. usa today.com/sports/college/football/2008-07-30-college-fantasy-game_N. htm

C.B.C. Distrib. & Mktg. v. Major League Baseball Advanced Media, L.P., 443 F. Supp. 2d 1077 (E.D. Mo, 2006), *aff'd,* 505 F.3d 818 (8th Cir. 2007).

Grady, I. (2007). Fantasy stats case tests limits of intellectual property protection in the digital age. *Sport Marketing Quarterly,* 16 (4), 230–232.

Humphrey v. Viacom inc., 2007 U.S. Dist. LEXIS 44679 (D. N.J., 2007).

Mohl, B. (2007. April 22). Diamonds (and free couches) are a Red Sox fan's best friend: Critics say local retailer's promotions violate state's gambling laws. *Boston Globe Online.* Retrieved October 26, 2008, from, http://www.boston.com/business/articles/2007/04/22/diamonds_and_free_couches_are_a_red_sox_fans_best_friend/

N.J.Stat..§2A:4O-1(2008). *State v. Am. Holiday Ass'n, Inc.,* 727 P.2d 807 (Ariz. 1986).

Tedesco, R. (2007, December 1). Jordan's Monster Deal: Rebate or lottery? *Promo.com.* Retrieved October 26, 2008, from http://promomagazinc.com/retail/jordans_monster_deal_promotion/

The Unlawful Internet Gambling Enforcement Act of 2006, 31 U.S.C. § 5361 et seq. (2006).

Bibliography

❖

Baert, Albert L., and Apostolos H. Karantanas. *Sports Injuries in Children and Adolescents*. Heidelberg: Springer, 2011. Print.

Batchelor, Bob, and Danielle Sarver Coombs. *American History through American Sports: From Colonial Lacrosse to Extreme Sports*. Santa Barbara: Praeger, 2013. Print.

Cahn, Susan K., and Jean O'Reilly. *Women and Sports in the United States: A Documentary Reader*. Boston: Northeastern UP, 2007. Print.

David, Paul. *A Guide to the World Anti-Doping Code: A Fight for the Spirit of Sport*. Cambridge: Cambridge UP, 2012. Print.

Davies, Richard O. *Sports in American Life: A History*. Chichester: Blackwell, 2012. Print.

Delaney, Tim, and Tim Madigan. *Sports: Why We Love Them!*. Lanham: UP of America, 2009. Print.

Fay, Gail. *Sports: The Ultimate Teen Guide*. Lanham: Scarecrow, 2013. Print.

Fuller, Linda K. *Sport, Rhetoric, and Gender: Historical Perspectives and Media Representations*. New York: Macmillan, 2006. Print.

Horne, John. *Understanding Sport: A Socio-Cultural Analysis*. Milton Park: Routledge, 2012. Print.

Hugenberg, Barbara S., Paul M. Haridakis, and Adam C. Earnheardt. *Sports Fans, Identity, and Socialization Exploring the Fandemonium*. Lanham: Lexington, 2012. Print.

Lapchick, Richard Edward. *New Game Plan for College Sport*. Westport: Praeger, 2006. Print.

Mitchell, Nicole, and Lisa A. Ennis. *Encyclopedia of Title IX and Sports*. Westport: Greenwood, 2007. Print.

Robinson, Tom. *Sportsmanship in Youth Athletics*. Edina: Abdo, 2009. Print.

Shropshire, Kenneth L., and Scott Rosner. *The Business of Sports*. Sudbury: Bartlett, 2011. Print.

Smith, Lauren Reichart, and Kenny D. Smith. "Identity in Twitter's Hashtag Culture: A Sport-Media-Consumption Case Study." *International Journal of Sport Communication* 5.4 (2012): 539–557.

Waddington, Ivan, and Andy Smith. *An Introduction to Drugs in Sport: Addicted to Winning?*. London: Routledge, 2009. Print.

Watson, Emily O., and Jack L. Murray. *Encyclopedia of Sports and Athletics*. New York: Nova, 2012. Print.

Websites

❖

American Medical Society for Sports Medicine (AMSSM)
http://www.amssm.org/

The AMSSM provides education, research, and advocacy in sports medicine for athletes and programs. The organization is one of the leading sources for research and resources to understand the effects of head injuries in athletes of all ages.

National Alliance for Youth Sports (NAYS)
http://www.nays.org/

A nonprofit agency, the NAYS offers programs for youth across America in the promotion of health and safety. The organization works to coordinate administrators, families, and volunteers in programs and services that add positive value to youth sports.

National Collegiate Athletic Association (NCAA)
http://www.ncaa.org/

A nonprofit governing agency for more than 1200 college sports programs, the NCAA represents the major athletic conferences in the nation. The NCAA regulates athletic programs according to core policies governing personnel, recruiting, eligibility, benefits, financial aid, and playing and practice.

National Council of Youth Sports (NCYS)
http://www.ncys.org/

Representing more than two hundred organizations, the NCYS promotes safe environments and healthy lifestyles in youth programs in communities across the nation. The programs are noted for their community-based approaches that emphasize grassroots building of youth sports programs.

President's Council on Sports, Fitness, and Nutrition
http://www.fitness.gov/

The President's Council promotes health, fitness, and education through programs and initiatives that join private and public sectors. Initiatives such as the President's Challenge and the President's Youth Fitness Program target specific age groups in the support of living healthy lifestyles. The website provides information on programs and resources for health and fitness.

The United States Collegiate Athletic Association (USCAA)
http://theuscaa.com/landing/index

The USCAA represents athletic program in small colleges and community colleges across the nation, organizing eleven National Championships in seven sports.

Title IX
http://www.titleix.info/

Title IX is a nonprofit organization dedicated to the promotion of equality for women in education and sports programs across the nation through education and the promotion of Title IX policies.

Title IX Handbook
United States Department of Justice
http://www.justice.gov/crt/about/cor/coord/ixlegal.php

Complete text of Title IX Education Amendment of 1972. Manual includes an overview of legislative history and the scope of influence on education and labor policy.

World Anti-Doping Agency (WADA)
http://www.wada-ama.org/en/

The WADA coordinates and monitors policies on drug testing in countries throughout the world. Charged by the World Anti-Doping Code, the organization works to coordinate national policies across borders and sports fields.

Index

❖